OECD Green Growth Studies

Material Resources, Productivity and the Environment

OECD
BETTER POLICIES FOR BETTER LIVES

Please cite this publication as:
OECD (2015), *Material Resources, Productivity and the Environment*, OECD Green Growth Studies, OECD Publishing, Paris.
http://dx.doi.org/10.1787/9789264190504-en

ISBN 978-92-64-19049-8 (print)
ISBN 978-92-64-19050-4 (PDF)

Series: OECD Green Growth Studies
ISSN 2222-9515 (print)
ISSN 2222-9523 (online)

PREFACE

Establishing a resource efficient economy is central to achieving green growth. It involves putting in place policies that improve resource productivity and that ensure a sustainable natural resource and materials management building on the principle of the 3Rs —reduce, reuse and recycle— and encouraging more sustainable consumption patterns. Better resource productivity can both help to improve the environment, by reducing the amount of resources that economic activity requires and diminishing the associated environmental burden, and help to sustain economic growth by securing adequate supplies of materials, investing in new technologies and innovation, and improving competitiveness.

To be successful resource efficiency and material productivity policies need to be founded on a good understanding of the material basis of the economy, of international and national flows of materials, and of the factors that drive changes in natural resource use and material productivity over time, across countries and in the different sectors of the economy. Some natural resources, such as water, energy, forests, are monitored internationally, but information is insufficient to give an integrated view of how minerals, metals, or timber flow through the economy throughout their life cycle. In addition, little is known about how this affects the productivity of the economy and the quality of the environment.

This report is a first step to fill some of these gaps. It describes the material basis of OECD economies and provides a factual analysis of material flows and resource productivity in OECD countries in a global context. It takes an economy-wide perspective and dwells upon major material categories such as metals, minerals, biomass and energy carriers. Some of the challenges and opportunities associated with selected materials and products that are internationally-significant, both in economic and environmental terms (aluminium, copper, iron and steel, paper, phosphate rock and rare earth elements) are also described. The report also highlights the most important information and knowledge gaps that need to be filled to effectively support resource efficiency and material productivity policies.

Building on this report, we plan to both deepen our analysis of trade-related material flows and flows of secondary raw materials, the links with commodity prices and recycling markets, and the links with natural and anthropogenic stocks of materials. We will also review the environmental consequences of material resource use, as well as the economic and environmental opportunities provided by improved resource productivity. We will do so by working closely with national and international partners, in particular the International Resource Panel steered by UNEP.

Simon Upton
OECD Environment Director

FOREWORD

This report is part of the OECD programme of work on material flows and resource productivity that supports the implementation of the 2004 and 2008 OECD Council recommendations related to material flows and resource productivity. It contributes to OECD work on monitoring progress towards green growth and to the OECD project on measuring economic performance and social progress.

A first version of this report was issued at the occasion of the Green Growth and Sustainale Development Forum in December 2012.

Its elaboration has been drawing upon the OECD's expertise with with environmental reporting, resource productivity and sustainable materials management. It benefitted from the financial support of Japan and from contributions by members of the OECD Working Parties on Environmental Information and on Resource Productivity and Waste. It has been drafted as a joint effort by a small group of experts from OECD countries led by the OECD Secretariat (Myriam Linster and Farah Huq). Task team members included: Mr Derry Allen (USEPA), Ms Kate Johnson and Mr. Jeff L. Doebrich (USGS), Ms Cheryl Beillard (Natural Resources Canada), Mr Pawel Kazmierzick (EEA), Mr Yuichi Moriguchi (Japan), Mr. John Atherton (BIAC), Mr Guido Sonnemann (UNEP), Mr Peter Borkey (OECD). Statistical and analytical support was provided by Pierpaolo Cazzola and Mauro Migotto.

Part I of the report provides the economic and policy context for the report by outlining the main issues and challenges arising from global patterns and trends in material use. It highlights the linkages between production and consumption, economic growth, international trade, technological development and environmental issues.

It further describes the material basis of the economy. It examines trends in the stocks and flows of materials worldwide and in OECD countries. It begins with an integrated analysis of trends in the extraction, consumption and trade of materials using economy-wide Material Flow Analysis (EW-MFA), distinguishing six groups of materials: 1) biomass for food and feed, 2) wood, 3) fossil energy carriers, 3) construction minerals, 5) industrial minerals, 6) metals and metal ores. It then looks at global and regional flows of waste and recycled materials and presents the latest state of the art on estimating material stocks, both natural and man-made.

Part II of the report presents a series of factsheets on selected materials and products that are internationally-significant, in both economic and environmental terms: aluminium, copper, iron and steel, paper, phosphorus and rare earth elements.

TABLE OF CONTENTS

EXECUTIVE SUMMARY

Natural resources are fundamental for the economy and for well-being. They provide essential raw materials, water and other commodities, and are an important source of income and jobs. With land and ecosystems, they form our society's natural capital.

Establishing a resource efficient and sustainable economy is central to achieving green growth. It is the way to ensure adequate supplies of materials; to manage the environmental impacts associated with their extraction, processing, transport, use and disposal; and to make sure that natural resources are not degraded.

To be successful resource efficiency policies need to be founded on a good understanding of the material basis of the economy, of international and national flows of materials, and of the factors that drive changes in resource use and productivity across time, countries and sectors. This report is a first step to provide some of this information.

Key messages

The last decades have witnessed unprecedented growth in demands for raw materials worldwide, driven in particular by the rapid industrialisation of emerging economies and continued high levels of material consumption in developed countries. At the same time, international commodity markets have expanded, with increasing international trade flows, and increasing mobility and fragmentation of production. This has been accompanied by increases in, and volatility of, commodity prices, and by growing competition for selected raw materials.

- The amount of **materials extracted from natural resources and consumed worldwide** doubled since 1980, an estimated ten-fold increase since 1900. It reached nearly 72 billion metric tonnes (Gt) in 2010, and is projected to reach 100 Gt by 2030.The annual per **capita material consumption** in OECD countries remains high, at about 60% above the world average. The average person living in an OECD country consumed roughly 46 kg of materials per day in 2011, including 10 kg of biomass, 18 kg of construction and industrial minerals, 13 kg of fossil energy carriers, and 5 kg of metals.
- Material **consumption in OECD countries** increased however more slowly than at the global level, and there are first signs of decoupling from economic growth and of improvements in **material productivity.** Today, OECD countries generate 50% more economic value per unit of material resources used than in 1990 and 30% more than in 2000. This is partly due to policy action: some countries managed to decrease material consumption while economic growth increased (absolute decoupling) with well-functioning waste management and extended producer responsibility schemes, and well-developed resource efficiency or 3R (Reduce, Reuse, Recycle) strategies.
- However, there are other factors to the improvement of material productivity: the rise of the **service sector**; **offshoring** resource- and pollution-intensive production; and the **economic crisis**. Much of the improvements in recent years can be attributed to the slowdown in industrial output and construction activities following the economic crisis, which led to a reduction in material demands across the OECD.
- An important aspect of the management of material resources is what happens *after* they have been used. It is estimated that about one fifth of the raw materials extracted worldwide end up as waste and that OECD countries account for about one third of global waste generation.

- Efforts to **transform waste into valuable resources** are starting to pay off. Recycling rates increased for some high-volume materials, such as glass, steel, aluminium, paper and plastics, but remain low for many other valuable materials, including precious or specialty metals.
- Markets for **secondary raw materials** have expanded, but have to cope with volatile commodity prices. Unexploited "**urban mines**", i.e. the materials locked in the economy that could one day be available for reuse or recycling free of technical or economic constraints (*e.g.* buildings, cars, electric and electronic equipment) represent a potentially important source of raw materials in the future.

By 2050, the world economy is expected to quadruple and the global population to grow to over 9.5 billion. A growing population with higher average income requires more food, more industrial products, more energy and more water, thus placing additional strain on the earth's material resources and the environment. This creates formidable **economic and environmental challenges**. As production and consumption have become displaced with increasingly globalised value chains, questions also arise about the distribution of the environmental burden associated with resource use.

- Confronting the scale of these challenges requires **more ambitious policies** to increase the resource productivity at all stages of the material life-cycle. This includes actions and investments to support technological change and innovations, and integrated life-cycle-oriented management approaches, such as 3R policies, **sustainable materials management** and circular economy initiatives.
- It requires the involvement of a large number of economic actors and **concerted action** by all ministries whose policies affect resource productivity. Governments have an important role in ensuring that all relevant policies and measures are coherent and well integrated, and in establishing proper framework conditions. This will in turn create **opportunities** for investment, for new products, new markets and employment.
- It also requires **better data and a better understanding** of the physical resource base of countries' economies. The **environmental consequences** and costs of material resource use are not yet fully understood, nor are the **economic opportunities** provided by improved resource productivity. More in-depth analysis is needed of specific resources and materials, and their interactions. Examples include trade-related resource flows and flows of secondary (recycled) raw materials and waste; and the way material flows interact with commodity prices and recycling markets, how they relate to natural resource stocks, to innovation and to materials stocks locked in the economy.
- Considerable progress has been made over the past fifteen years to develop methods to analyse material flows and measure resource productivity. Important **information gaps** remain to be filled and are highlighted in this report:
  - Harmonised data on material flows that do not enter the economy as transactions, but that are relevant from an environmental point of view, including **indirect flows associated with international trade**.
  - Information on **secondary raw materials**, which is essential to assess resource productivity and move towards circular business models.
  - Disaggregated information on resource use and productivity **by industry**, which is essential to identify opportunities for efficiency gains along the supply chains.
  - Information on the quality and deterioration of **natural resource stocks**, and compatible data on **critical materials** that raise economic and environmental concerns.

The OECD will continue to assist countries in improving natural resource and material flow data and indicators, and report on the state of resources and resource productivity in OECD countries and beyond. This is done in collaboration with UNEP and its International Resource Panel, Eurostat and several research institutes.

READER'S GUIDE

OECD work on material flows and resource productivity

This report is part of the OECD programme of work on material flows and resource productivity that aims to (i) develop a better understanding of the physical resource base of countries' economies, including the international and environmental dimensions, (ii) monitor progress with resource productivity, and (iii) foster the implementation of effective policy mixes that improve resource productivity, reduce negative environmental impacts of natural resources, materials and product use, and promote integrated life-cycle oriented approaches to natural resource, waste and materials management. The work encompasses:

- The development of an international knowledge base on material flows and resource productivity (data, indicators, accounts, and subsequent analyses and reporting). This is done in collaboration with UNEP and its International Resource Panel, Eurostat and several research institutes.
- The development of policy guidelines and best practices, with emphasis on sustainable materials management (SMM). It is complemented with work on trade, innovation and sustainable manufacturing. Progress is evaluated on a regular basis in country peer reviews.

OECD work on material flows and resource productivity
Main streams of work and building blocks

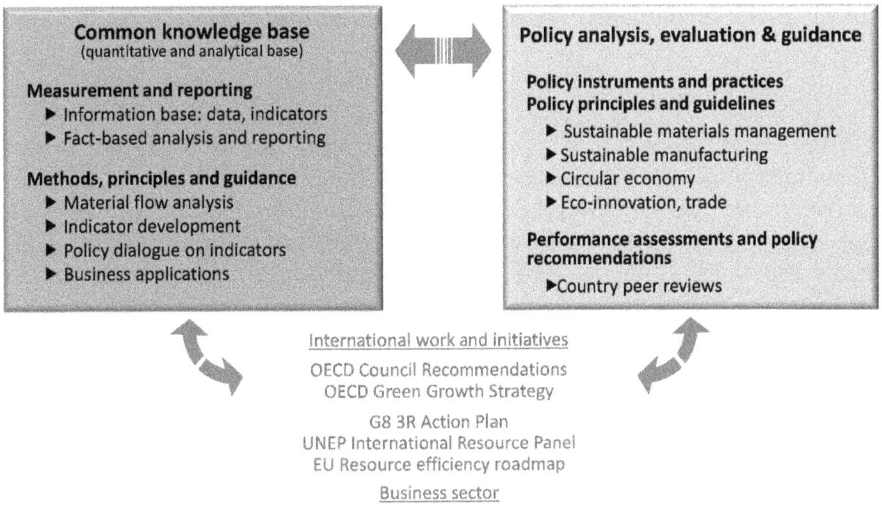

Objectives of this report

This report applies the concepts and methods described in the OECD guidance documents on *Measuring material flows and resource productivity* released in 2008. It:

- Gives an *overview* of material use and resource productivity in OECD countries, and identifies *main trends and challenges,* placing them within the global context.

- Describes the *stocks and flows* of selected materials that are of particular importance for the environment and for economic development.
- Describes some of the *environmental implications* of current trends in resource use and material consumption.

Future work will deepen the analysis of trade-related flows and flows of secondary raw materials, the links with commodity prices and recycling markets, and the links with natural and anthropogenic stocks of materials. It will also review the environmental consequences of material resource use, as well as the economic and environmental opportunities provided by improved resource productivity.

Scope of this report

Resources and materials covered

This report uses an integrated approach to natural resource use and material flows, but pays particular attention to those natural resources, and the materials and products derived from them whose extraction, processing, use and disposal are internationally-significant, in both economic and environmental terms, and that are not yet or insufficiently monitored in other international work. Emphasis is placed on the "material" aspect of resources, and on minerals (metallic and non-metallic industrial minerals) and biomass. Energy, water, land and fish resources are only covered to the extent that they are part of an integrated approach to the entire resource cycle. Given their importance in global material flows, fossil energy carriers are covered together with other major material groups in the report.

Countries and regions covered

The report examines trends and patterns in material use in OECD countries, placed in a global context. Given their growing importance as users and suppliers of raw materials, the report looks at developments in the BRIICS countries: Brazil, Russia, India, Indonesia, China and South Africa.

Selecting key material resources

The environmental implications associated with the use of different natural resources, materials and products vary, each presenting unique challenges and opportunities for improving resource productivity. The factsheets presented in Part II of this report aim to illustrate some of these challenges and opportunities by focusing on a selection of materials and products whose extraction, processing and disposal are internationally-significant, both in economic and environmental terms. Consistent with the definition used in the 2008 OECD Council Recommendation on Resource Productivity, the scope of selection was limited to minerals (metallic and non-metallic industrial minerals), and biomass (wood fibre).

- **Environmental significance**: Particular attention was paid to materials whose use is associated with significant adverse environmental effects. All aspects of the lifecycle were considered, from extraction and processing, to transportation and end of life. Given the environmental implications of international trade (e.g. indirect flows, greenhouse gas emissions from transportation), the weight and patterns of international flows were also selection criteria. The positive contributions of raw materials (and/or their applications) to the environment, in terms of recyclability, energy efficiency and green growth, were also considered. Consideration was also given to those materials and products relevant in the context of the 2008 Kobe 3R Action Plan, the work of the OECD's Working Party on Resource Productivity and Waste (WPRPW) on Sustainable Materials Management (SMM) and the work of the UNEP International Resource Panel.

- **Economic significance**: Materials were selected on the basis of their economic importance, assessed in terms of contribution to the global economy (e.g. GDP, employment, production, consumption, and international trade) as well as the diversity and significance of end-use applications. Consideration was also given to other international and national initiatives to identify materials that are critical to the economy, including the European Commission's report on critical raw materials and work by the U.S. Geological Survey (USGS).

Table 1: Economic and environmental significance of selected key materials

Selected Material/ Product	Environmental Significance	Economic Significance
Aluminium	♦ Lightweight (transportation fuel efficiency) ♦ Infinitely recyclable ♦ Energy intensive production (GHG emissions) ♦ Solid waste (red mud)	♦ Widely used esp. in transportation, construction, electricity ♦ Increasing global demand ♦ Price volatility ♦ Consumption strongly coupled with economic growth
Copper	♦ Infinitely recyclable ♦ Energy intensive production ♦ E-waste	♦ Widely used esp. in electrical transmission & construction ♦ Increasing global demand ♦ Price volatility
Iron and Steel	♦ Infinitely recyclable ♦ well-developed scrap markets ♦ Energy intensive production	♦ Most widely used and traded metal in the world ♦ Increasing global demand ♦ Price volatility
Rare Earth Elements	♦ Used in clean energy & energy efficiency technologies ♦ Recycling extremely challenging ♦ Chemically-intensive processing ♦ E-waste	♦ Used in wide range of high tech electronics ♦ Lack of substitutes ♦ Increasing global demand, recent supply chain issues ♦ Price volatility
Phosphorus	♦ Eutrophication ♦ Waste (phosphogypsum) and emissions (fluorine) ♦ Recyclable (with losses)	♦ Food security ♦ Supports agricultural production
Paper	♦ Renewable / recyclable (with losses) ♦ Carbon sequestration, habitat (forests) ♦ Potential (competing) source of energy (wood biomass) ♦ Energy and water consumption	♦ Demand growing esp. in emerging economies ♦ Wide variety of products

Table 2: Priority materials identified by other international and national studies

List of Critical Raw Materials at the EU Level *(supply security perspective)*	UNEP International Resource Panel Priority Materials *(environmental perspective)*	OECD Case Studies on Sustainable Materials Management *(environmental perspective)*
1. Antimony 2. Beryllium 3. Cobalt 4. Fluorspar 5. Gallium 6. Germanium 7. Graphite 8. Indium 9. Magnesium 10. Niobium 11. Platinum-Group Metals 12. Rare earth elements 13. Tantalum 14. Tungsten	1. Fossil fuels 2. Agricultural biomass (especially animal products) 3. Metals (specifically iron, steel and aluminium)	1. Aluminium 2. Critical metals for mobile phones (antimony, beryllium, palladium and platinum) 3. Wood fibres 4. Plastics (non-packaging)

Information basis and data quality

The report brings together findings from OECD and other international work, and from work in member countries. It builds in particular on OECD work on *Measuring Material Flows and Resource Productivity* (2008b), and on *Sustainable Materials Management* (SMM), complemented with information from work on export restrictions for raw materials. Findings from relevant international and national studies, including the work of the UNEP International Panel for Sustainable Resource Management (International Resource Panel - IRP), work by the European Environment Agency on resource efficiency and studies by research institutes were also drawn upon.

This report thus reflects the state of the art concerning information on the state of resources, material flows and resource productivity in member countries and in international organisations. First results were presented in the 2011 OECD report on *Resource Productivity in the G8 and the OECD* in the framework of the Kobe 3R Action Plan.

Databases

- The OECD **database on material flows,** established further to the adoption in 2004 of the OECD Council Recommendation on material flows and resource productivity, serves as the primary information basis for Part 2 of the report.
  - The dataset covers the period 1980-2010/11, all 34 OECD countries and the BRIICS countries. The focus is on material resources, i.e. metals and metal ores, construction minerals, industrial minerals, energy carriers (oil, coal, gas), and biomass (food, feed, wood). Water as a natural resource is excluded. (see *Glossary*). It builds on and expands Eurostat's economy-wide material flows database, and makes use of various other international and national sources (e.g. OECD Trade Database and UN COMTRADE, U.S. Geological Survey, FAO).
  - It is complemented with data from the SERI/WU Global Material Flows Database, set up and administrated by *SERI (Sustainable Europe Research Institute)* and the *Vienna University of Economics and Business (WU Vienna)*, in cooperation with the *Institute for Energy and Environmental Research (IFEU)* and the *Wuppertal Institute for Climate, Environment, Energy*; with OECD data on waste flows, UN COMTRADE data on physical trade flows and information on mineral reserves from the *U.S. Geological Survey*.
  - Original calculations were made by the Wuppertal Institute on behalf of the OECD. Eurostat conventions for establishing direct material flows accounts have been followed. Unused materials flows were calculated based on the Wuppertal's database of coefficients developed with the Sustainable Resources Europe Institute (SERI) as part of the EU-funded projects EXIOPOL and INDI-LINK.

Many of the indicators shown in this publication are expressed on a per unit of GDP basis. The GDP figures used are expressed in USD and in 2005 prices and purchasing power parities (PPPs). PPPs are the rates of currency conversion that equalise the purchasing power of different countries by eliminating differences in price levels between countries. When converted by means of PPPs, expenditures on GDP across countries are expressed at the same set of prices, enabling comparisons between countries that reflect only differences in the volume of goods and services purchased. The data for OECD countries come from the OECD Economic Outlook (OECD (2012), "OECD Economic Outlook No. 91", *OECD Economic Outlook: Statistics and Projections* (database), *http://dx.doi.org/10.1787/data-00606-en* and the *OECD Annual National Accounts Statistics* (database). The data for the BRIICS come from the World Bank (World Development Indicators, The World Bank, Washington D.C.).

The population data used in this report come from the "OECD population statistics, historical population data and projections", *OECD.Stat* (database), *http://dx.doi.org/10.1787/data-00285-en.*

Website and online data

- OECD data on material flows (includes experimental data on unused flows): "Material resources", *OECD Environment Statistics* (database). *http://dx.doi.org/10.1787/data-00695-en.*
- OECD Green growth indicators: *www.oecd.org/greengrowth/indicators.*
- Selected OECD environmental data and indicators: *OECD Environment Statistics* (database). *http://dx.doi.org/10.1787/env-data-en.*

Comparability and interpretation

The indicators presented here are of varying relevance for different countries and should be interpreted taking account of the context in which they were produced. It should be borne in mind that national averages can mask significant variations *within* countries. In addition, care should be taken when making international comparisons:

- The data **coverage and completeness vary** by variable and from country to country; gaps remain in particular for the 1980s up to the 1990s for the former centrally-planned economies in Southeast and Eastern Europe, and for emerging economies. In general, caution needs to be exercised when drawing conclusions based on country-level data. Differences exist among countries in both the **definitions and measurement methods** applied and the policy approaches used to increase resource productivity. Hence inter-country comparisons may not compare the same things.
- There is a level of **uncertainty** associated with the data sources and measurement methods on which the indicators rely. Differences between two countries' indicators are thus not always statistically significant; and when countries are clustered around a relatively narrow range of outcomes, it may be misleading to establish an order of ranking.

It should also be noted that:

- Although considerable progress was made in the past decade to set up **material flow** accounts, *missing information*, including on physical flows of international trade, and a *lack of consensus* on conversion factors limit the calculation of some material flow indicators at the international level. The most significant gaps concern *indirect and unused flows* of materials and flows of *recycled or secondary raw materials.*
- Gaps in information on **waste flows** and their management constrain the analysis of trends and the tracking of progress. These gaps stem from a number of issues, including different definitions of waste across countries and inconsistent or non-existent tracking and reporting of waste streams. The waste data used here are part of the OECD core set of environmental data; they have been updated based on country replies to the OECD questionnaire on the state of the environment, and on other national and international sources, including Eurostat and the United Nations Statistics Division (UNSD).
- The data presented in this report reflect the impact of the 2008 global **financial crisis**. In most OECD countries, the economic slowdown caused material extraction and consumption to level off or decrease (sometimes significantly) after 2007. This should be

taken into consideration when reviewing and interpreting the trends in material flows and resource productivity outlined in this report.

Acronyms and abbreviations

Signs

The following signs are used in the figures:

n.a. or .. : not available
n. app.: not applicable

Country aggregates

OECD	This zone includes all member countries of OECD, *i.e.* countries of OECD Europe plus Australia, Canada, Chile*, Israel*, Japan, Mexico, New Zealand, the Republic of Korea and the United States
OECD Europe	This zone includes all European member countries of the OECD, *i.e.* Austria, Belgium, the Czech Republic, Denmark, Estonia*, Finland, France, Germany, Greece, Hungary, Iceland, Ireland, Italy, Luxembourg, the Netherlands, Norway, Poland, Portugal, the Slovak Republic, Slovenia*, Spain, Sweden, Switzerland, Turkey and the United Kingdom.
OECD Americas	This zone includes Canada, Mexico, the United States, and Chile.
OECD Asia	This zone includes Japan, South Korea and Israel.
OECD Oceania	This zone includes Australia and New Zealand.
OECD Asia-Oceania	This zone includes all OECD member countries in Asia and Oceania.
BRIICS	This grouping includes OECD Key Partner countries, *i.e.* Brazil, India, Indonesia, China, and South Africa, and the Russian Federation.

* Chile became a member of the OECD on 7 May 2010; Slovenia on 21 July 2010; Israel on 7 September 2010; and Estonia on 9 December 2010.

Country aggregates include Secretariat estimates and may refer to partial totals.

The statistical data for Israel are supplied by and under the responsibility of the relevant Israeli authorities. The use of such data by the OECD is without prejudice to the status of the Golan Heights, East Jerusalem and Israeli settlements in the West Bank under the terms of international law.

Cut-off date

This report is based on information available to the OECD Secretariat up to September 2013 for data on material flows and January 2014 for other data. The material resources factsheets are based on data available up to January 2012.

Country codes

AUS - Australia	FRA - France	NLD - Netherlands	BRA - Brazil
AUT - Austria	GBR - United Kingdom	NZL - New Zealand	CHN - China, People's Republic of
BEL - Belgium	GRC - Greece	NOR - Norway	IND - India
CAN - Canada	HUN - Hungary	POL - Poland	IDN - Indonesia
CHE - Switzerland	ISL - Iceland	PRT - Portugal	RUS - Russian Federation
CHL - Chile	IRL - Ireland	SVK - Slovak Rep.	ZAF - South Africa
CZE - Czech Republic	ITA - Italy	SVN - Slovenia	
DEU - Germany	ISR - Israel	SWE - Sweden	
DNK - Denmark	JPN - Japan	TUR - Turkey	
ESP - Spain	KOR - Korea, Rep.	USA - United States	
EST - Estonia	LUX - Luxembourg		
FIN - Finland	MEX - Mexico	EU - European Union	

Abbreviations

BGS	British Geological Survey
BIAC	The Business and Industry Advisory Committee to the OECD
BIR	Bureau of International Recycling
cap	Per Capita
DEU	Domestic Extraction Used
DMC	Domestic Material Consumption
DMI	Direct Material Inputs
EEA	European Environment Agency
EOL	End-of-life
EU	European Union
EUROSTAT	Statistical Office of the European Commission
FAO	Food and Agricultural Organisation of the United Nations (U.N.)
FAOSTAT	FAO Statistical Databases
GDP	Gross Domestic Product
GGKP	Green Growth Knowledge Platform
GHG	greenhouse gas (emissions)
Gt	billion metric tonnes (t = tonnes)
IAI	International Aluminium Institute
ICSG	International Copper Study Group
IEA	International Energy Agency
IFA	International Fertilizer Industry Association
IFEU	Institute for Energy and Environmental Research
IFPTB	Indirect Flow Physical Trade Balance
IOA	Input-Output Analysis
IPP	Integrated Product Policies
ISIC	International Standard Industrial Classification
IRP	International Resource Panel (UNEP)
kg	Kilograms
LCA	Life-Cycle Assessment
LED	Light-emitting Diode
LSA	Local System Analysis
MFA	Material Flow Analysis (EW – economy wide – MFA)
MSA	Material System Analysis
MSW	Municipal Solid Waste
Mt	Million tonnes (t = tonnes)
NGL	Natural Gas Liquids
PCFs	Per fluorocarbons
PPP	Purchasing Power Parities
PTB	Physical Trade Balance
REE	Rare Earth Elements
R&D	Research and Development
RoW	Rest of the World (statistical, residual, category)
SCP	Sustainable Consumption and Production
SEEA	System of Environmental-Economic Accounting
SERI	Sustainable Europe Research Institute
SFA	Substance Flow Analysis
SITC	Standard International Trade Classification
SMM	Sustainable Materials Management
toe	Tonnes of Oil Equivalent
TMC	Total Material Consumption
TMR	Total Material Requirement
TPES	Total Primary Energy Supply
UDE	Unused Domestic Extraction
UNCTAD	United Nations Conference on Trade and Development
UNEP	United Nations Environmental Programme
UNSD	United Nations Statistics Division
USD	United States Dollar
USEPA	United States Environmental Protection Agency
USGS	United States Geological Survey
WB	World Bank
WPEI	OECD Working Party on Environmental Information
WPRPW	OECD Working Party on Resource Productivity and Waste
WTO	World Trade Organisation

Part I: The material basis of the economy and resource productivity

Chapter 1. Natural resources: The material basis of the economy

Natural resources are fundamental for the economy and for well-being. They provide essential raw materials, water and other commodities, and are an important source of income and jobs. With land and ecosystems they form the society's natural capital.

The use of materials from natural resources in human activities and the associated production and consumption processes have many environmental, economic and social consequences that often extend beyond the borders of individual countries or regions, and that affect future generations.

Using natural resources and materials in an efficient and sustainable manner all way through the economy is important from an environmental perspective as well as from an economic and trade perspective. It is important for ensuring adequate supplies of materials to economic activities, managing the environmental impacts associated with their extraction, processing, transport, use and disposal, maintaining essential environmental services and preventing the degradation and depletion of natural resources.

A development pattern that depletes the economy's natural asset base without providing secure, long-term substitutes for the goods and services that it provides, is unlikely to be sustainable and entails risks to future growth.

THE ROLE AND FUNCTIONS OF NATURAL RESOURCES

Natural resources are fundamental to economic activity and human well-being

Natural resources are a major foundation of the economy and human welfare. Together with land and ecosystems, they form the society's natural capital, and support the provision of environmental and social services that are necessary to develop man-made, human and social capital.

Natural resources provide the raw materials required to meet basic human needs: food, shelter, water and medicine. As factor inputs into the production process, natural resources are transformed into the goods and services that support our quality of life. Energy resources are harnessed to power industries, homes and mobility. Minerals and metals are extracted from the earth's crust and used in the construction of buildings, roads and communications networks. Wood products, pulp and paper are produced from forests. Land, water and soil are used to grow food for human and livestock consumption.

The use of natural resources bears important environmental, economic and social consequences

The use of materials from natural resources in human activities and the associated production and consumption processes have many environmental, economic and social consequences that often extend beyond the borders of individual countries or regions, and that affect future generations. They have consequences on:

- The rate of exploitation and the productivity of **natural resource stocks**.
- The **environmental pressures** associated with the extraction, processing, transport, use and disposal of materials; and their effects on environmental quality, including ecosystem services and human health.
- International **trade and market prices** of raw materials and other goods.
- The **availability of raw materials** and products to support economic activity; and the productivity and the competitiveness of the economy.

The environmental consequences of the use of natural resources and materials occur at different stages of the resource cycle and affect the quantity and quality of natural resource stocks and the quality of ecosystems and environmental media. The type and intensity of these consequences depend on the kind and amounts of natural resources and materials used, the way these resources are used and managed, and the type and location of the natural environment from where they originate.

Natural resources make important contributions to the economy in terms of income and of employment

The extraction of materials from natural resources and their use in human activities make important **direct and indirect contributions** to the economy.

The direct contributions vary from country to country and depend on a number of factors, including a country's natural endowment and economic structure. In 2008, the primary resources sector (forestry, fisheries, agriculture, and mining and quarrying activities, including energy carriers) contributed for example less than 1% to the GDP of Belgium and Luxembourg, but over 30% to that of Norway. The manufacture of finished and semi-finished natural resource-based products and materials, excluding food and agro-food products, (e.g. papermaking, petroleum refining, metal casting and glass production) contributes an additional 2-6% to the economies of OECD countries in terms of GDP.

The natural resources sector is also an important source of **employment** in OECD countries. In 2008, over 30 million people were directly employed in the primary natural resource sectors in OECD member countries, with another 16 million employed in the manufacturing of finished and semi-finished natural resource-based products and materials.[1] This represents between 4 and 16% of total employment in OECD countries. This does not include indirect employment generated by the natural resource sector (i.e. jobs created by natural resource activities, but outside of the sector, such as transportation, engineering and financial services), nor does it cover the entire supply chain. The economic value of the secondary raw materials market has been estimated to represent about 500 billion dollars annually and to provide an income for about 20 million people (Bureau of International Recycling, BIR).

From an economic point of view, the way natural resources are used and managed has consequences (i) on short term costs and long term economic sustainability, (ii) on the supply of strategically important materials, (iii) on the costs associated with the downstream management of materials, and (iv) on the productivity of economic activities and industrial sectors.

Natural resources provide non commercial ecosystem services and social benefits

The importance of natural resources goes beyond satisfying human material needs. Some natural resources play a much larger role in supporting human **wellbeing** and provide important benefits when left in their natural state. As an integral part of the environment, biotic natural resources support the effective functioning of the ecosystem and the provision of **ecosystem services**, including regulating functions (e.g. climate regulation, water purification) and cultural services (i.e. recreation, spiritual, aesthetic) (Millennium Ecosystem Assessment, 2005). Many abiotic natural resources (minerals and metals) are required by plants, animals and humans, for enzyme and metabolic function where either too little (deficiency) or too much (toxicity) can have adverse effects (NRCan, 1997).

NATURAL RESOURCES AND NATURAL CAPITAL

There are important **characteristics** that distinguish natural capital from other forms of capital, such as human and physical capital (OECD, 2008):

Exhaustibility

Natural capital, unlike physical and human capital, cannot be produced by human activity meaning that if depleted or degraded, it is often difficult to replace or restore.

- *Non-renewable resource stocks* cannot be regenerated once exploited or can only be replenished through natural cycles that are relatively long at human scale (e.g. mineral deposits (OECD, 2001). It is important, however, to distinguish between non-renewable resource stocks whose materials are dissipated with consumption (e.g. fossil fuels) and those whose materials have the potential to be recycled (e.g. refined metals).

- *Renewable resource stocks* can regenerate over a relatively short-period of time through natural processes such as fish, freshwater and forests. But their exploitation must take place at a rate that does not compromise the resources' ability to regenerate naturally. If overexploited, renewable resource stocks can be exhausted.

Geographic distribution

Many natural resources are unevenly distributed across countries and regions. Unlike other factors of production that are generally mobile, the distribution of natural resources is geographically determined. For example:

- Nearly 60% of the world's arable land is located in ten countries.[2,3]
- Half of the world's forest area is found in Russia, Brazil, Canada, the United States and China, the world's five largest countries. Ten countries have no forest at all and in another 54 countries forests cover less than 10 % of their total land area. (FAO, 2011).
- Ninety percent of the world's proven oil reserves are found in 15 countries and 99% of all oil reserves are located in 40 countries (WTO, 2010).
- Fifty percent of global reserves of rare earth elements are found in China, over 75% of the world's phosphate rock reserves are located in Morocco and the Western Sahara, and nearly 95% of reserves of platinum group metals are found in South Africa (USGS, 2011).[4]

Trade has helped to alleviate some of these disparities by allowing natural resources to be redistributed from countries with excess supply to countries with limited or no domestic supplies. Many countries that are relatively resource-poor are dependent on imports of natural resources (commodities) to maintain a high quality of life and as inputs into their production processes. Other countries that are relatively resource-rich rely on the export of natural resources as an important source of income. This is particularly true for countries with less diversified export economies[5].

Availability and accessibility

The availability of materials needed to support economic activity depends both on a country's endowment in natural resources and on the accessibility of external sources of material inputs (via imports). The extent to which this availability is a constraint for economic growth depends on the efficiency with which the resources are used and on a country's capacity to innovate and develop new technologies. At international level, the availability of materials is further influenced by their geographical distribution, by worldwide demands and market prices for materials, as well as by political, institutional and regulatory factors. When development relies heavily on a particular resource that is geographically concentrated (such as certain minerals or oil) this can put the supply of that resource to economic activities at risk (e.g. in case of political instability or weak governance, in case of natural or industrial disasters) (OECD 2008).

Externalities and pricing

Natural resources are associated with both positive and negative externalities, resulting in the economic undervaluation of natural capital. When natural resources are used as inputs in the economy, they generate a **commercial return**, which is captured and priced by the market. But natural resources can also generate benefits when left in their natural state (e.g. recreational use of a body of water and ecosystem services from waste assimilation, carbon sequestration, fish habitat and flood control). These indirect or **non-use benefits** are more difficult to value. Non-use values incorporate the concept of "existence values" - values that people attach to a good or service even though he or she does not have (or foresee) any actual, planned or possible use for the food or service himself or herself (OECD, 2011a). Since these non-use benefits cannot be captured, they are not reflected in market prices and even if estimated may have little relationship to the price determined by markets.

The production and consumption of natural resources can have negative spillover effects for the environment, including air and water pollution, waste and pressures on biodiversity and habitats. The market prices of natural resources and materials reflect the cost of their direct use in the economy, but do not incorporate the cost of using other environmental assets (ecosystem services) or changes in the condition of those assets. See also the section on the environmental implications of natural resource use.

THE RESOURCE CYCLE AND THE MATERIALS BALANCE

Inputs from natural stocks

Material resources used in an economy originally stem from raw materials extracted from domestic natural resource stocks or extracted from natural resource stocks abroad and imported in the form of raw materials, semi-finished materials and materials embodied in manufactured goods.

Material resources are extracted from the sub-soil and water bodies, or harvested from forests and farm land. The usable parts of these resources enter the economy as material inputs where they become priced goods that are traded, processed and used. Other parts remain unused in the environment. These materials are called "*unused materials*" or "unused extraction". Examples include mining overburden, soil and rock excavated during construction and not used elsewhere, dredged sediments from harbours, harvest residues.

Outputs from production and consumption

After use in production and consumption activities, materials leave the economy as an output either to the environment in the form of *residuals* (pollution, waste), or to the rest of the world as exports in the form of raw materials, semi-finished materials and materials embodied in manufactured goods.

Accumulation in man-made stocks

Some materials accumulate in the economy where they are stored in the form of buildings, transport infrastructure or durable and semi-durable goods, such as cars, industrial machinery or household appliances. These materials are sooner or later released in the form of demolition waste, end-of-life vehicles, e-waste, bulky household waste, etc., that if not recovered flow back to the environment.

Indirect flows

When materials or goods are imported for use in an economy, their upstream production is associated with *unused materials* that remain abroad, with *raw materials* that were needed to produce the goods, and with the generation of *residuals* (pollution, waste). These "*indirect flows*" of materials take into account the life-cycle dimension of the production chain, but are not physically imported. Their environmental consequences occur in countries from which the imports originate.

Closing the loop

Materials that have accumulated in the economy (buildings, infrastructure, cars, electric and electronic equipment, machinery, etc.) constitute important man-made stocks that can be exploited through recycling to gain secondary raw materials from waste, and through reuse and remanufacturing to keep products in the commercial life-cycle. The same applies to materials that have been accumulating in landfills or in mine containment ponds and that could be recovered in future. These "*urban mines*" offer a potential future source of raw materials for industry.

Box 1.1. Characteristics and values of natural capital and natural resources

Natural capital comprises **natural resource stocks** or assets (i.e. mineral and energy resources, soil resources, water resources, biological resources), **land and ecosystems**. All these resources are considered essential to the long-term sustainability of development for their provision of "functions" and "services" to the economy, as well as to humankind outside the economy and other living beings.

Natural resources are characterised by **three features** that distinguish them from other types of capital:

- Natural resources are not produced.
- If depleted or degraded their natural stocks cannot easily be replaced or restored.
- They form an integral part of larger ecosystems, and their depletion and degradation can lead to environmental degradation and reduced ecosystem services.

Natural resources are commonly divided into **non-renewable and renewable** resources:

- **Non-renewable** natural resources are exhaustible natural resources whose natural stocks cannot be regenerated after exploitation or that can only be regenerated or replenished by natural cycles that are relatively slow at human scale. Examples include metals and other minerals such as industrial and construction minerals, and fossil energy carriers, such as oil.
- **Renewable** natural resources are natural resources that, after exploitation, can return to their previous natural stock levels by natural processes of growth or replenishment. Examples include timber from forest resources, freshwater resources, soil resources, wildlife resources such as fish, agricultural resources. Conditionally renewable resources are those whose exploitation eventually reaches a level beyond which regeneration will become impossible at human scale (e.g. tropical forests).

Their **value** depends both on:

- The **commercial return** from their use as inputs into the production of economic goods and services. These **use values** are generally captured in commercial markets. Most non-renewable resources (fossil fuels, minerals, metallic ores) and certain renewable resources (e.g. timber, agricultural products), once extracted or harvested, become priced goods with market values.
- Environmental, recreational and **other services** they provide. These **non-use values** are generally not captured in markets or are not valued for the full service provided, and their determination is complex.

Functions and services of natural capital (natural resource stocks or assets, land and ecosystems)

Values	*Functions*	*Services*	
Use values	*Resource functions*	*Productive or provisioning services*	Refers to the capacity of natural capital to provide: -- Natural resources (water, energy, and other raw materials including medicinal resources) and space (land) for use as inputs in the economy where they are used in the production of goods and services. Examples are mineral deposits, timber from natural forests, deep sea fish and land. -- Ecosystem inputs, such as water and other natural inputs (e.g. nutrients, carbon dioxide) required by plants and animals for growth, and oxygen and other gases needed for combustion and production processes.
Non-use values	*Sink functions*	*Regulating services*	Refers to the capacity of natural capital to absorb the unwanted by-products of production and consumption and to regulate air, water and soil quality and natural processes. This includes: -- the absorption of pollution and waste, and the sequestration and storage of carbon; -- the provision of flood and disease control, and the moderation of extreme natural events; -- the provision of other functions such as pollination support.
	Service functions	*Supporting services*	Refers to services that underpin almost all other services, i.e., the capacity of natural capital to provide living spaces (habitats) for plants, animals and man, and to maintain biological diversity (genetic diversity). This includes: -- functions that are essential to life, such as the provision of clean air or clean water or protection against UV rays (survival functions).
		Cultural services and amenities	-- functions that are less essential but improve the quality of life, i.e. the non-material benefits that people obtain from contact with ecosystems, for example recreational, aesthetic and leisure benefits (amenity functions), or spiritual and psychological benefits (cultural functions).

Source: Based on OECD (2001) *Sustainable development – Critical issues* ; United Nations *et al.* (2013), *System of Environmental-Economic Accounting - Central Framework*; and on TEEB (2010) *The Economics of Ecosystems and Biodiversity: Mainstreaming the Economics of Nature: A synthesis of the approach, Conclusions and recommendations of TEEB.*

Figure 1.1. Economy-wide material balance and flow scheme

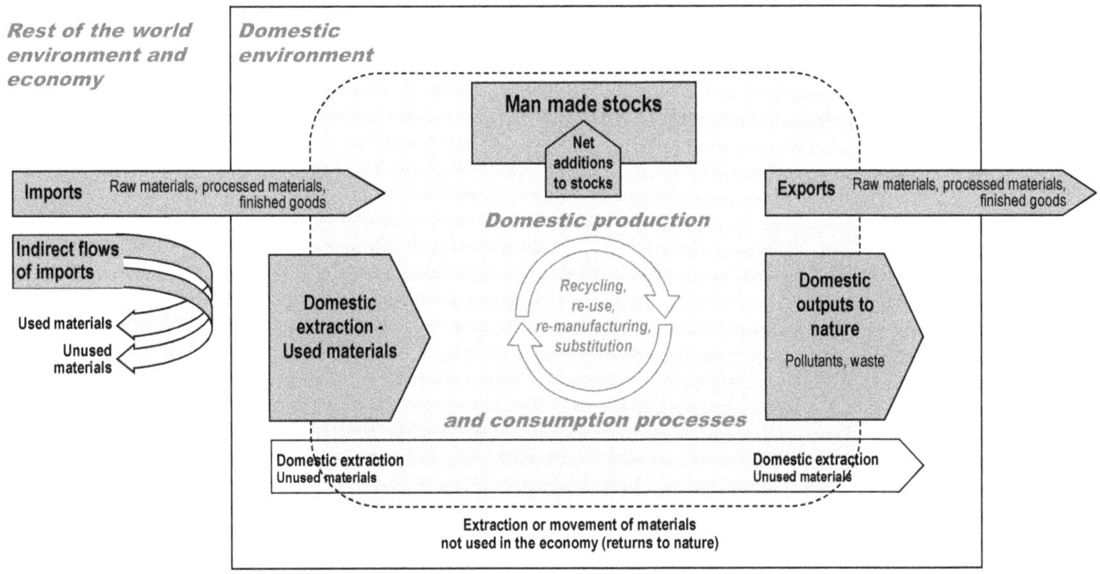

Source: Based on OECD (2008).

Figure 1.2. Flows of materials through the commercial lifecycle

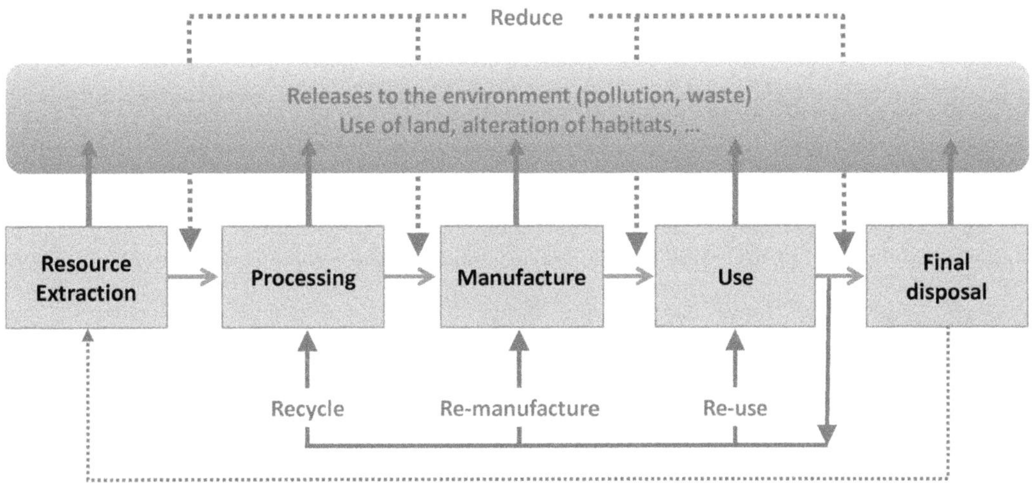

Source: Based on OECD (2008).

THE ENVIRONMENTAL IMPLICATIONS OF RESOURCE USE

Resource use bears important consequences for the environment

The generation of pollution and waste, and alteration of habitats resulting directly or indirectly from the activities related to the extraction and production of material resources have the potential to impair the provision of ecosystem services by altering the environment's natural balance.

Air pollutants produced during industrial processes and released into the environment can disrupt the ecosystems' capacity to regulate air quality. Toxic substances released as waste can accumulate in the environment, posing a risk to human health and to the health of other living organisms. Deforestation due to agriculture and urbanisation reduces the earth's natural carbon sinks and hinders its ability to regulate the climate.

In the case of resources from renewable natural stocks, unsustainable management practices can lead to the resource degradation and depletion, threatening its natural productivity and regenerative capacity (e.g. fisheries, soil nutrients). It can also impair the provision of recreation and non-market ecosystem services.

In the case of resources from non-renewable natural stocks, unsustainable management practices can lead to excessive resource depletion and supply disruptions in the longer term and increase environmental pressures associated with their extraction and economic use. Absent other factors such as improvements in technology or the discovery of new deposits, depletion will reduce the environmental and economic productivity of the resource, as lower cost stocks are typically extracted first (i.e. higher-grade ores). Lower quality stocks often require more energy to extract and process, resulting in increased environmental pressures (e.g. greenhouse gas emissions, air pollution, waste).

Box 1.2. Resource use and environmental sustainability

The OECD has defined four criteria for "environmental sustainability" that are in many respects relevant to material flows and resource productivity.

Regeneration: Renewable resources shall be used efficiently and their use shall not be permitted to exceed their long-term rates of natural regeneration.

Substitutability: Non-renewable resources shall be used efficiently and their use limited to levels which can be offset by substitution by renewable resources or other forms of capital.

Assimilation: Releases of hazardous or polluting substances to the environment shall not exceed its assimilative capacity;

Avoiding Irreversibility: Irreversible adverse effects of human activities on ecosystems and on biogeochemical and hydrological cycles shall be avoided. The natural processes capable of maintaining or restoring the integrity of ecosystems should be safeguarded.

Source: OECD (2001), OECD Environmental Strategy for the first decade of the Twenty First Century.

The environmental consequences of resource use vary by type of materials

Material resources have different characteristics and the activities associated with their extraction, management and use have different potential environmental impacts.

Mining can have a number of environmental effects, both at operational sites and beyond them. These effects include air and water pollution, waste generation and pressures on biodiversity and wildlife habitats. Mining and refining mined ores into metal is also often energy and water-intensive (see *Part II*, factsheets on aluminium, copper, and iron and steel).

The environmental effects of **oil and gas exploitation** include pollution at the extraction sites and during transportation, and habitat disruption. The combustion of fossil fuels to generate energy produces carbon dioxide emissions that account for more than half of total made-man greenhouse gas (GHG) emissions (UNEP, 2010b). Non-energy uses of fossil energy carriers in (e.g. plastics, chemicals) have a very different set of environmental implications often related to waste and toxics management.

The **production of biomass** for food and feed can contribute to the loss of habitat and biodiversity. Unsustainable agricultural practices can result in soil degradation if mineral content is not replenished. The environmental impacts of marine fishing include by-catches (marine mammals, birds and non-commercial fish species), damage to ocean and sea floors, and waste and pollution. Aquaculture can reduce some of the pressure on marine fisheries, but it can also contribute to sedimentation and water pollution and can have negative impacts on wild fisheries from their use as sources of seed and feed inputs for fish farms (OECD, 2001 and 2011b).

Unsustainable **forest management** can contribute to increased soil erosion, habitat destruction and loss of biodiversity. Forests improve water and soil quality by filtering airborne pollutants and enriching soil. They act as carbon sinks and temperature buffers, providing climate change mitigation and adaptation mechanisms. The production of pulp and paper from wood fibre is water and energy intensive (IEA, 2008) (see *Part 3*, factsheet on paper for further detail).

The environmental consequences of resource use vary by material properties

The **physical and chemical properties** of the material are also important. When analysing material flows, a distinction is commonly made between **toxic and bulk flows** (OECD, 2008b). Toxic flows are associated with certain industrial raw materials or substances, such as mercury, lead, and plastics, which have very specific potential environmental impacts stemming from their toxic properties. Although used in relatively small amounts, if allowed to accumulate in the environment, these materials can have significant damage to human and ecosystem health (e.g. mercury, pesticides). Other materials, though non-toxic and with low environmental impacts per unit mass, flow in large volumes through the economy (so-called bulk flows) that the cumulated potential environmental impacts of this group of materials can be very high (e.g. fossil energy carriers, agricultural biomass, construction minerals).

The environmental consequences of resource use vary throughout the resource lifecycle

Each stage of the resource cycle – from extraction to end of life – carries its own, often differing, environmental implications which also vary by the type of resource:

- The extraction (or harvesting) of raw materials generally requires energy and water, generating pollution and waste, and often permanently or temporarily altering the surrounding habitat. The type and magnitude of these pressures depends on the extraction or harvest rate, the reserves or available stocks of the resource, and technology and management practices.
- The processing and consumption stages generate pollution and waste, both processing-related and accidental. The type and magnitude of these pressures depend heavily on management practices and technology, on the level of compliance and enforcement and on consumer behaviour and consumption patterns.
- There is also potential for negative environmental impacts during transportation, including accidents or leakages, such as oil spills. Transport fuel consumption also generates atmospheric emissions, which can contribute to air pollution and climate change. The type and magnitude of

the potential environmental impacts of transportation depend on a number of factors, including mode of transport, regulatory regime and level of compliance, distance travelled and weight of the material.

- The environmental implications associated with the post-consumption stage depend on what happens to the product at the end of its life. Some materials are recycled, re-entering the economy as secondary production (e.g. glass, paper and metals such as steel, copper and aluminium), whereas other materials are disposed of based on prevailing waste management practices and may get lost for the economy.
- The environmental consequences of resource use extend beyond borders.
- Impacts can be widely distributed geographically if resources are traded internationally, either in the form of raw materials or the products embodying them. Most environmental pressures associated with natural resource extraction (e.g. habitat alteration, waste) remain in the country of extraction, but some impacts, such as air pollutants and greenhouse gas emissions have implications that do not respect borders. When resources are exported, other environmental pressures occur in the countries where resources are transformed into materials or products and where those same materials and products are disposed.

Figure 1.3. Schematic presentation of materials flows, environmental impacts and policies

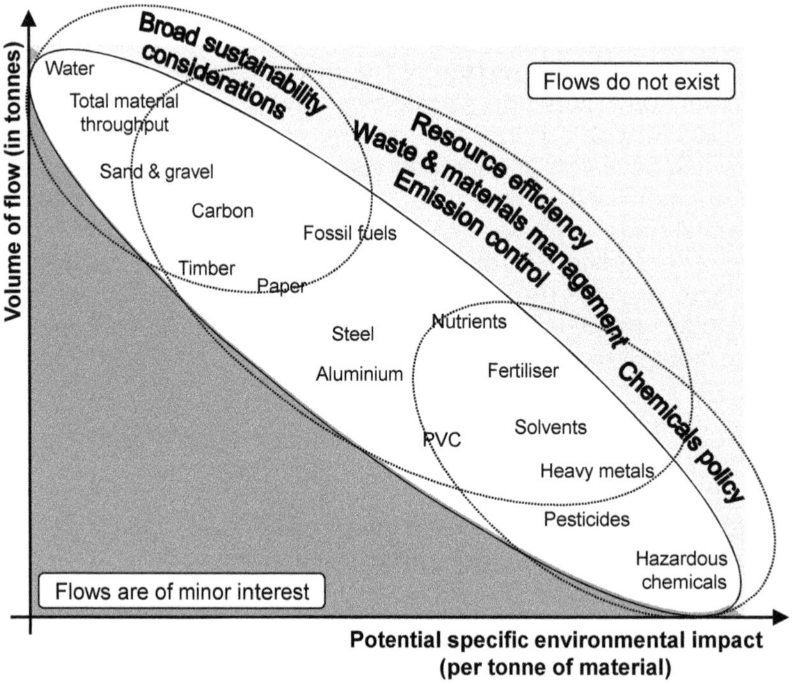

Source: OECD (2008).

Table 1.1. Potential environmental impacts by material group

Material Group	Potential Environmental Impacts
Biomass for food and feed	Intensification of land use, soil degradation, groundwater contamination, disintegration of nutrient cycles, food chain contamination through pesticides, acidification, loss of biodiversity, habitat loss, water use *Specifically associated with biomass from pastures*: eutrophication, overgrazing, bush encroachment, methane gas emissions *Specifically associated with fish:* overexploitation of natural stocks, biodiversity loss, marine pollution
Wood	Intensification of land use, soil erosion, loss of biodiversity, forest degradation, habitat alteration, carbon sink depletion, desertification, alteration of watersheds
Metals and metal ores	Resource availability, entropy, toxicity, habitat alteration, mining overburden, air emissions, water usage, tailings, radioactivity
Fossil energy carriers	Resource availability, air pollutants, carbon dioxide emissions, habitat alteration, overburden, toxic chemicals for processing, water usage
Industrial minerals	Resource availability, entropy, toxicity, habitat alteration, mining overburden, air emissions, waste water, tailings
Construction minerals	Loss of biodiversity, habitat alteration, soil compaction, carbon dioxide emissions (e.g. cement manufacturing), transport intensity, sealing of land area, soil compaction

Source: Based on OECD (2008).

Prioritising environmental pressures

Given the consumption and use of virtually every raw material is associated with a range of environmental impacts, where should attention be focused?

The International Panel for Sustainable Resource Management of the United Nations Environment Program (International Resource Panel) addressed this question in a report assessing the environmental impacts of consumption and production (see UNEP, 2010a). The Resource Panel examined economic activities from three perspectives: production, consumption and material groups, and identified six priority pressures on natural resources and the environment:

- Three impacts are associated with ***emissions***: (1) climate change and greenhouse gas emissions; (2) eutrophication of water bodies due to excess nitrogen and phosphorus from fertilizers; and (3) human and eco-toxic effects caused by air pollution and other toxic emissions.
- Three impacts are associated with the use of ***resources:*** (4) the depletion of non-renewable primary resources, metallic minerals and fossil energy carriers in particular; (5) degradation of renewable resources, notably fisheries and forests; and (6) the alteration of habitat and resource competition stemming from land and water use.

Consistent with the International Resource Panel's assessment of priority materials, this report places specific emphasis on the use of materials that are associated with one or more of the priority pressures, such as metals (aluminium, iron and steel, among others), materials that can contribute to eutrophication (phosphate rock), materials used in consumer electronics and appliances (rare earth elements, copper, steel), and energy and water-intensive materials (aluminium, paper).

Table 1.2. Summary of the UNEP Resource Panel's Assessment of the Environmental Impacts of Consumption and Production

Main Environmental Pressures	Production Perspective	Consumption Perspective	Priority Materials
Which environmental and resource pressures need to be considered in the prioritisation of products and materials?	*Which production processes contribute most to environmental pressures and impacts?*	*Which products and consumption categories have the greatest impacts across their life cycle?*	*Which materials have the greatest impacts across their life cycle?*
• Climate change • Eutrophication • Human and ecotoxic effects • Depletion of non-renewable resources • Degradation of renewable resources • Habitat change and resource competition	• Production processes involving fossil fuels combustion • Agriculture and biomass using activities • Fisheries	• Household consumption: o Food o Housing o Mobility o Manufactured products (particularly electrical appliances) • Government consumption and capital expenditure • Imports and exports	• Fossil fuels • Agricultural biomass (especially animal products) • Metals (specifically iron, steel and aluminium)

Source: Adapted from UNEP (2010).

ENDNOTES

1 Based on ISIC rev. 3 classification of economies activities. Primary natural resources sectors include: A – agriculture, hunting and forestry; B- fishing, and C – mining and quarrying. Natural resources manufacturing sectors include: D20 - Manufacture of wood and of products of wood and cork, except furniture; manufacture of articles of straw and plaiting materials; D21 - Manufacture of paper and paper products; D23 - Manufacture of coke, refined petroleum products and nuclear fuel; D26 - Manufacture of other non-metallic mineral products; D27 - Manufacture of basic metals; D28 - Manufacture of fabricated metal products, except machinery and equipment. Data is from OECD STAN database, supplemented by the International Labour Organisation's Laborstat database.

2 Arable land includes land defined by the United Nations Food and Agriculture Organisation (FAO) as land under temporary crops (double-cropped areas are counted once), temporary meadows for mowing or for pasture, land under market or kitchen gardens, and land temporarily fallow. Land abandoned as a result of shifting cultivation is excluded.

3 Based on data from the World Bank's World Development Indicators database (accessed 16 December 2010).

4 The platinum group metals are: platinum, palladium, rhodium, ruthenium, iridium, osmium.

5 In Angola, Iraq, Bolivia, Sudan, Nigeria, Yemen, and Libya natural resources make up over 90% of merchandise exports in monetary terms (WTO, 2010).

REFERENCES

- EEA (European Environment Agency) (2010), The European Environment: State and Outlook 2010 –Material Resources and Waste, *http://www.eea.europa.eu/soer/europe/material-resources-and-waste.*
- *European* Commission, Resource Efficiency, *http://ec.europa.eu/environment/resource_efficiency/about/index_en.htm*
- European Commission, Sustainable use of natural resources, *http://ec.europa.eu/environment/natres/index.htm* .
- OECD (2014), *Green Growth Indicators 2014*, OECD Green Growth Studies, OECD Publishing, Paris, *http://dx.doi.org/10.1787/9789264202030-en.*
- OECD (2011), "Resource Productivity in the G8 and OECD: A Report in the Framework of the Kobe 3R Action Plan", OECD, *http://www.oecd.org/document/14/0,3746,en_2649_34395_47926478_1_1_1_1,00.html.*
- *OECD* (2011), *Towards Green Growth: Monitoring Progress: OECD Indicators*, OECD Green Growth Studies, OECD Publishing, Paris, *http://dx.doi.org/10.1787/9789264111356-en.*
- OECD (2008), *Measuring Material Flows and Resource Productivity.* http://*www.oecd.org/environment/resourceefficiency.*
- *OECD* (2001), *Sustainable development: Critical issues,* OECD Publishing, Paris, *http://dx.doi.org/10.1787/9789264193185-en.*
- OECD work on Green Growth, *http://www.oecd.org/greengrowth/gg-sd-2012.htm.*
- OECD project on measuring economic performance and social progress, *http://www.oecd.org/statistics/measuring-economic-social-progress/aboutthehigh-levelexpertgroup.htm.*
- TEEB (2010) The Economics of Ecosystems and Biodiversity: Mainstreaming the Economics of Nature: A synthesis of the approach, Conclusions and recommendations of TEEB.
- United Nations et al. (2013), System of Environmental-Economic Accounting - Central Framework, New York.
- UNEP (United Nations Environment Programme) (2013), *International Resource Panel. http://www.unep.org/resourcepanel.*
- UNEP (2010a), *Assessing the Environmental Impacts of Consumption and Production: Priority Products and Materials, A Report of the Working Group on the Environmental Impacts of Products and Materials to the International Panel for Sustainable Resource Management.* Hertwich, E., van der Voet, E., Suh, S., Tukker, A., Huijbregts M., Kazmierczyk, P., Lenzen, M., McNeely, J., Moriguchi, Y., UNEP, Paris.
- WTO (2010), *World Trade Report 2010: Trade in Natural Resources*, WTO Secretariat, Geneva.

Chapter 2. An evolving economic context and new environmental challenges

The last decades have witnessed unprecedented growth in demands for raw materials worldwide, driven in particular by the rapid industrialisation of emerging economies and continued high levels of material consumption in developed countries. At the same time, international commodity markets have expanded, with increasing international trade flows, and increasing mobility and fragmentation of production. This has been accompanied by increases in, and volatility of, commodity prices, and by growing competition for selected raw materials.

These developments have implications for the ways in which natural resources are supplied to and used in the economy. Hence, natural resource consumption and the economic efficiency of materials use have become important issues, and the nature of the environmental challenges with which governments are confronted has changed.

RISING DEMAND FOR NATURAL RESOURCES AND COMMODITIES

Demand for material resources has accelerated over the last decade

The last century has witnessed strong growth in the use of natural resources worldwide. Growth in demand has been virtually continuous with only a few instances of stagnation coinciding with periods of global economic downturn – the economic crisis of the 1930s, two World Wars, the oil price shocks of the 1970s – revealing the strong link between resource use and economic development. In the last 10 to 20 years there has been a marked acceleration in the demand, spurred by the rapid industrialisation in the large emerging economies.

Metals

The production of **major industrial metals** has risen particularly rapidly over the past 30 years, although with important differences between different metals. Between 1980 and 2010 the production of aluminium rose by 170%, copper production by 125% and the production of steel, zinc and nickel by around 100%. With the exception of copper, all of these metals saw the strongest growth in production in the last decade. Conversely, the production of lead and tin grew more modestly.

Fossil energy carriers

The production of **coal and natural gas** has doubled since 1980. Natural gas production has been trending steadily upward since the 1970s. Coal production grew steadily until the 1990s then remained flat until the beginning of the 2000s when it began to expand at an accelerated rate. Although concerns over coal's high carbon content and CO_2 emissions have lead to declining consumption in some developed countries, coal's abundance and low costs make it a fuel of choice in other countries particularly in light of the increasing price of oil.

Compared to coal and natural gas, the production of **crude oil** and NGL has grown relatively modestly; global production increased by 35% between 1980 and 2012. Energy consumption varies significantly around the world. A person living in an OECD country consumes on average more than 3.4 tonnes of oil equivalent (toe) per year compared to less than 0.9 toe per person in low-income regions (Africa and parts of Asia and Latin America) (OECD, 2011d).

Wood

Global harvesting of **wood** decreased in the 1990s, but has since returned to previous levels – 3.4 million cubic metres per year globally (FAO, 2010b).[1] Over two-thirds of wood harvesting takes place in OECD countries. However, most of the loss of forest continues to occur in countries and areas in the tropical regions.

Food

Food production has also been growing, expanding at a rate faster than the world's population. Global **fish** production reached 156 million tonnes in 2011 (FAO, 2012a). Capture fisheries continue to provide the largest share of fish supply (94.5 million tonnes in 2011), but most of the growth in global fish production has come from fish farming, which increased at an annual rate of 7.4% between 1990 and 2011 (compared to 0.5% for capture fisheries). Over the last decade the production of **cereals and meat** expanded by over 2% per year while the global population increased by 1.3% annual. Since 1980 meat production has more than doubled while cereal production has risen by 64%.

A CHANGING GEOGRAPHY OF DEMAND AND SUPPLY

Material resources represent an important and growing share of international trade

The globalisation of resource consumption has increased with the expansion of international trade over the last century. Important improvements in transportation technology, which dramatically reduced the costs of shipping, and the liberalisation of natural resource markets contributed to a massive expansion in the volume and range of raw materials traded internationally.

Today almost every commodity is being traded internationally, allowing countries with limited natural stocks to benefit from the use of these materials. The proximity of natural resource supplies is not as important today as it was a century ago, freeing up industries to establish themselves in the most cost-efficient locations (e.g. aluminium refineries in Iceland and the Middle East) and accelerating the trend towards international specialisation (i.e. as resource suppliers or demanders) (WTO, 2010).

In 2012, the dollar **value** of global trade in raw, semi-finished and finished materials reached USD 3.6 trillion, a more than 4-fold increase from the beginning of decade.[2] The value of global trade in these materials has been growing faster than manufactured goods, increasing their share of total trade from 8% to 17% from 2000 to 2012; however, manufactured goods continue to dominate world merchandise trade in dollar terms.[3]

Looking at trade flows in terms of **weight** rather than dollar value reveals that much of the growth in the monetary value of trade in materials over the last decade has been driven by prices as opposed to increased physical trade volumes. The weight of global trade in raw, semi-finished and finished materials reached an estimated 6.3 billion tonnes in 2012, a 60% increase relative to 2000 (compared to a 360% increase in terms of monetary value).[4] While the value of material trade contracted by a third in 2009, the weight of trade decreased more modestly (-10%).

In 2008, **OECD** countries accounted for half of the world's exports of raw materials, semi-finished and finished products, **BRIICS** countries represented roughly 30% and the rest of the world the remaining 20%.

For OECD countries, intra-regional trade is significant – in 2012 roughly 60% of all materials exported by OECD countries were to other member countries. However, intra-OECD trade has been declining in favour of increased exports to BRIICS countries. The global financial crisis, which contracted consumer demand in many OECD countries, amplified this trend. Between 2000 and 2012, the weight of intra-OECD trade declined from 76% to 58% of total OECD country exports. Exports to BRIICS countries more than quadrupled, increasing from 7% to 26% of total OECD material exports.

Figure 2.1. Trade in selected raw, semi-finished and finished materials, by region and by material groups, 2000-2012

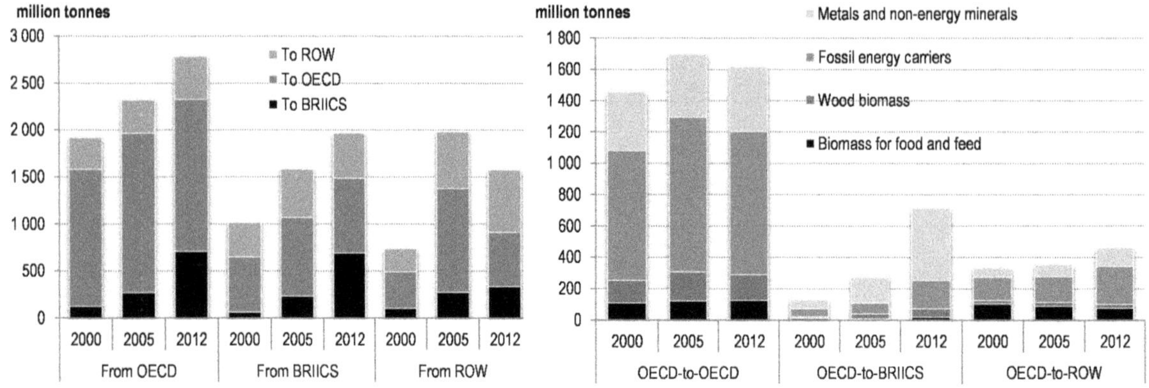

Notes: For definition of raw, semi finished and finished products see footnote 2.
Source: OECD based on UN COMTRADE.

Box 2.1. Is trade good or bad for the environment?

The expansion of international trade has both positive and negative implications for the environment. Trade liberalisation can allow for more efficient use of resources in one country, but can also exacerbate resource extraction in other countries. For example, increased Chinese imports of timber relieves pressures on the country's forests; on the other hand, China's huge demand for raw materials is putting more pressure on exporting countries, and can result in overall negative impacts. Trade also facilitates the dissemination and development of environmental goods, services and technologies, as well as the substitution of materials, which can help mitigate negative environmental externalities For example, through trade, countries primarily reliant on oil or coal for energy production can gain access to cleaner burning natural gas imports. A growing number of regional trade agreements include environmental provisions (most commonly environmental co-operation mechanisms and standards).

Source: Adapted from World Bank (2010) and OECD (2008c).

Demand is shifting from developed to developing and emerging economies

Demand for raw materials has been historically driven by the economies of the United States, Europe and Japan – traditionally the largest consumers of the world's raw materials. But rapid economic growth in the emerging and developing economies over the last decade has shifted global demand for material resources. This is particularly true for **non-renewable resources** that are integral to industrial development (i.e. fossil energy carriers and metals).

Between 2000 and 2012 OECD economies grew on average by 1.5% annually (GDP 2005 USD PPP) while the BRIICS economies expanded by nearly 7% per year, led by China, India, Indonesia and Russia. China surpassed the United States as the world's largest consumer of metals. Between 2000 and 2008, China's consumption of metals like aluminium, copper, lead, nickel, tin, and zinc grew on average by around 15% a year, while in the rest of the world demand for metals grew by less than 1% annually (World Bank, 2010b). China is also now the second largest consumer of energy behind the United States. India is the fourth.

But this shift in demand is not isolated to non-renewable resources. Rising incomes and increased urbanisation in the large emerging economies and population growth in less developed countries are contributing to an unprecedented expansion of **global food markets** and a change in global **dietary patterns**. Demand for animal protein, especially from meat, milk, eggs and fish products, is rising while the share of basic cereals (except rice) is decreasing. Annual global per capita consumption of meat almost doubled in the period 1961–2011, rising from 23 kg to 42 kg (FAOSTAT), with growth led by the rapidly industrialising emerging economies and less developed countries. As dietary habits are fairly established in developed countries and protein levels already saturated, growth in food demand is expected to continue to be led by emerging and developing economies.

Many OECD countries continue to feel the lingering effects of the crisis and real GDP growth is modest – 2.3% in 2011, 2.8% in 2012 and 1.3% in 2013. As a result, growth in demand for raw materials continues to be fuelled by economic expansion in the BRIICS countries, led by the Chinese economy which grew by 9.0% in 2011 followed by India (8.5%) and Indonesia (6.6%).

The last decade has witnessed sharp increases and volatility of commodity prices

Growing demand for raw materials began to propel **commodity prices** sharply upward starting in the early 2000s, with some commodity prices reaching record highs in 2008 prior to the financial crisis. Between 2000 and 2010 the price of minerals and metals increased by 12% annually on average and crude oil prices increased by 10% a year compared to annual growth rates of 4.5% for minerals and metals and 7.6% for crude oil since 1960 (when expressed at current prices).[5] Similarly the price of food and non-food agricultural raw materials rose more rapidly over the last decade (over 8% annually) than over the last 40 years (3% annually) The strong upward trend broke with the 2008 financial crisis, but prices of many commodities have since rebounded and remain at historically elevated levels. However, in real terms, the prices of many raw materials – with the exception of crude oil – remain well below peaks reached in the early 1970s.

Fluctuations and volatility in the market prices of raw materials have a number of important **environmental implications**. Manufacturing, mining and agriculture are typically more responsive to demand and supply shocks, while non-financial services are less so. Swings in economic activity are thus likely to be more correlated with swings in environmental pressures when countries are orientated towards energy-intensive manufacturing and resource-intensive primary sectors (OECD 2011).

Figure 2.2. Commodity prices, world price index, 1990-2012

Index 1990-100

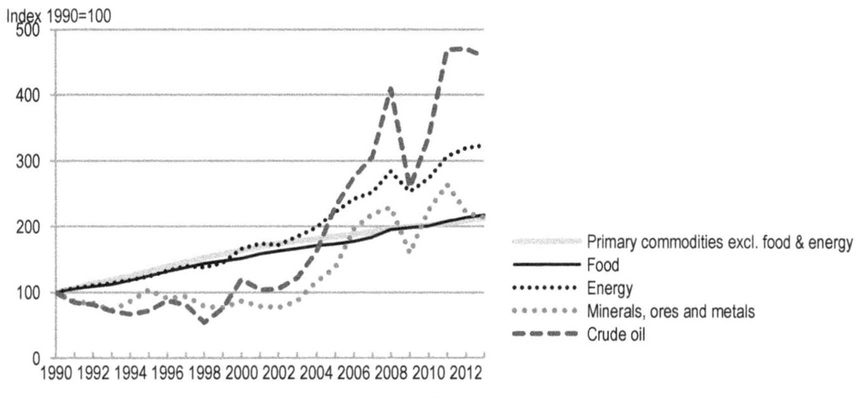

Source: OECD Main Economic Indicators, *http://dx.doi.org/10.1787/mei-data-en*

Higher prices for raw materials increase the cost of production; this can encourage greater efficiency in the use of more expensive materials and the development of more cost effective substitutes. Changes in the prices of primary commodities also alter the relative costs of recycling and secondary production. Rising copper prices have led to higher prices for secondary copper and increasing instances of copper theft from rail lines, telephone lines, electrical substations, highway infrastructure and residential homes.

Fluctuations in the prices of raw materials can also have **socio-economic consequences**. Increases in raw material prices are often passed directly onto consumers, particularly for food and energy where demand is fairly inelastic. Also for resource-based export economies, lower resource prices mean decreased export earnings.

NEW ENVIRONMENTAL CHALLENGES AND POLICY DIRECTIONS

These developments have implications for the ways in which natural resources are supplied to and used in the economy. Hence, natural resource consumption and the economic efficiency of materials use have become important issues, and the nature of the environmental challenges with which governments are confronted has changed. This influences the policies put in place in many countries.

The nature of the environmental implications of resource use has evolved

The extraction of resources was once primarily viewed of as a **local** issue, with the most immediate environmental impacts occurring around the area of extraction. Climate change, air and water pollution, and loss of biodiversity have broadened the scope of environmental policies issues. Today the environmental consequences of resource use extend well beyond national orders and many are **global** in nature (e.g. climate change).

The environmental burden is shifting between regions with potential displacement effects to emerging economies

The **expansion of international trade** in raw materials over the last century has added an important new dimension, changing the nature of the environmental implications of their use and raising concerns regarding the distribution of **environmental impacts**. Associated with trade and foreign investment are changes in the international chain of value-added and a trend towards greater specialisation. The stages of the material life cycle have thus become '**displaced**'. Today the extraction, production, consumption, and recycling and/or final disposal of a material often take place at great distances from one another and/or in completely different countries. This process has allowed companies to take advantage of costs savings by outsourcing to countries where the necessary factors of production are plentiful and cheaper (e.g. labour, energy, land). This process has also displaced the potential environmental impacts associated with each stage of the material life cycle, shifting the environmental burden between regions of the world.

Resource exploration and extraction are moving afield

At the same time, **resource extraction has grown** to meet ever-increasing demand for raw materials. Projects are increasing in size while exploration and harvesting activities are **moving farther afield** (e.g. high seas fisheries, seafloor mining, Arctic oil and gas exploration). Moving extraction into these new environments poses new challenges. The rights to the resources in these areas are sometimes not yet well defined (e.g. outer continental shelf) leading to international disputes or tensions. Our scientific knowledge of the ecology of these less developed areas is also often limited.

FROM WASTE TO RESOURCES: CLOSING THE MATERIAL CYCLE

Growing material use is raising waste management issues
Many valuable materials get lost for the economy when disposed of as waste

With rising global demand for raw materials and economic growth, the **amount of waste** generated by economic activity is growing. Waste can be generated at any stage of the material cycle – during the extraction of raw materials, in the processing of raw materials into intermediate or final products, during the consumption of final products or post-consumption when the product is recycled or disposed of. The amount and composition of waste generated depends on a number of factors, including production processes, consumption patterns, waste and materials management approaches, population growth and wealth.

Waste management is also a resource management issue. Many **valuable materials** are disposed of as waste, or in waste, and are **potentially lost to the economy**. This is particularly true for e-waste (electric and electronic waste) as modern electronics can contain up to 60 different elements, including precious and special metals (UNEP, 2009). E-waste is creating an increasingly important management challenge in both developed and developing countries. Markets in electronic equipment change rapidly and the useful life of such appliances is constantly shrinking, resulting in an exponential growth in e-waste. Globally, some 50 million tonnes of e-waste are estimated to be generated every year[6]. This represents an important source of secondary raw materials for industry.

Despite renewed focus, recycling rates for key materials remain low

Reducing the waste of raw materials, reusing products and recycling materials contained in waste can reduce pressure on landfills, virgin stocks of resources and the environment by reducing waste and saving both energy and water.

International initiatives, such as the 2008 G8 Kobe **3R Action Plan**, as well as a variety of policies and programmes by national, sub-national and municipal governments (e.g. public collection schemes, deposit-refund systems, take-back programs, product standards on minimum standards of recycled content, and bans), the private sector (e.g. take-back programs, cradle-to-cradle product design, recycling targets) and non-governmental organisations (e.g. charitable collection programs), have been put in place to encourage the 3Rs.

Some materials and products have already experienced considerable **success in terms of recovery,** recycling and re-use rates, such as glass, beverage containers, automobiles, lead-acid batteries, paper and paperboard, and waste recycling rates continue to improve in OECD countries. However, recycling **rates for some key materials remain low**, particularly specialty metals used in a wide variety of emerging technologies (UNEP, 2011b).

Increasing recycling is not always straightforward. The amount of materials and products being recycled depends on the existence of well functioning recycling markets. The growth of markets for recyclable materials faces a number of challenges:

- Predicting how much recyclable material will be available, where and when, is difficult, since it is by its very nature the by-product of other decisions. The life-span of end-uses, the rate of in-use dissipation, the efficiency of collection and recycling processes, and commodity prices, all affect the development of secondary material markets.
- Product design determines the ease, and hence cost, with which scrap can be recovered. Both products and materials are becoming increasingly complex, driving up the costs of recovering recyclable materials and often times making it prohibitively expensive (e.g. post-consumer electronics, plastics).

- Post-consumer scrap is of variable quality and can contain impurities and contaminants, including substances that could be hazardous if handled improperly. As a result, secondary producers must incur additional costs to sort, clean and purify recovered scrap.

Recycling and re-use may not always be the most appropriate option in terms of reducing environmental impacts. As with primary production, the environmental implications of secondary (recycled) production need to be considered from a **life cycle perspective**. Although recycled production often requires less energy, water and other raw material inputs than production from virgin materials, the collection and transportation of recovered materials to recycling facilities may result in greater transportation fuel consumption. Keeping or reusing electric appliances helps to reduce pressure on virgin materials, but older appliances are typically less energy efficient than newer models and may consume more energy over their lifetime.

The rationale for end of life recycling also depends on local conditions that determine the access to recycling infrastructure and the availability of appropriate technologies, which change and improve over time. In some cases improving the quality of the separating and sorting stages of the recycling process helps increase recovery of materials embodied in products, particularly in complex consumer appliances (e.g. platinum in notebooks) and reduce harmful chemicals involved in the treatment processes (e.g. when separating ink from paper).

Technology development and innovation

Technology offers opportunities for improved resource productivity …

Technology and innovation play important roles in improving resource productivity and mitigating the negative environmental impacts of resource use and material consumption. Their role is complex, with the power to alter both supply and demand for primary and secondary raw materials.

More **efficient extraction and production** processes can reduce waste and alleviate pressure on natural stocks, as can improvements in the **recyclability, re-usability and substitutability** of materials and products. In addition to increasing the supply of materials for recycling, advances in geological science and technology can lead to the discovery of new resource stocks and unlock stocks whose extraction was previously considered unfeasible for technical or economic reasons (e.g. unconventional gas, bitumen, sea floor mining, deepwater offshore oil and gas).

… and presents new challenges

How we use resources and materials evolves over time with developments in science and technology. Many new technologies have the potential to generate additional **environmental pressures** or to **strain material availability**. New technologies frequently involve the use of new materials or the substitution of materials and the consequences of using these new materials need to be known.

Materials can fall in and out of favour with the products that embody them, making long-term demand predictions challenging. For example, new insights from medical science, particularly with regard to the human health effects of some substances (e.g. BPA, asbestos, cadmium, PCBs), can reduce their demand. Concerns regarding climate change are increasing demand for certain materials, such as those used in energy efficiency and renewable energy technologies (e.g. lithium in rechargeable batteries, platinum in fuel cells, rare earth elements in LED light bulbs and wind turbines, aluminium in automobiles to improve fuel efficiency, biomass for biofuels).

New products and applications, and their increasing complexity, also bring new environmental considerations, many of which relate to waste management and recycling (e.g. e-waste, plastics, compact fluorescent light bulbs, portable batteries), others to air pollution and chemical safety. Environmental and product standards have a role in influencing the material composition and recyclability of new products. All these externalities and their consequences need to be understood and addressed.

Consumption patterns and consumer behaviour

Attention is shifting to consumption-based approaches

In 2010, each person on earth directly and indirectly consumed approximately 29 kg of material resources each day (SERI/WU material flows database). But how much we each actually consume varies significantly between countries and regions of the world. Developed countries consume significantly more on a per capita basis than less developed countries. Per capita consumption in OECD member countries is nearly 60% above the global average. There is also wide variation among OECD member countries, ranging from over 100 kg per person per day in resource-rich exporting countries to an average 38 kg in the OECD Europe region.

The decisions made by individual consumers on how, what, and how much to consume can support sustainable resource use. In many countries household consumption accounts for 60% or more of the environmental impacts associated with final consumption (UNEP, 2010b). In industrialised countries, housing, mobility, food and manufactured products determine about 70% of the impacts of household consumption, while in developing and emerging economies, consumption related to food and housing is responsible for most of the impact, while mobility is less of a factor.

Consumption patterns are complex and changing consumer behaviour is challenging. The consumption of one product is often linked to the consumption of other products, or determined by history or national circumstance.

ENDNOTES

1 According to the FAO (2010b) the figure is "undoubtedly higher" considering that informally and illegally removed wood is not captured. Wood fuel is the most commonly under-reported category. Wood fuel accounts for about half of the wood removed globally.

2 Data based on OECD analysis of UN COMTRADE data. Trade is measured as one-way trade (i.e. exports). The sample includes 178 countries. "Raw, semi-finished and finished products" are defined materials and products falling under the following broad material categories: cereals, wood, paper, fish, meat, dairy, fossil fuels, ferrous and non-ferrous metals and phosphates as well as products mainly derived from these materials. This list corresponds largely with the material categories outlined in Eurostat's questionnaire on economy-wide material flow accounts, with the exception of non-metallic, non-energy minerals and some types of food biomass (e.g. fruits, vegetables). Save for phosphate rock, non-metallic minerals are rarely traded between countries and their inclusion/exclusion is not expected to materially influence trade flows (when expressed in terms of weight or volume).
(*http://epp.eurostat.ec.europa.eu/portal/page/portal/environmental_accounts/methodology/data_collections*)

3 These findings are consistent with World Bank (2010), which found that in the decade prior to the global economic and financial crisis, the value of global trade in natural resources had been growing 20% annually, rising from USD 0.6 trillion in 1998 to 3.7 trillion in 2008 and increasing its share of total trade from 11% to 24% over the time period. Results from the OECD's analysis differ from World Bank results due to differing definitions of natural resources. The World Bank defines natural resources as including the following product groups according to revision 3 of the Standard International Trade Classification (SITC): fish (division 03); raw hides, skins and fur skins (21); crude rubber (23); cork and wood (24); wood pulp (25); textile fibres (26); crude animal and vegetable materials, n.e.s. (29); Crude fertilizers, other than those of division 56, and crude minerals, excluding coal, petroleum and precious stones (27); metalliferous ores and metal scrap (28).

4 Figures have been estimated using physical trade volume data (i.e. weight) from the UN Commodity Trade Statistics Database (Comtrade). Although Comtrade is regarded as the most comprehensive source of information on international trade flows, physical trade volume data are incomplete. Our analysis found coverage fairly complete for OECD and BRIICS countries (over 95% from 2000-2009), but significantly lower for other countries (around 40% of weight values are missing between 2000 and 2009). OECD and BRIICS countries account for the bulk of world trade so coverage of trade flows overall is expected to be fairly complete, except for certain materials such as phosphate rock and tin where other countries are important global suppliers.

5 Price of metals and minerals: annual price index for minerals, metals and ores calculated by UNCTAD. Price of crude petroleum: average of UK Brent (light), Dubai (medium), and Texas (heavy) equally weighted USD/barrel.

6 *www.step-initiative.org/index.php/overview-world.html*

REFERENCES

- EEA (European Environment Agency) (2010), The European Environment: State and Outlook 2010 –Material Resources and Waste. www.eea.europa.eu/soer/europe/material-resources-and-waste.
- OECD (2014), *Green Growth Indicators 2014*, OECD Green Growth Studies, OECD Publishing, Paris, *http://dx.doi.org/10.1787/9789264202030-en.*
- OECD (2011), *Towards Green Growth: Monitoring Progress: OECD Indicators*, OECD Green Growth Studies, OECD Publishing, Paris, *http://dx.doi.org/10.1787/9789264111356-en.*
- OECD (2011), Resource Productivity in the G8 and the OECD: A Report in the Framework of the Kobe 3R Action Plan, ENV/EPOC/WPRPW/WPEI(2011)1/FINAL, OECD, Paris, *http://www.oecd.org/env/waste/47944428.pdf.*
- OECD (2008a), Recommendation of the Council on Resource Productivity [*C(2008)40*], OECD, Paris, available at *http://webnet.oecd.org/oecdacts/.*
- OECD (2008b), *Measuring Material Flows and Resource Productivity. www.oecd.org/environment/resourceefficiency.*
- OECD (2008c), *OECD Environmental Outlook to 2030*, OECD Publishing, Paris, *http://dx.doi.org/10.1787/9789264040519-en.*
- OECD (2004), Recommendation of the Council on Material Flows and Resource Productivity [*C(2004)79*], OECD, Paris available at *http://webnet.oecd.org/oecdacts/.*
- OECD (n.d.), "International trade", *Main Economic Indicators* (database) , *http://dx.doi.org/10.1787/data-00045-en.*
- OECD project on measuring economic performance and social progress, *www.oecd.org/statistics/measuring-economic-social-progress/aboutthehigh-levelexpertgroup.htm.*
- OECD work on Green Growth, *www.oecd.org/greengrowth/gg-sd-2012.htm* .
- SERI/WU (Sustainable Europe Resource Institute/Vienna University) (2014), *Global Material Flow Database.* 2014 Version. Available at *www.materialflows.net.*
- UNEP (United Nations Environment Programme) (2013), *International Resource Panel. www.unep.org/resourcepanel.*
- UN (2014), *System of Environmental-Economic Accounting 2012: Central framework*, European Commission, FAO, IMF, OECD, UN, the World Bank, United Nations, New York. *http://unstats.un.org/unsd/envaccounting/seeaRev/SEEA_CF_Final_en.pdf.*
- World Bank, World Development Indicators, *http://data.worldbank.org/data-catalog/world-development-indicators.*

Chapter 3. Sustainable resource use and resource productivity

By 2050, the world economy is expected to quadruple and the global population to grow to over 9.5 billion. A growing population with higher average income requires more food, more industrial products, more energy and more water, thus placing additional strain on the earth's material resources and the environment. As production and consumption have become displaced with increasingly globalised value chains, questions also arise about the distribution of the environmental burden associated with resource use.

Confronting the scale of these challenges requires more ambitious policies to increase the resource productivity at all stages of the material life-cycle. This includes actions and investments to support technological change and innovations, and integrated life-cycle-oriented management approaches, such as 3R policies, sustainable materials management and circular economy initiatives. It requires the involvement of a large number of economic actors and concerted action by all ministries whose policies affect resource productivity. Governments have an important role in ensuring that all relevant policies and measures are coherent and well integrated, and in establishing proper framework conditions. This will in turn create opportunities for investment, for new products, new markets and employment.

It also requires better data and a better understanding of the physical resource base of countries' economies. The environmental consequences and costs of material resource use are not yet fully understood, nor are the economic opportunities provided by improved resource productivity. More in-depth analysis is needed of specific resources and materials (trade-related material flows, flows of secondary raw materials and waste, etc.) and the way material flows interact with commodity prices and recycling markets, how they relate to natural resource stocks, to innovation and to materials stocks locked in the economy.

THE POLICY AGENDA

It is expected that by 2050, the world economy will have quadrupled and the world's population will have grown from 7 billion today to over 9.5 billion people (OECD, 2011d). Most of the growth in both income and population will be in the rapidly industrialising economies of Brazil, Russia, India, Indonesia, China and South Africa (the BRIICS) and in developing countries. This will place additional strains on a variety of material and energy resources and the global environment. A growing population with higher average income requires more food, more industrial products, more energy and more water for domestic purposes. The OECD Environmental Outlook 2012 projected that:

- World energy demand in 2050 will be 80% higher, with most of the growth to come from emerging economies and still 85% reliant on fossil fuel-based energy.
- Global water demand will increase by some 55%, due to growing demand from manufacturing (+400%), thermal power plants (+140%) and domestic use (+130%).

This creates both formidable economic and environmental **challenges** for policy- and decision-makers, as well as new **opportunities** for efficiency gains through technical change and innovation, and for new products and markets.

There is growing consensus that the current trajectory is not sustainable

Whether the earth's finite natural resources will be sufficient to meet humanity's future needs remains an ongoing debate. Dire predictions regarding the exhaustion of non-renewable resources have failed to materialise. A complex interaction between population and economic (e.g. commodity prices, economic shocks) dynamics, public policies, technological change, and consumer behaviour drive the demand and supply of natural resources.

Beyond the resource scarcity debate, there is growing consensus that the current consumption path is not environmentally sustainable. Although OECD countries have made **considerable progress** in addressing many environmental challenges and improving resource productivity, these **gains have been outpaced** by the pressures of population and economic growth. Climate change, biodiversity loss, the unsustainable management of water resources and the health impacts of pollution and hazardous chemicals remain pressing issues.

It raises the question as to how to **sustain economic growth** and welfare in the longer term while **keeping negative environmental impacts under control** and preserving natural resources. Among the key issues relating to the use of non-renewable resources is whether the rate of discovery of new resources will continue to match the rate of use these resources and to what extent innovation will help developing alternative substitute materials. Experience indicates that in the longer term sustainable resource use and technological progress help decoupling economic growth, increases in resource consumption and environmental degradation.

Improving resource productivity and implementing life cycle based management approaches is critical.

Against this background, **improving resource productivity** and ensuring that the flows of materials are managed in an effective and sound way through the economic system is critical, not only from an environmental perspective but also from an economic perspective. It has a bearing on decisions cutting across many policy areas, ranging from economy, trade, innovation and technology development, to natural resource and environmental management, and to human health.

The OECD puts "resource productivity" in a welfare perspective. It is understood to contain both a *quantitative* dimension (e.g. the quantity of output produced with a given input of natural resources) and a *qualitative* dimension (e.g. the environmental impacts per unit of output produced with a given natural resource input).

Resource productivity encompasses aspects linked to the economic efficiency and environmental effectiveness of resource use at the various stages of the production and consumption chain, as well as related social aspects. The aim is to optimise the net benefits from resource use within the context of economic development, by:

- Ensuring adequate supplies of renewable and non-renewable resources to support economic activities and economic growth.
- Managing the environmental impacts associated with the extraction, processing, use and end-of-life disposal of materials, to minimise adverse effects on environmental quality and human health.
- Preventing natural resource degradation and depletion.
- Maintaining non-commercial environmental services.

Improving the resource productivity of the economy and implementing integrated life-cycle based approaches to natural resource use and materials management building on the principle of the 3Rs, is of increasing importance to many **governments and businesses**, as are instruments aimed at stimulating technological change, and integrated supply chain management.

OECD countries bear a special responsibility for leadership, worldwide, historically and because of the weight they continue to have in the global economy and environment.

Table 3.1. The weight of OECD countries in the world in 2011*

OECD countries share of global....			
Gross Domestic Product [a]	~ 50 %	Domestic material extraction [d]	~ 27 %
Population [b]	18 %	Total waste generation [e]	~ 30 %
Total primary energy supply [c]	40 %	Municipal solid waste generation [e]	30-50 %
CO_2 emissions [c]	39 %	Freshwater abstractions	~ 30 %
Natural resource stocks: [f]			
Bauxite reserves	21 %	Tin reserves	5 %
Copper reserves	53 %	Zinc reserves	35 %
Iron ore reserves (crude ore)	23 %	Crude oil reserves	14 %
Lead reserves	47 %	Natural gas reserves	10 %
Nickel reserves	37 %	Coal reserves	44 %
Phosphate rock reserves	3 %	Forest land	26 %
Rare earth reserves	13 %	Agricultural land	25 %
Trade in material resources: [g]		*Trade in material resources:* [g]	
Physical exports	44 %	Physical exports	44 %
Monetary exports	47 %	Monetary exports	47 %

Sources and notes:
*or most recent year available
(a) OECD, Environmental Outlook to 2050.
(b) OECD.stat and World Bank World Development Indicators
(c) IEA (2009), CO2 Emissions from Fuel Combustion
(d) SERI/WU material flows database.
(e) OECD environmental data, national data, Chalmin & Gaillochet (2009) and UNSD
(f) U.S. Geological Survey, 2011 Mineral Commodity Summaries; BP Statistical Review of World Energy 2013; FAO 2010 Forest Resources Assessment, World Bank World Development Indicators.
(g) OECD based on UN COMTRADE; includes intra regional trade.

NATIONAL AND INTERNATIONAL INITIATIVES

Resource productivity and sustainable resource use are high on the international policy agenda

There are a growing number of **initiatives at the international level** that focus on resource productivity, sustainable resource use and management and the circular economy, and that encourage international cooperation in these areas.

Heads of State and Government of **G8 countries** paid specific attention to these issues at their summits in 2003, 2004, 2006, and 2006. At their 2004 summit in Sea Island, the endorsed the **3R initiative** (Reduce, Reuse, and Recycle). At their 2008 meeting in Kobe, Japan, G8 Environment Ministers' adopted the **3R Action Plan**. As requested, the OECD has been following up on the progress of work related to resource productivity and provided an interim report at 2011 G8 meeting.[1]

OECD countries are committed to improve resource productivity and have signed up to two **OECD Council recommendations** in 2004 and 2008 to this effect[2]. The first one was to improve information on material flows and resource productivity. The second one to analyse material flows and the associated environmental impacts, to promote the use of resource productivity indicators, and to develop and implement policies to improve resource productivity and reduce negative environmental impacts of materials and product use. EU member states are further committed to implement European policy and law.

Improving resource productivity is key to achieving green growth

Improving resource productivity is also a central element in the move towards **green growth** and in the OECD's Green Growth Strategy released at the 2011 OECD Ministerial Council Meeting. The strategy outlines a policy framework and practical tools to help OECD member and partner countries identify ways to move towards greener growth, including the policy packages needed to remove barriers and correct market failures and distortions to green growth. It calls for incentives for increased efficiency in the use of resources and natural assets to enhance productivity, reduce waste and energy consumption, and make resources available to their highest value use (OECD, 2011b). It also includes a conceptual framework and a set of indicators to monitor progress (OECD 2011c; OECD 2014c).

Several other international bodies have embarked on work on green growth. The United Nations Environment Program (UNEP) launched its Green Economy Initiative in late 2008, including a framework for assessing progress. To achieve synergies at international level, the OECD, the Global Green Growth Institute, UNEP and the World Bank work together within the framework of the Green Growth Knowledge Platform (GGKP).

Many initiatives encourage international cooperation in these areas

Resource productivity issues are also being addressed by **UNEP** and the **European Commission**. Examples include:

- The UNEP International Panel on Sustainable Resource Management (International Resource Panel), established in 2007 to provide independent scientific assessment on the sustainable use of natural resources and of their environmental impacts over the full life cycle. First results from its work were published in 2010.

- The EU Thematic strategy on the sustainable use of natural resources (adopted in 2005), complemented with a strategy on the prevention and recycling of waste, integrated product policies (IPP), an Environmental Technology Action plan, and a Sustainable Consumption and Production and Sustainable Industrial Policy Action Plan (2008).
- The EU Raw Materials Initiative (November 2008) and Strategy (February 2011) that set out measures to secure access to non-energy raw materials for the EU, to boost resource efficiency and promote recycling including through improvements in recycling markets, in waste treatment, in statistics on waste and materials flows.
- These objectives are also part of the EU 2020 Flagship Initiative on Resource Efficiency (announced in January 2011). The initiative provides a long-term framework for actions in many policy areas aiming at increasing certainty for investment and innovation and ensuring that all relevant policies factor in resource efficiency in a balanced manner. It encompasses a RE Roadmap and a set RE indicators (the Ressoure Efficicency Scorboard), whose implementation is supported by the European Resource Efficiency Platform.
- The EU has also developed criteria to distinguish secondary raw materials from waste so as to create greater legal certainty and a level playing field for the recycling sector, and works towards establishing a common market for "green products". A communication from the Commission "Towards a circular economy: a zero waste programme for Europe" was released in July 2014

These initiatives are supported by international efforts to promote good **governance in the raw materials sector** and to make the management of natural resource rents more transparent (e.g. the Extractive Industries Transparency Initiative, and the OECD Due Diligence Guidance for Responsible Supply Chains of Minerals from Conflict-Affected and High-Risk Areas); and by international efforts to promote sustainable consumption and production (SCP) such as the 10-year framework of programmes on SCP under the UN Commission on Sustainable Development.

Improving resource efficiency and productivity is of increasing importance to many governments and businesses

Improving resource productivity is of increasing importance to governments. Many countries have included resource productivity and efficiency issues in their sustainable development strategies, green growth strategies or environmental plans, have established programmes on sustainable production and consumption, sustainable manufacturing, stewardship programmes for raw materials and natural resources, integrated waste and materials management policies such as the 3Rs or circular economy approaches, and green public procurement policies. In several countries, policies to improve resource productivity are interwoven with energy efficiency policies. Many have set national targets for waste management focusing on end-of-life management and recycling. Some have set targets for material productivity and sustainable use of natural resources. Many initiatives are taken in Europe, stimulated by the policies, regulations and action plans of the European Union. This encompasses national strategies or action plans on resource efficiency and on raw materials, as well as waste management plans and targets[3].

3R and circular economy initiatives aim at closing materials loops and extending the lifespan of materials through longer use and the increased use of secondary raw materials. These initiatives also aim at material substitution: using materials with smaller environmental impact, and replacing the environmentally most damaging materials.
See Glossary.

While differing in their level of ambition and their specific focus, these programmes and policies all share:

- the need to move towards policies and measures that build on an integrated approach to natural resource and materials management over the full resource cycle, such as Sustainable Materials Management (SMM);
- the need for greater efficiency in the way natural resources and materials are used in the economy; and
- the recognition that a life cycle approach is needed to maximise the net benefits from natural resource and materials use, and minimise negative impacts on the environment.

Several of these initiatives call for moving away from the traditional linear economic and business models towards circular models and a green economy[4]. Countries also work in partnership with industry to move towards more sustainable use of natural resources and raw materials, reduce the amounts of waste that go to final disposal, and establish new more circular business models[5].

Many businesses address these issues by establishing stewardship programmes for raw materials (e.g. in mining industries) and products, investing in R&D and using advanced technologies to increase materials and energy efficiency, enhancing environmental management, promoting eco-design and coherent materials supply and use systems along the supply chain, including sustainable sourcing of raw materials.

Many businesses are seeking new profits from better management of materials that were once regarded as waste, and fom producing higher-value products with less material inputs. "Design-for-Environment" targets are triggering companies to re-design their products to reduce material use and toxic inputs, and to make products more recyclable. And interest in new "circular" business models and system innovation that encourage resource efficiency is increasing. These initiatives are driven by concerns about reducing costs, but also by consumer demand for greener management of materials. The findings of a McKinsey study show that resource efficiency can drive competitiveness and job creation, and represents a business opportunity of USD 3500 billion (McKinsey, 2012).

Initiatives in the field of corporate performance reporting and accounting that integrate natural resource and materials use are also expanding.

Box 3.1. OECD references to material flows and resource productivity issues

The *Council of the OECD* has adopted several policy and legal texts of relevance to sustainable resource use and resource productivity and concerning actions that Member countries agreed to carry out in the framework of the Organisation.

In 2001, OECD Environment Ministers and the OECD Council at ministerial level adopted the *OECD Environmental Strategy for the First decade of the 21st Century* that includes two relevant objectives: (i) maintaining the integrity of ecosystems through the efficient management of natural resources; (ii) decoupling environmental pressure from economic growth and making integrated efforts to address consumption and production patterns, including by encouraging more efficient resource use and hence increases in resource productivity.

This follows on the recommendations formulated in 1997 of the High Level Advisory Group on the Environment to the Secretary General of the OECD: "*... it is now time for the OECD to concentrate* ***on increasing resource productivity*** *with the same effectiveness it applied to labour productivity. This should be done not just for environmental reasons, but also for economic and social reasons*" (OECD, 1997)

In 2004, the Council of the OECD adopted a *Recommendation on material flows and resource productivity* asking OECD countries to improve information and knowledge on material flows and resource productivity and to develop common methodologies and measurement systems, with emphasis on areas in which comparable and practicable indicators can be defined.

In 2008, the Council of the OECD adopted a *Recommendation on resource productivity* asking OECD countries to (i) strengthen their capacity for analysing material flows and the associated environmental impacts, and for measuring resource productivity, and (ii) to take actions to improve resource productivity and reduce negative environmental impacts of materials and product use, by encouraging environmentally effective and economically efficient uses of natural resources and materials at the macro, sectoral and micro levels.

In 2011, the OECD *green growth strategy* called for policies that "foster economic growth and development while ensuring that the natural assets continue to provide the resources and environmental services on which our well-being relies".

In 2011, the Council of the OECD adopted a *Recommendation on due diligence guidance for responsible supply chains of minerals from confict-affected and high-risk areas.* It provides detailed recommendations to help companies respect human rights and avoid contributing to conflict through their mineral purchasing decisions and practices. It is for use by any company potentially sourcing minerals or metals from conflict-affected and high-risk areas, and is one of the only international frameworks available to help companies meet their due diligence reporting requirements.

Box 3.2. Other International references to material flows and resource productivity issues

G8 summits

In 2003, the Heads of State and Government of G8 countries adopted an Action Plan on "Science and Technology for Sustainable Development" stating that G8 members *"will enhance their understanding of resource material flows and continue work on resources productivity indices, notably in the OECD"*. (Evian summit, 1-3 June 2003, France). This followed on the communiqué by G8 Environment Ministers who recognised "that it is essential to improve resource productivity" and noted "that a common approach has to be elaborated in order to identify and develop indicators ... to monitor the shift in consumption and production patterns". They invited *"the OECD to play a supportive role in that respect"*. (Communiqué adopted by G8 Environment Ministers, Paris, 25-27 April 2003).

In 2004, the Heads of State and Government of G8 countries endorsed the "Reduce, Reuse and Recycle" (3Rs) initiative proposed by Japan as part of the follow-up to the Action Plan on "Science and Technology for Sustainable Development" adopted in 2003. (Sea Island summit, 9-10 June 2004, United States).

In 2006, the Heads of State and Government of G8 countries adopted a Plan of Action on Global Energy Security emphasising the importance of energy efficiency and stating that "*As part of an integrated approach to the entire resource cycle we reaffirm our commitment to comprehensive measures to optimise the resource cycle within the 3Rs Initiative (Reduce, Reuse, Recycle). In furthering these efforts, we will set targets as appropriate taking account of resource productivity.*" (St Petersburg summit, 15-17 July 2006, Russia).

In 2007, the Heads of State and Government of G8 countries agreed to increase transparency and good governance in the raw materials sector as a contribution to sustainable growth, and stated that "*based on sound life cycle analyses, we will ... encourage conservation, recycling and substitution of raw materials, including rare metals, for sustainable growth.*" (Heiligendamm summit, 6-8 June 2007, Germany).

In 2008, the Heads of State and Government of G8 countries endorsed the Kobe 3R Action Plan in which G8 Environment Ministers agreed to take action to improve resource productivity, establish an international sound material-cycle society, and collaborate for 3R capacity development in developing countries. The Action Plan requests the OECD to follow up on the progress of work related to resource productivity (Kobe, 24-26 May 2008, Japan).

European Union references

In 2005, the *European Union adopted* a thematic *strategy on the sustainable use of natural resources,* complemented with a strategy on the prevention and recycling of waste, and with integrated product policies (IPP) aiming at improving environmental performance of products through their full life-cycle. Other EU texts of relevance include an Environmental Technology Action plan, and a Sustainable Consumption and Production and Sustainable Industrial Policy Action Plan (2008).

The *EU Raw Materials Initiative* (November 2008) and Strategy (February 2011) set out measures to secure access to non-energy raw materials for the EU, to boost resource efficiency and promote recycling including through improvements in recycling markets, in waste treatment, in statistics on waste and materials flows.

These objectives are also part of the EU 2020 Flagship Initiative on *Resource Efficiency* (January 2011) that includes a Resource Efficiency Roadmap specifying policy goals and targets, and indicators to measure progress.

United Nations

The *UN Conference on Sustainable Development* in June 2012 (Rio+20), reaffirmed that changing unsustainable consumption and production patterns is one of the three overarching objectives of, and essential requirements for, sustainable development, and adopted the 10-Year Framework of Programmes on *Sustainable Consumption and Production Patterns* (10YFP). UNEP acts as Secretariat of the 10YFP, and administers a Trust Fund to support SCP implementation in developing countries and countries with economies in transition.

UNEP works to promote resource efficiency and sustainable consumption and production (SCP). This includes the promotion of sustainable resource management in a life cycle perspective for goods and services. In 2007, UNEP established an International Panel on Sustainable Resource Management (International Resource Panel) to provide independent, coherent and authoritative scientific assessment on the sustainable use of natural resources and the environmental impacts of resource use over the full life cycle.

IMPROVING KNOWLEDGE AND INFORMATION FOR DECISION MAKING

To be successful resource efficiency and material productivity policies need to be founded on a good *understanding* of the material basis of the economy, of international and national flows of materials, and of the factors that drive changes in natural resource use and material productivity over time, across countries and in the different sectors of the economy. Some natural resources, such as water, energy, forests, and selected subsoil assets are monitored internationally, but information is insufficient to give an integrated view of how minerals, metals, or timber flow through the economy throughout their life cycle. In addition, little is known about how this affects the productivity of the economy and the quality of the environment.

The analytical approaches and measurement tools that have been developed to support *Material Flow Analysis* (MFA) are particularly useful to fill these gaps and inform decision making.

Since 2004 OECD countries have been working together with the OECD Secretariat and other international partners to improve their knowledge about resource productivity and material flows, and to develop common measurement systems and indicators to inform policy debates. The results of this work are grouped in a series of OECD guidance documents on measuring material flows and resource productivity that were released on the occasion of the 2008 OECD-UNEP Conference on Resource Efficiency.

MEASURING AND ANALYSING MATERIAL FLOWS

Material Flow Analysis: A family of tools to study how flows of materials interact with the economy and the environment

Material flows can be measured and analysed at various scales and with different instruments depending on the issue of concern and on the objects of interest of the study. The analysis can be applied to the complete collection of all resources and products flowing through a system to single chemical elements. It can be applied to the global or the national economy, an industry, an enterprise, a city or a river basin. The term MFA therefore designates **a family of tools** encompassing a variety of analytical approaches and measurement tools. Each type of analysis is associated with MF accounts or other measurement tools, and can be used to derive various types of indicators. Often a combination of tools is necessary to gain the required insights. (Box 3.3).

To provide a comprehensive assessment of resource productivity and the environmental challenges associated with material resource use, MFA can be used in conjunction with other tools, including economic and other environmental accounts and modelling, information on market prices, and resource rents, qualitative environmental impact assessments, cost-benefit analysis, and value chain analysis.

A holistic approach

The most complete applications of MFA take a holistic approach and capture so-called unused and indirect flows flows that do not enter the economy, but that are relevant from an environmental point of view. The underlying rationale is that every movement or transfer of materials or energy from one place to another has repercussions on the environment and has the potential to alter the environmental balance. These flows can add to the pollution burden, disrupt habitats or alter landscapes, but do not enter the economy as priced goods (e.g. mining overburden; pollutants and waste generated upstream in a production process and that occur outside the system under review).

Much of these flows are hidden and not seen in economic accounts or in trade and production statistics. (See *Glossary*).

Box 3.3. Material Flow Analysis (MFA): a multi-purpose family of tools

What is Material Flow Analysis?

Material Flow Analysis is the study of physical flows of natural resources and materials into, through and out of a given system (usually the economy). It is based on methodically organised **accounts** in physical units, and uses the principle of **mass balancing** to analyse the relationships between material flows (including energy), human activities (including economic and trade developments) and environmental changes.

The principle of **mass balancing** is founded on the first law of thermodynamics (called the law of conservation of matter), which states that matter (mass, energy) is neither created nor destroyed by any physical process.

Material flow accounts are part of the physical flow accounts described in the System of Environmental-Economic Accounting (**SEEA**). They provide data on the material inputs taken from the environment into the economy (e.g. resources extracted or harvested from the surrounding natural environment or imported from other countries), the transformation and use of inputs within the economy (from production to final consumption) and the material outputs from the economy to the environment as residuals (waste, pollutants) or to other countries in the form of exports. The data are compiled from available production, consumption and trade data, and from environment statistics (on waste, emissions, etc.).

A material flow analysis can cover any set of materials at various scales and levels of detail and completeness.

Emphasis can be put on:

- ❶ **all materials entering and leaving the national economy;**
- ❷ the industry level, enterprise level, and product level, from product groups down to specific products;
- ❸ certain materials and substances, from the national down to the local level;
- ❹ **a combination of specifications.**

Overall architecture of MFA and the associated tools

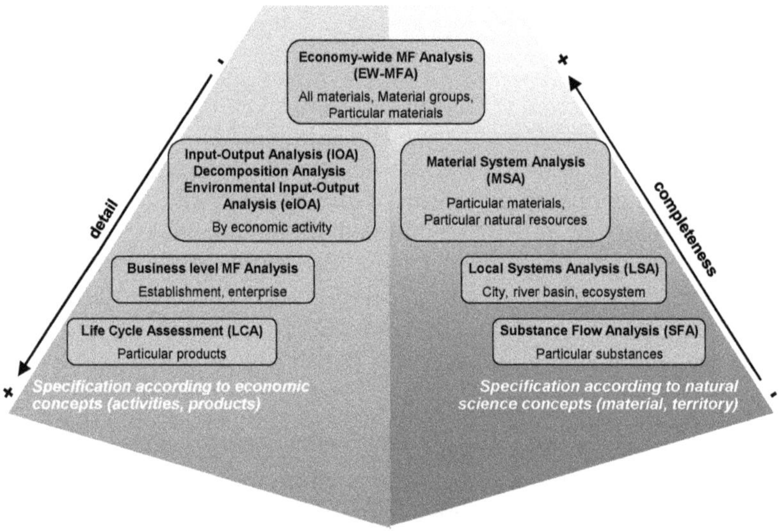

Source: OECD 2008b.

Table 3.2. Material Flow analysis: Overview of policy applications

Policy areas		Relevant MFA functions	Appropriate MFA tools
Economic, trade and technology development policies	Economic policies	♦ Measure aspects of the physical performance of the economy. ♦ Analyse the materials requirements for activities that involve construction, reconstruction, maintenance and disposal of infrastructure. ♦ Measure the degree of "decoupling" between direct and indirect environmental pressures (pollution, waste, primary resource inputs) and economic growth	♦ Economy-wide MFA ♦ Physical I-O analysis *In conjunction with*: ♦ Productivity measures ♦ Economic modelling ♦ Analysis of energy requirements
	Trade aspects & supply patterns	♦ Support structural analysis of the global economy in physical terms: effects of globalisation on international material flows; substitution of domestic raw materials with imported ones; interaction with production & consumption patterns. ♦ Monitor the structural effects of trade and environment measures on international materials markets and on flows of environmentally significant materials (e.g. hazardous materials; secondary raw materials, recyclable materials). ♦ Monitor the environmental implications of changes in international material flows, including (i) environmental pressures from indirect flows abroad associated with trade; (ii) environmentally significant materials embedded in imported goods; (iii) environmental risks related to international transport of materials, etc.	♦ Economy-wide MFA covering trade flows by origin/destination; ♦ Physical I-O analysis; ♦ Environmental I-O analysis; *In conjunction with:* ♦ Monetary I-O tables; ♦ International trade statistics; ♦ International transport statistics.
	Technology development	♦ Guide the development of new technologies and identify those that would severely strain material availability or generate excessive additional environmental pressures. ♦ Identify potential areas for research on substitutions of materials and on the availability of materials for the development of new technologies. ♦ Detect opportunities for new technologies that help reduce inefficiencies in energy and materials use, increase domestic reuse or recycling and the use of alternative materials.	♦ Material system analysis & material specific accounts; ♦ Life cycle analysis of products *In conjunction with:* ♦ Value chain analysis
Natural resource management policies		♦ Assess the status and trends of a country's natural resources. Monitor sustainable production levels (e.g. forest resources) and support related management plans. ♦ Examine the demand, scarcity and raw material requirements, based on the full material cycle and understand what is behind price and production trends in commodities over extended periods of time. ♦ Assess mineral systems by tracking (i) raw materials used in the economy, (ii) the flow of a specific material in the economy as a commodity (iii) the flow of different materials as a product, (iv) material stocks in use, reuse and disposal in a country. ♦ Assess energy systems by tracking energy carriers used in the economy, by giving insights into multiple uses, including non-fuel uses (e.g. plastics, synthetic fibres).	♦ Material system analysis and resource specific accounts; *In conjunction with:* ♦ Natural resource accounts ♦ Information on proven reserves & rates of discovery. ♦ Energy accounts & statistics ♦ Modelling
Environmental policies	Integrated pollution prevention & control	♦ Map the flows of nutrients or contaminants in a region, country or river basin and identify whether, where and to what extent these flows contribute to environmental degradation "downstream". ♦ Estimate environmental pressures from metal extraction and production, the part due to inefficiencies in production technologies and the benefits that could be gained from new technologies and from improved recovery and recycling. ♦ Monitor and help understand indirect and unused materials flows and their effects on the environment, at home and abroad.	♦ Economy-wide MFA with detailed breakdown of materials. ♦ Substance flow analysis. ♦ Material system analysis and material specific accounts. *In conjunction with:* ♦ Waste statistics & accounts
	Integrated waste & materials management	♦ Analyse trends in waste generation, and how they affect opportunities for (i) resource conservation, (ii) resource productivity, and (iii) material recovery and recycling. ♦ Assess the economic benefits and costs to keeping materials in the active materials stream and to minimising the amounts going to final disposal. ♦ Assess developments in markets for reused and recyclable materials. ♦ Identify areas for research on (i) energy conservation and recovery, (ii) materials recycling, (iii) alternative materials and (iv) new technologies.	♦ Various MFA tools distinguishing between primary & secondary raw materials, and recyclable materials. *In conjunction with:* ♦ Waste statistics & accounts ♦ Cost benefit analysis ♦ Modelling
	Product related policies	♦ Examine source reduction, substitution, and recyclability of the materials composing a product and help understand the synergistic nature of the flows of these materials. ♦ Examine environmental impacts of products, in particular products with toxic ingredients (e.g. lead paint, asphalt roofing, batteries with cadmium). ♦ Explore design issues that affect the environment at end of product life, and identifying leverage points for green design and pollution prevention, and implications of a policy shift (e.g. ban on use of certain materials in particular products).	♦ Life cycle analysis & assessments
	Other	♦ Analyse the effects of environmental policy instruments on material flows and on the material supply mix. ♦ Analyse the benefits of government purchasing policies (e.g. for the availability of recycled or redesigned products to the market), and how they affect material flows ♦ Monitor environmental performance targets with industry and government.	♦ Various MFA tools *In conjunction with:* ♦ Cost benefit analysis ♦ Modelling ♦ EMS

Source: based on OECD (2008b)

When applied at economy-wide level, MFA gives an integrated view of material flows through the economy, and reveals how flows of materials shift among countries, and how this affects the economy and the environment within and beyond national borders.

When applied at a more granular level, MFA reveals how flows of materials shift among sectors and industries, and within countries. This helps identify inefficiencies in the use of natural resources, energy and materials in process chains or in the economy at large that would go undetected in conventional economic or environmental monitoring systems

MFa provides information useful for a variety of policies

These characteristics make it a useful tool for a variety of public and private policies and for examining trade-offs between policies and for understanding the implications of decisions that depend on interrelationships in the economy and the environment. It can be used to analyse issues that cut across different media and policy areas and support decisions that have economic, environmental and social implications.

Experience suggests MFA is particularly useful in three broad policy areas: (i) economic, trade and technology development policies; (ii) natural resource management policies; and (iii) environmental policies. The three policy areas overlap because they are all concerned with particular aspects of resource use and management. Potentially, a wide range of government agencies, ministries and departments will find use for these types of analysis. (Table 3.1).

Filling knowledge gaps and advancing the measurement

Considerable progress has been made

A considerable amount of work on MFA has been carried out in the past decade, much of it focusing on the development of methodologies and the necessary "spade work" to set up accounts required for calculating material flow (MF) indicators and carrying out the analysis. About two-thirds of OECD countries have developed MFA initiatives, mostly focussing on their economically and environmentally most important resources and materials. Recent efforts in Europe to promote the implementation of economy-wide MF accounts in EU countries have led to mandatory reporting.

This is supported with international efforts led by the UN to develop the System of environmental-economic accounting (SEEA). The SEEA Central Framework was adopted by the United Nations Statistical Commission in 2012, as the first international standard for environmental-economic accounting. The implementation of physical flow accounts in line with the SEEA is expected to progressively broaden the information basis for analysing material flows and the associated monetary flows.

Countries are also increasingly interested in monitoring progress with regard to resource productivity and sustainable use of resources/materials on the basis of indicators and quantitative objectives or targets. (e.g. Finland, Germany, Japan, Netherlands, Sweden).

Important gaps remain

However important gaps remain. Missing information and inconsistencies still limit the tracking of progress with resource productivity in many countries and hence at international level. The most important gaps that remain to be filled relate to:

- Material flows that do not enter the economy as transactions, but that are relevant from an environmental point of view, including unused materials and **indirect flows** associated with international trade. Estimates of the *indirect* flows of **raw materials embedded in traded**

goods are currently available for a few countries and the European Union as a whole, and often only for the most recent years. The main challenges in estimating such indirect demand-based materials flows are: gaps in reliable data on the physical volume of international trade; lack of an international consensus about the calculation method to be used; lack of an agreement to use a **common international database** (multi-regional input-output tables) on which to base the estimates. Distinguishing between the materials and products directly used in an economy and the raw materials that are required upstream to produce these products is important to understand the full raw material requirements of an economy, to detect the effects of domestic policies on resource productivity, and to become aware of the environmental consequences that may occur abroad.

- Flows of materials that are important to a circular economy and the 3Rs, including flows of **secondary raw materials** (recycled materials) and of **waste**. The main challenges are: conceptual and methodological differences between material flow accounts and waste statistics; gaps in physical and monetary data on international trade in secondary raw materials. Distinguishing between primary and secondary raw materials is crucial for assessing resource productivity and decoupling trends, and for understanding the economic benefits of a circular economy.
- Material resource use and productivity disaggregated **by industry** and by type of material, and information on the **processing levels** of the materials (raw materials, semi-finished products, finished products). Such information is indispensable to indicate opportunities for improved performance and efficiency gains in production and consumption processes and along the supply chain.
- Compatible international data for **key materials and substances**, i.e. those that are economically and environmentally most important, to support a more granular analysis of material flows. This includes critical raw materials, and materials or substances that are environmentally harmful or that play a role in global geochemical cycles or raise global concerns.
- Reliable data on the availability, quality and deterioration of **natural resource stocks and reserves**. Such information remains scarce and is often not comparable.
- Comparable information about the **economic opportunities**, in terms of jobs and competitiveness, arising from improved resource productivity remains scarce. This is because the dynamic aspects of resource productivity policies are difficult to capture statistically, and because many measurement efforts have been focusing on the waste management phase, rather than on the overall efficiency of the economy and of supply chains.

Gaps also remain as regards the size and value of **future urban mines**, i.e. the material stocks locked in the economy. With the exception of the some of the most common industrial metals, there are insufficient estimates of these anthropogenic stocks to form a reliable picture of their potential to contribute to future supply. Capitalising on the potential of the urban mine will require not only better knowledge of its size, but also its dynamics, how it evolves over time and in relation to virgin stocks.

Other important gaps include information on economic and fiscal instruments in use, including **subsidies** for resource extraction and use, beyond those for fossil fuels, and other market-based instruments. Also, links between trends in material flows and trends in **market prices** for these materials, or trends in related **resource rents** remain largely unexplored.

Efforts are needed to better assess environmental impacts, to establish compatible databases on key materials and natural resources and to provide industry-level information

There is considerable scope for deeper analysis of particular resources and materials, and the interactions between these resources. Future work will need to deepen the analysis of trade-related flows and flows of secondary raw materials, the way they interact with commodity prices and recycling markets, and and how they relate to natural and anthropogenic resource stocks, to supply security and to innovation. Future work will also need to explore the environmental impacts and costs of natural resource use, and the economic and environmental opportunities provided by improved resource productivity.

More specifically, efforts are needed to:

- Develop methods to assess the **environmental impacts** of materials use throughout the entire life cycle of materials and the products that embody them (i.e. from natural resource extraction, manufacturing and use to end-of-life management). This should include impacts from resources that have been traded, possibly including indirect effects in terms of natural resource use, pollution and waste induced by countries' demand for traded raw materials and products.
- Implement **natural asset accounts** for key natural resources and **material flow accounts** by material and by industry.

Required also are compatible databases for key material flows and key natural resources, the further development of MF and resource productivity indicators, and the sharing of good practices within countries, among countries and among enterprises.

Better information will in turn help make a strong case for policies aimed at improving resource productivity by showing the full benefits of such policies, and will contribute to a better analysis of progress towards green growth.

The OECD will continue to develop internationally harmonised material flow and resource productivity data and indicators (both at macro level and for selected materials such as critical raw materials and materials raising particular environmental concerns) and to promote the exchange of related experience among countries. This is done in collaboration with UNEP and its International Resource Panel, Eurostat and several research institutes. International cooperation has also been established to advance the measurement and knowledge of green growth (GGKP, OECD, WB, UNEP).

ENDNOTES

1 The report *Resource Productivity in the G8 and OECD: A Report in the Framework of the Kobe 3R Action Plan* is available at: *www.oecd.org/document/14/0,3746,en_2649_34395_47926478_1_1_1_1,00.html*

2 OECD (2008), Recommendation of the Council on Resource Productivity [*C(2008)40*], Paris; OECD (2004), *Recommendation of the Council on Material Flows and Resource Productivity [C(2004)79]*, Paris.

3 For instance, some EU Member States are developing national strategies or action plans on resource efficiency, such as the Raw Materials Strategies and the Resource Efficiency Action Plans in Austria and

Germany; the *circular economy roadmap* in France; the *National Programme on Natural Resources* in the Netherlands; and the *Resource Security Action Plan* in the United Kingdom.

4 For instance, the *green growth strategy* of Chile; the *circular economy roadmap* in France; and the *Green Economy Action Plan* in Switzerland.

5 For instance, the United States *Sustainable Manufacturing Initiative* (SMI) and Public-Private Dialogue launched by the Department of Commerce to support United States companies in their sustainable manufacturing efforts; the *Material-efficiency Centre* in Finland; or the *Resource efficiency network* set up by the German Ministry of the Environment.

REFERENCES

- European Commission, Resource Efficiency, *http://ec.europa.eu/environment/resource_efficiency/about/index_en.htm*
- European Commission, Sustainable use of natural resources, *http://ec.europa.eu/environment/natres/index.htm*
- EEA (European Environment Agency) (2010), The European Environment: State and Outlook 2010 –Material Resources and Waste, www.eea.europa.eu/soer/europe/material-resources-and-waste.
- OECD (2014), *Green Growth Indicators 2014*, OECD Green Growth Studies, OECD Publishing, Paris, *http://dx.doi.org/10.1787/9789264202030-en.*
- OECD (2011) Resource Productivity in the G8 and OECD: A Report in the Framework of the Kobe 3R Action Plan, *www.oecd.org/document/14/0,3746,en_2649_34395_47926478_1_1_1_1,00.html.*
- OECD (2011), *Towards Green Growth: Monitoring Progress: OECD Indicators*, OECD Green Growth Studies, OECD Publishing, Paris, *http://dx.doi.org/10.1787/9789264111356-en.*
- OECD (2008), Recommendation of the Council on Resource Productivity [*C(2008)40*], OECD, Paris, available at available at *http://webnet.oecd.org/oecdacts/.*
- OECD (2008b), *Measuring Material Flows and Resource Productivity. www.oecd.org/environment/resourceefficiency.*
- OECD (2008c), *OECD Environmental Outlook to 2030*, OECD Publishing, Paris, *http://dx.doi.org/10.1787/9789264040519-en.*
- OECD (2004), Recommendation of the Council on Material Flows and Resource Productivity [*C(2004)79*], Paris, available at *http://webnet.oecd.org/oecdacts/.*
- OECD project on measuring economic performance and social progress, *www.oecd.org/statistics/measuring-economic-social-progress/aboutthehigh-levelexpertgroup.htm*
- OECD work on Green Growth, *www.oecd.org/greengrowth/gg-sd-2012.htm.*
- SERI/WU (Sustainable Europe Resource Institute/Vienna University) (2014), *Global Material Flow Database.* 2014 Version. Available at *www.materialflows.net.*
- UN (2014), *System of Environmental-Economic Accounting 2012: Central framework*, European Commission, FAO, IMF, OECD, UN, the World Bank, United Nations, New York. *http://unstats.un.org/unsd/envaccounting/seeaRev/SEEA_CF_Final_en.pdf.*
- UNEP (United Nations Environment Programme) (2013), *International Resource Panel, www.unep.org/resourcepanel.*

Chapter 4. The material basis of the global economy

This chapter examines global trends in material flows and resource productivity using tools from Material Flow Analysis (MFA) and data from Material Flow Accounting (see the Reader's Guide for data sources). In MFA, the term "materials" is often used in a broad sense, so as to encompass all material-related flows arising at all stages of the material cycle. It refers to both materials and products derived from natural resources that are used as inputs into human activities, as well as residuals (such as waste or pollutant emissions) arising from their extraction and use, and ecosystem inputs (such as nutrients, carbon dioxide, and oxygen) required for their extraction and use. Here the focus is on "material resources" that designate the usable materials or substances (raw materials, energy) produced from natural resources. These usable "materials" include energy carriers (gas, oil, coal), metal ores and metals, construction minerals and other minerals, soil and biomass. Ecosystem inputs and pollutant outputs are not considered.

MATERIAL EXTRACTION RATES

Domestic extraction used (DEU) measures the flow of materials that originate from the environment and physically enter the economy to be transformed into or incorporated in products. These materials are usually of economic value.

Domestic material consumption (DMC) provides a measure of the amount of materials directly consumed by economic activities within an economic system (e.g. a country). DMC equals DEU plus imports minus exports. *At the global level DEU and DMC are equivalent.*

See Glossary.

Global extraction of material resources continues to grow

The amount of materials extracted, harvested and consumed worldwide reached nearly 72 billion metric tonnes (Gt) per year in 2010. This is twice as much as in 1980 when global material extraction was 36 Gt, and an estimated ten-fold increase since the early 1900s when extraction was estimated at around 7 Gt (SERI/WU material flows database; Krausman *et al.*, 2009). Based on these global figures, OECD countries accounted for 27% of domestic extraction of used materials (DEU) worldwide in 2010 (compared to 46% in 1980), while the BRIICS countries (Brazil, Russia, India, Indonesia, China and South Africa) accounted for 51% (compared to 30% in 1980).[1] Although more updated global figures are not currently available, given the limited growth of the global economy since the 2008 financial crisis, material use likely stays at around 72-75 Gt today.

Material use is expected to continue growing, in line with economic activity, with one projection expecting it to reach 100 Gt by 2030.[2]

Figure 4.1. Global material resource extraction, trends and materials mix, 1980-2010

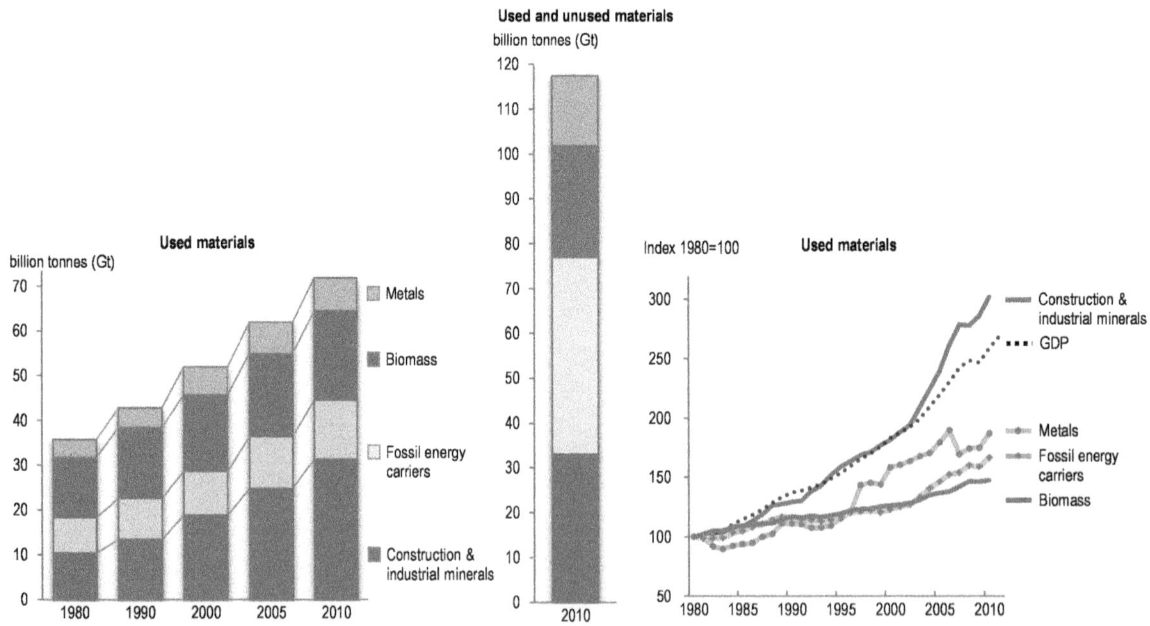

Source: SERI/WU (2014) material flows database, *www.materialflows.net.*

Figure 4.2. Global material resource extraction, geographical distribution and materials mix, 1990-2010

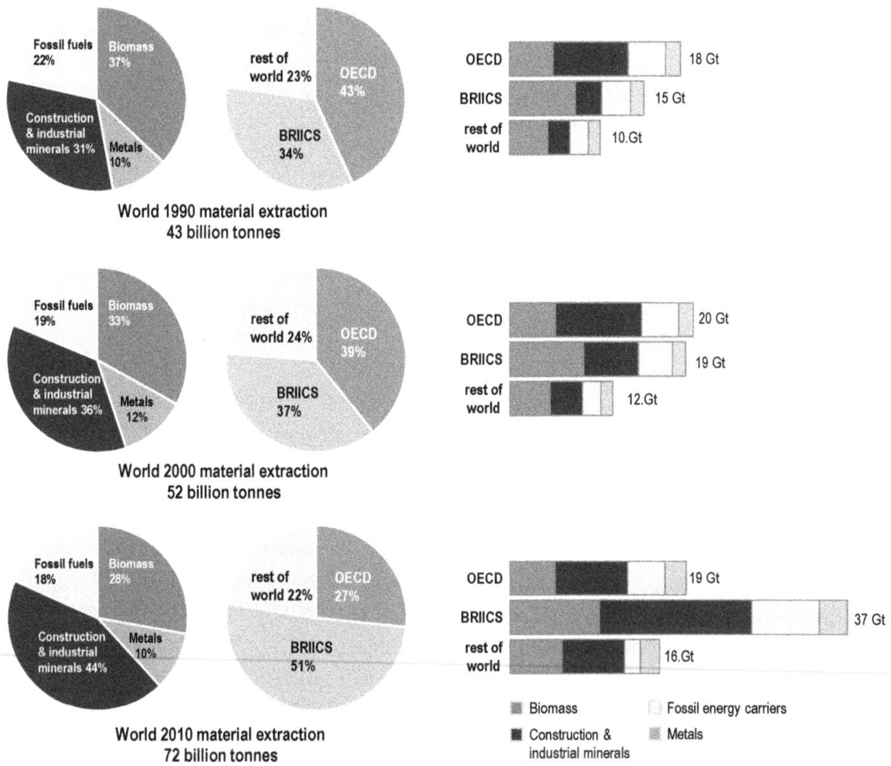

Source: SERI/WU (2014) material flows database, *www.materialflows.net*

Figure 4.3. Global material extraction, population and GDP, by material group, 1980-2010

Index 1980=100

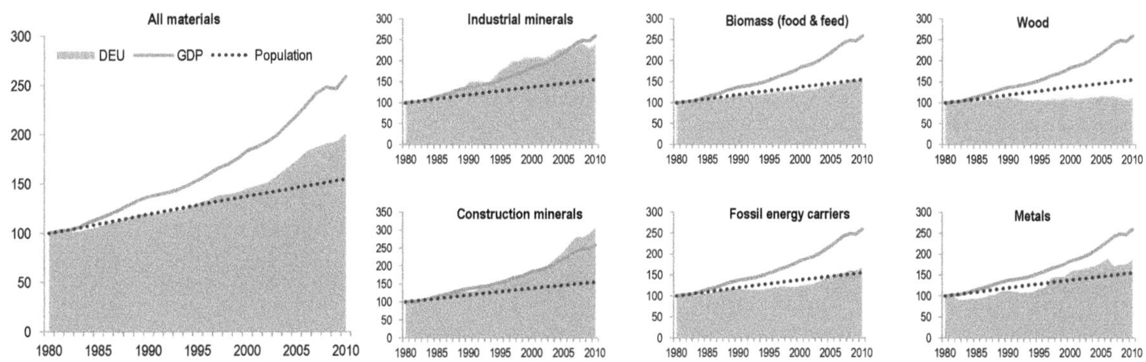

Note: GDP in USD at 2005 prices and PPPs. Material extraction: used materials only
Source: SERI/WU (2014) material flows database, *www.materialflows.net*

Figure 4.4. Decoupling trends, OECD and world, 1980-2010

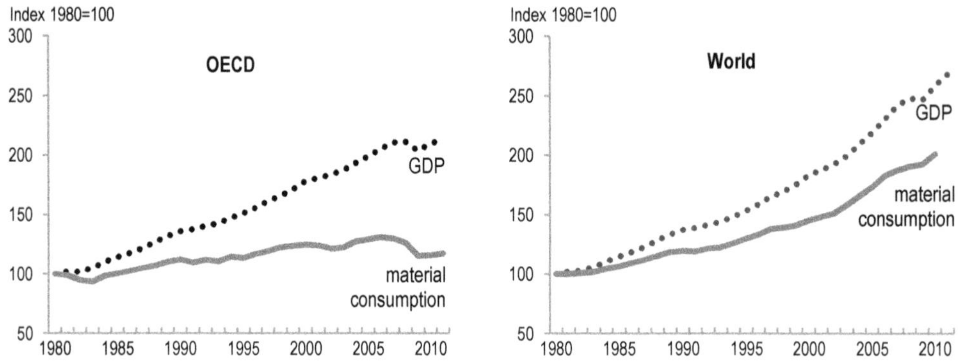

Source: SERI/WU (2014) material flows database. *www.materialflows.net*

Growth has been uneven across materials and over time

Growth has been primarily driven by increased global demand for construction minerals, biomass for food and feed, fossil energy carriers. These three material groups account for 80% of total global material extraction.

Over last century extraction of resources from non-renewable stocks has grown while extraction from renewable stocks has declined, reflecting the shift in the base of the global economy from agriculture to industry. Once accounting for an estimated 75% of global material extraction, biomass accounts for less than a third of total extraction today (Krausman *et al.*, 2009; SERI/WU material flows database). Non-renewable resource extraction now represents over two-thirds of global material extraction with construction minerals making up 42% of global DEU in 2010 (compared to 34% in 2000), fossil energy carriers 18%, and metal and metal ores 10%. Industrial minerals account for around 2% of global extraction.

Although global material use has been increasing steadily overall, growth has varied across material groups, pointing to differences in the way economic and demographic factors are driving their evolution.

Metals

Over the last 30 years, growth in raw material demand (in relative terms) has been strong for **metal ores**, reflecting the importance of economic growth as a demand driver. Global metal extraction rose from 3.9 to 7.4 Gt or by 87% between 1980 and 2010. But growth has not followed a steady upward trajectory; after declining in the early 1990s, the rate of metal extraction witnessed a significant upswing beginning in the late 1990s and the early 2000s. This acceleration was due to the high demand from economies entering their energy- and material-intensive development phase, coupled with the ongoing high levels of consumption in developed economies.

Construction minerals

The strongest growth has been in demand for **construction minerals**. It has expanded rapidly, growing by 20Gt, a threefold increase between 1980 and 2010. As with metal ores, global extraction of construction minerals began to accelerate in the early 2000s; it grew on par with global economic growth till the early 2000s, and much faster since.[3] Economic growth and the associated expansion of the construction sector (building industries, commercial facilities and transportation and other infrastructure) have a strong influence on demand. But the need for construction minerals is related to both changes in demographics (e.g. the amount and type of housing needed) and in average wealth (e.g. the size of dwellings), as well as a number of country specific factors (i.e. geography, urban planning, consumer preferences). In recent years, these economic factors appear to have become the driving force.

Fossil energy carriers

Global extraction of **fossil energy carriers** expanded less than metal ores and construction minerals – growing by 4.8 Gt or 66% between 1980 and 2010. Throughout the 1990s when real crude oil prices were relatively low, the extraction of fossil energy carriers stabilised and in some years even declined. But by the early 2000s, as in the case of metal ores and construction minerals, extraction began to trend upward again driven by an expanding global economy.

Biomass for food and feed

From 1980 to 2010, both the world's population and the extraction of agricultural biomass increased by about 55%. Because food is essential to sustain human life, it is not surprising that changes in the amount of **biomass for food and feed** harvested are closely related to changes in population. But income also influences demand, although generally to a lesser extent. Changes in wealth typically bring changes in dietary habits, including both in the types of foods eaten and the total food intake. Meat consumption, in particular, tends to increase with wealth. More biomass (in terms of feed) is required to support a meat-based diet relative to a vegetarian diet.

Wood

Wood harvesting experienced the slowest rate of growth. The harvesting of wood grew by 11% between 1980 and 2010, significantly lower than population growth. Increased paper recycling and competition from digital media have likely contributed to flat demand for wood fibre.

Industrial minerals

Growth in the extraction of industrial minerals is more volatile than other material groups. This group consists of variety of minerals ranging from phosphate rock to diamonds, and demand is likely driven by the interaction of a number of factors. Trend data must be interpreted with caution since there are many uncertainties associated with the underlying estimates.

Material extraction increases by two-thirds when unused materials are considered

Along with 72 Gt of material resources that were extracted and entered the global economy in 2010, an additional 45 Gt of materials were extracted as a consequence, but **not used in the production process**. These materials – referred to as unused domestic extraction (UDE) – include mining overburden, harvest residues and fisheries by-catch. Soil erosion from agriculture is another important unused flow, but is not considered in this report.[4] They generally have low or no economic value. Although these materials are unused from the perspective of direct consumption and production, they often end up having other uses. Mining overburden is stored for later use in land reclamation, as is waste rock, which can also be used in road construction. Harvest residues can be used as biofuels. Fisheries by-catch can be sold as food or processed into feedstock or organic fertilizer.

Unused extraction is important, particularly for some materials; it accounts for almost 70% of the total extraction associated with **fossil energy carriers** (due to the large volume of unused materials associated with coal extraction) and more than half for **metals**, but much less for biomass and construction minerals. With unused extraction taken into account, fossil energy carriers overtake both biomass and construction minerals as the dominant material resource extracted globally, accounting for almost 40% of extraction in 2010.

Unused domestic extraction has grown almost on a par with domestic used extraction. Increased coal production, particularly in Australia, China, India and Indonesia from 2002 onwards, likely was a factor behind this growth in the amount of unused material extracted globally, as is increased metal ore extraction.

DECOUPLING AND MATERIAL PRODUCTIVITY

What is resource productivity? Resource productivity refers to the effectiveness with which an economy uses materials extracted from natural resources (physical inputs) to generate economic value (monetary outputs).

Decoupling is breaking the link between "environmental bads" and "economic goods". Absolute decoupling occurs when environmental degradation is decreasing while the economy is expanding. Decoupling is relative when environmental degradation is growing, but at a slower rate than the economy. In practice, the **measurement** of decoupling refers to the relative growth rates of a direct pressure on the environment and of an economically relevant variable to which it is causally linked.

See Glossary.

There are signs of a relative decoupling in material use from global economic growth

Global material use continues to grow in absolute terms, but progress is being made in decoupling material extraction and consumption from economic growth. Between 1980 and 2010 the material productivity of the global economy improved by amost 30%, rising from $0.70 per kilogram (2005 USD and PPPs) in 1980 to $1/kg by 2010 – meaning that the global economy generated 30% more economic value with a kilogram of material resources in 2010 than in 1980.

Productivity levels are reduced once **unused materials** are taken into account. With unused materials, in 2010 each kilogram of material resource generated $0.6 compared to $0.4/kg in 1980, a productivity loss of 40%.

But material use per capita remains high

The average person is using more material resources today than thirty years ago. Throughout the 1980s and the early 1990s per capita DMC (DEU) remained fairly stable around 8 tonnes (t) per person per year, but has been rising over the last fifteen years. In 2010 per capita DMC reached over 10 t per year, meaning that on average each person is using 29 kg of material resources per day, including 12 kg of construction minerals, 7 kg of biomass for food and feed, 5.3 kg of fossil energy carriers and 3 kg of metals. If unused domestic extraction (UDE) is included, per capita material use rises to nearly 17 tonnes per person per year in 2010 (46.6 kg per person per day), up from 13.6 tonnes in 1980.

Figure 4.5. Global material productivity and intensity per capita, 1980-2010

Global material productivity (used and unused materials), 1980, 1990, 2010

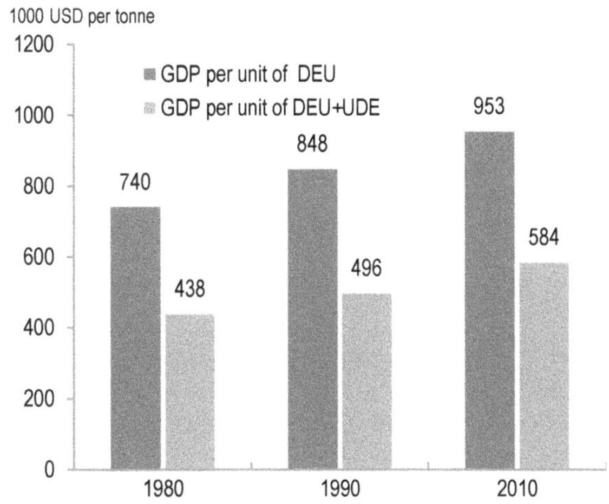

Global per capita material resource extraction (used materials), 1980-2010

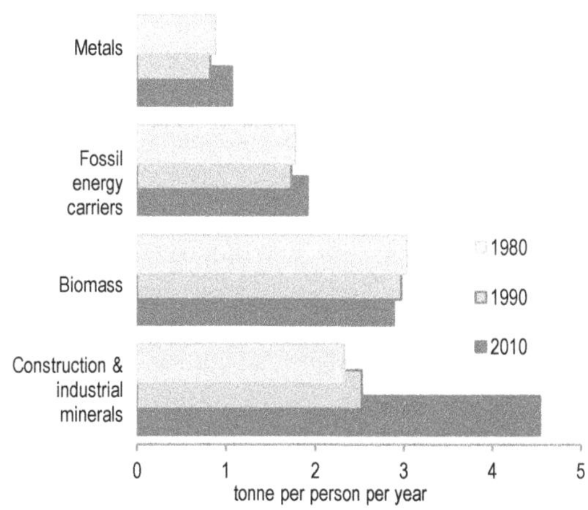

Notes: GDP in 2005 USD and PPPs.

Source: SERI/WU material flows database (www.materialflows.net), OECD (2013), OECD (2013), "Material resources", *OECD Environment Statistics* (database)

ENDNOTES

1 The OECD material flows database includes information on all 34 OECD member countries and BRIICS countries, but does not include world totals. The material flows database by the Sustainable Europe Research Institute (SERI) and the Vienna University (available at *www.materialflows.net*) has data on domestic extraction used (DEU) and unused domestic extraction (UDE) for 188 countries from which world totals were estimated. For consistency, OECD and BRIICS countries' global shares were calculated based on SERI/WU data rather than data from the OECD material flows dataset.

2 Projection by Wuppertal Institute based on business as usual scenario.

3 In the case of construction minerals, information sources have estimated missing data from non-missing values and trends in GDP (e.g. in SERI, 2010). As a result, correlations between the supply or demand of construction minerals and macroeconomic data as GDP must be interpreted with caution (Dittrich, 2010).

4 SERI has estimated that global soil erosion from agricultural land ranges between 25-50 billion tonnes a year. The indicator UDE in the OECD material flow database does not account for soil erosion. Estimating soil erosion is complex and beyond the scope of this report.

REFERENCES

- Dittrich, M. (2010), Physische Handelsbilanzen. Verlagert der Norden Umweltbelastungen in den Süden? Kölner Geographische Arbeiten 91, Köln.
- Dittrich, M. and S. Bringezu (2010), "The physical dimension of international trade, Part 1: Direct global flows between 1962 and 2005," Ecological Economics, Vol. 69, pages 1838-1847.
- EEA (2010), The European Environment: State and Outlook 2010 –Material Resources and Waste, *www.eea.europa.eu/soer/europe/material-resources-and-waste.*
- OECD (2014), *Green Growth Indicators 2014,* OECD Green Growth Studies, OECD Publishing, Paris, *http://dx.doi.org/10.1787/9789264202030-en.*
- OECD (2013), "Material resources", *OECD Environment Statistics* (database), *http:*//dx.doi.org/*10.1787/data-00695-en.*
- SERI/WU (Sustainable Europe Resource Institute/Vienna University) (2014), *Global Material Flow Database*, 2014 Version, available at *www.materialflows.net.*
- Giljum, S. et al. (2010), "Resource Use and Resource Productivity in Asia: Trends Over the Past 25 Years," SERI Working Paper, No. 11, SERI, Vienna, *http://seri.at/wp-content/uploads/2010/05/SERI-Working-Paper-11.pdf.*
- UNEP (2013), *International Resource Panel, www.unep.org/resourcepanel.*
- World Bank, World Development Indicators, *http://data.worldbank.org/data-catalog/world-development-indicators.*

Chapter 5. The material basis of OECD economies

This chapter examines trends in material flows and resource productivity in OECD countries using tools from Material Flow Analysis (MFA) and data from Material Flow Accounting (see the Reader's Guide for data sources). In MFA, the term "materials" is often used in a broad sense, so as to encompass all material-related flows arising at all stages of the material cycle. It refers to both materials and products derived from natural resources that are used as inputs into human activities, as well as residuals (such as waste or pollutant emissions) arising from their extraction and use, and ecosystem inputs (such as nutrients, carbon dioxide, and oxygen) required for their extraction and use. Here the focus is on "material resources" that designate the usable materials or substances (raw materials, energy) produced from natural resources. These usable "materials" include energy carriers (gas, oil, coal), metal ores and metals, construction minerals and other minerals, soil and biomass. Ecosystem inputs and pollutant outputs are not considered.

* The statistical data for Israel are supplied by and under the responsibility of the relevant Israeli authorities. The use of such data by the OECD is without prejudice to the status of the Golan Heights, East Jerusalem and Israeli settlements in the West Bank under the terms of international law.

TRENDS IN MATERIAL USE

Material extraction and consumption in OECD countries are growing at a slower pace than at global level

Material extraction in OECD countries has grown, but at a pace slower than global material extraction. It reached 21 Gt in 2007, a 28% increase from 1980, and then decreased to 19.7 Gt in 2011.[1] But even prior to the 2008 financial crisis, domestic extraction used (DEU) in OECD countries had begun to slow and was showing signs of stabilising around 20 Gt per year. The growth that has taken place between 1980 and 2007 has been primarily driven by greater extraction of **construction minerals**, which accounted for more than half of the increase, while **metal ore** extraction accounted for less than a quarter. The dominance of construction minerals is not surprising given their importance in the material mix of OECD countries (about 40% of total extraction) and their high weight to volume ratio.

The use of construction minerals has increased universally across all OECD regions since 1980, while growth in metal ore extraction was mainly isolated to Chile and Australia. In Chile copper ore extraction grew from 70 million tonnes (Mt) in the early 1980s to well over 500 Mt by 2010. In Australia metal ore extraction grew from under 200 Mt to over 600 Mt between 1980 and 2010, with the extraction of iron ore, copper and zinc more than doubling. Precious metal extraction increased by a factor of 12.[2] Aside from construction minerals and metals, growth in material extraction in OECD countries since 1980 has been modest, increasing by less than 1% annually and in some cases even decreasing (i.e. industrial minerals).

Roughly half of all material resource extraction in the OECD area takes place in the Americas (i.e. Canada, Chile, Mexico and the United States). OECD countries in Europe account for 35% of extraction while member countries in Asia-Oceania are responsible for the remaining 16% of extraction. Among OECD countries, the United States is the single largest extractor of material resources with 6.3 Gt extracted in 2010 – one third of all materials extracted in OECD countries. Australia, Canada, Mexico and Germany follow, each extracting between 1 and 1.8 Gt in 2010.

Domestic material consumption (DMC) in the OECD area has largely followed the same trends as DEU, growing by 30% between 1980 and 2007, with a stabilisation around 22 Gt per year, and then decreased to 20.7 Gt in 2011. The composition of material extraction and consumption are similar, with the exception that fossil energy carriers account for a slightly larger share of consumption than extraction in OECD countries, due to significant imports. In terms of regional shares in the OECD area, OECD Europe's share of consumption is slightly higher than the region's share of extraction, while the inverse if true for the OECD America region. The OECD Asia-Oceania region's share of consumption is the same as its share of extraction.

Figure 5.1. Domestic extraction used (DEU), by OECD region, 1980-2011

(billion tonnes)

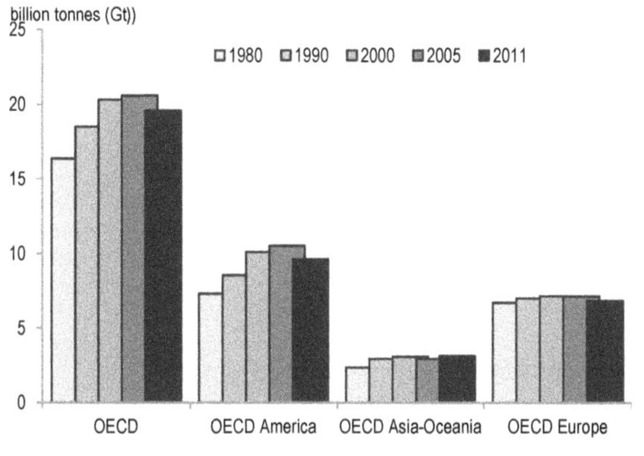

Source: OECD (2013), "Material resources", *OECD Environment Statistics* (database)

Figure 5.2. Domestic material consumption (DMC), by material group, OECD, 1980-2010

(billion tonnes)

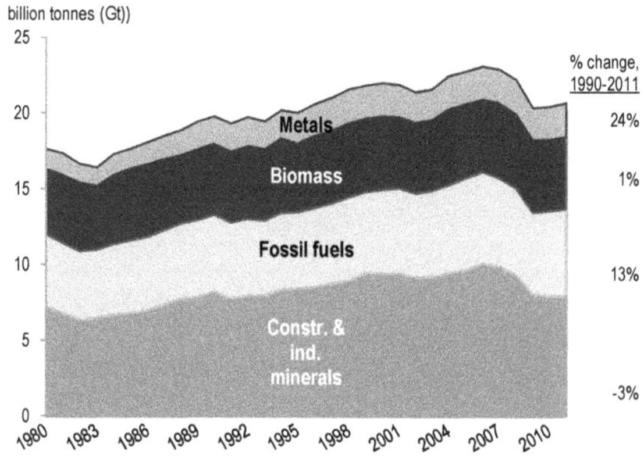

Figure 5.3. Used versus unused material extraction, by material group and by OECD region, 2010/11

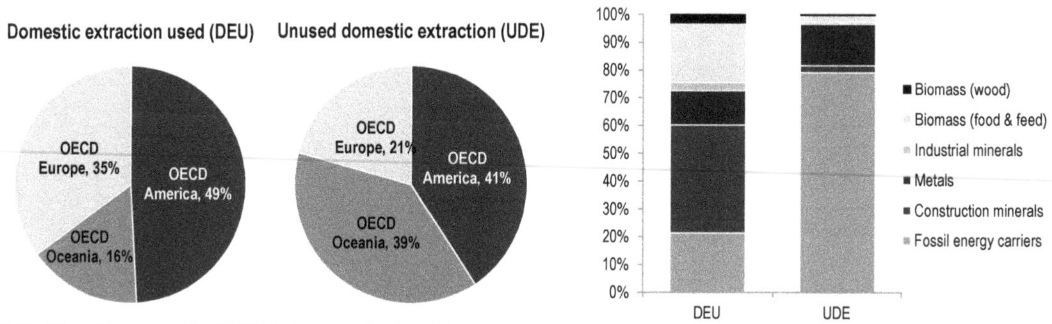

Source: OECD (2013), "Material resources", *OECD Environment Statistics* (database)

Figure 5.4. Material extraction, productivity and intensity per capita, OECD, 1980-2010

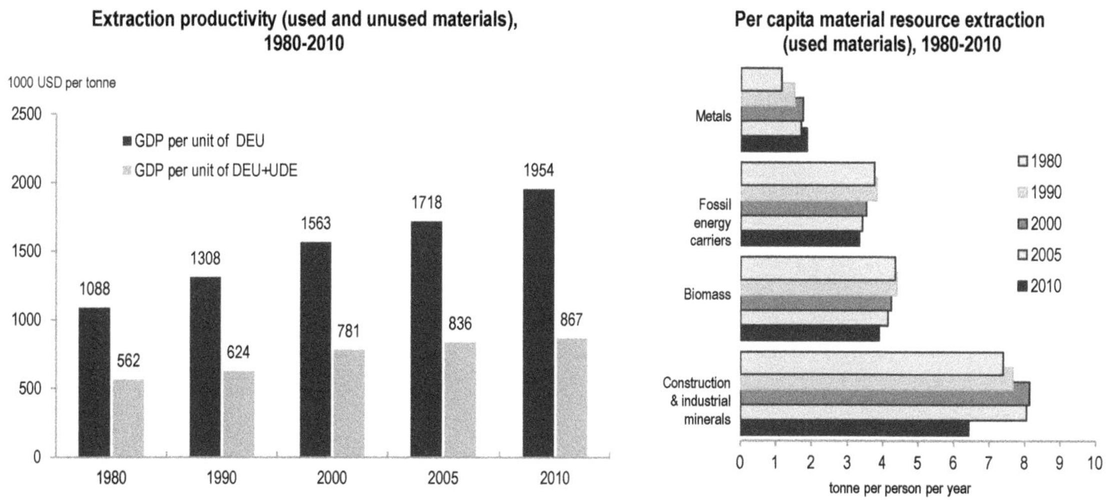

Notes: GDP in 2005 USD and PPPs.

Source: SERI/WU material flows database (www.materialflows.net); OECD (2013), "Material resources", *OECD Environment Statistics* (database).

Figure 5.5. OECD material consumption per capita, 1980-2010

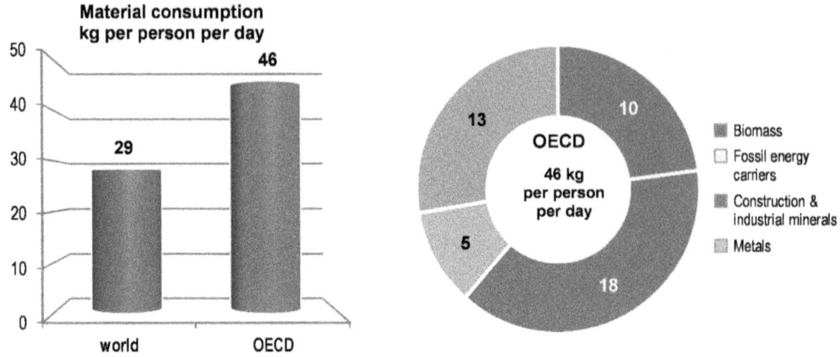

Notes: GDP in 2005 USD and PPPs.
Source: SERI/WU material flows database (www.materialflows.net OECD (2013), "Material resources", *OECD Environment Statistics* (database).

Figure 5.6. Change in domestic extraction used (DEU) and per capita GDP, 1990-2011, OECD countries

(Change, % 1990/92-2009/11)

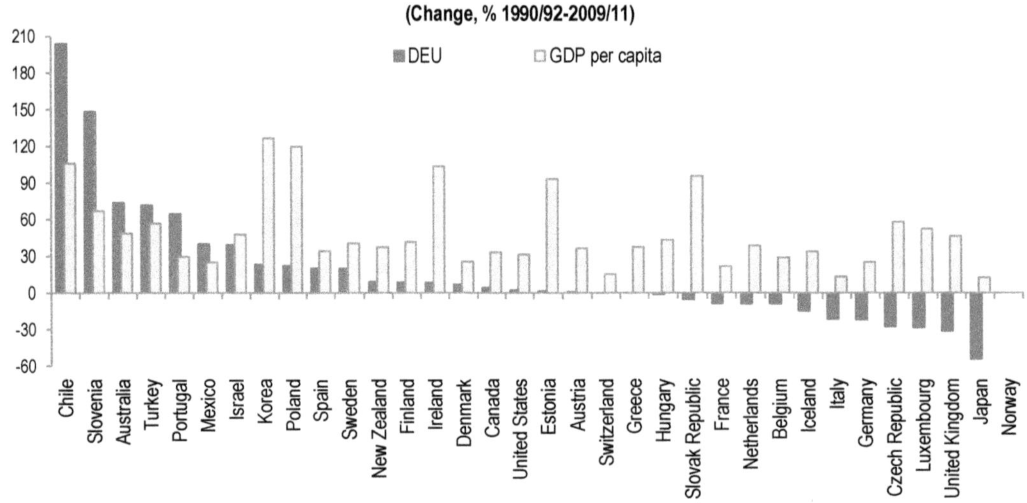

Note: GDP in 2005 USD and PPPs.
Source OECD (2013), "Material resources", *OECD Environment Statistics* (database)

Figure 5.7. GDP trends and structure, OECD, BRIICS and world, 1990-2009

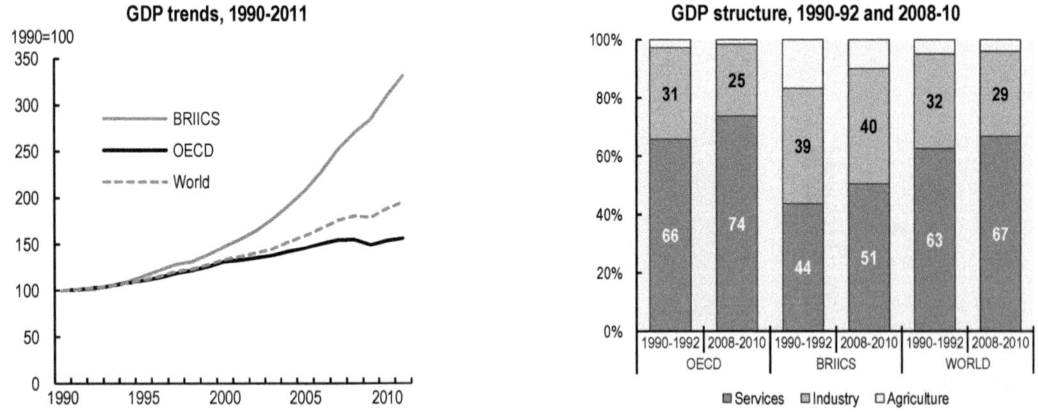

Source: OECD (2014a), *OECD Economic Outlook: Statistics and Projections* (database); *OECD National Accounts Statistics* (database), World Bank; *World Development Indicators.*

OECD economies are becoming less resource-intensive and more service-based

A number of other factors influence the amount of materials extracted and consumed in a specific country, including natural resource endowments, geography, population, average income, geopolitical stability, openness to trade and investment, and its ability to innovate and develop new technologies. Average income plays a particularly important role.

While material **extraction in OECD member countries is stabilising**, it is rising in countries experiencing rapid economic expansion and where incomes are rising, such as the **BRIICS** countries. Most of these countries experienced a **strong upswing** in material extraction starting the early 2000s, although China's surge began much earlier. By the early 1990s China had overtaken the United States as the world's largest extractor of material resources. With the exception of South Africa all of the BRIICS countries experienced large increases in material extraction when average income rose indicating that material extraction rises rapidly at relatively low levels of income when average income grows. This is likely attributable to the high rates of population growth typical of lower income countries and to the strong connection between the size of the population and the use of materials, especially those required to fulfil basic needs.

Conversely in OECD countries, where average incomes are higher, material extraction is growing less quickly. But there appears to be **two distinct trends for OECD countries** with average incomes exceeding 20 000 USD.

- In one case, material **extraction remains flat or decoupled** entirely from growth in average income. This could be because an increasing share of value added is being generated by economic activities that are not material intensive, such as the services sector, while material-intensive manufacturing is being outsourced to non-OECD countries. The share of value added from the services sector in OECD countries increased from around 50% in 1970 to 66% in the eraly 1990s and to over 70% today (OECD, 2014). The decoupling is absolute when population is decreasing faster than material extraction per capita. With the exception of Japan, all of the member countries in this group are located in Europe.
- In the other case, material **extraction continues to increase with GDP per capita**, remaining coupled with it. The growth of material extraction is weaker than in lower income countries, implying that incremental value added remains dependent on resource extraction. This group is generally characterised by, but not limited to, large resource-rich countries with relatively low population densities.

Material extraction in OECD countries doubles when unused materials are considered

The volume of unused materials extracted in OECD countries reached 24 Gt in 2011 – a level that is slightly above the volume of used extraction. Close to 80% of unused extraction is related to **fossil energy carriers** (70% of which is from coal extraction in Australia and the United States) followed by **metals**, which account for 15%. Relatively small volumes of unused extraction are associated with biomass and construction and industrial minerals.

Counter to the global trend, over the 1980-2010 period unused extraction in OECD countries has grown faster than used extraction. While it might be expected that unused extraction in OECD countries would decrease over time with improvements in extraction and processing technologies, a number of factors influence the generation of unused materials. For **minerals and metals** unused extraction actually tends to increase over time. Higher grade deposits or those that are easily accessible are usually found and extracted first. As those deposits are depleted, more must be extracted or extraction must go deeper in order to get the same amount of valuable materials from lower grade deposits (SERI, 2011). This would seem to be in the case in the OECD area.

DECOUPLING AND RESOURCE PRODUCTIVITY

Global material intensities have declined substantially in the last 30 years; energy intensity is 30% less than it was in 1970, and CO_2 intensity has dropped by almost 27% since 1980[3]. Global relative decoupling has occurred spontaneously at a rate of 1-2% per annum, mainly due to the fact that markets for bulk infrastructures, buildings and other resource intensive economic activities have been saturated in the advanced nations. In order to make the just transition to a greener, more social inclusive global economy, absolute reductions in resource use will be required in industrialised economies, while developing economies will need to face the challenge of relative decoupling (making sure that resource consumption rates are lower than economic growth rates over the long term).

Relative decoupling has been achieved, but there have been only a few instances of absolute decoupling

Although domestic material consumption has continued to increase in OECD countries since 1980, thanks to strong economic growth over the last 30 years, domestic material productivity (measured as GDP/DMC) has improved and material consumption has decoupled from economic growth in relative terms. Between 1980 and 2010 domestic material productivity of OECD economies improved, rising from 1 dollar per kilogram (2005 USD PPP) to over 1.8 USD/kg. Today, OECD countries generate 50% more economic value per unit of material resources used than in 1990 and 30% more than in 2000. Relative decoupling has occurred across all material groups and OECD regions, but there are only a handful of instances of absolute decoupling. In the OECD Asia-Oceania region, the consumption of wood and of construction and industrial minerals has decoupled from economic growth in absolute terms, as has biomass (food and feed) and fossil energy carriers consumption in the OECD Europe region.

The largest improvements have come in recent years ...

For OECD countries as a whole, the largest improvements in material productivity have come in recent years. Domestic material consumption remained relatively flat between 2000 and 2007, but decreased by 11% between 2007 and 2011.

- The strongest decoupling occurred in **wood, industrial minerals and construction minerals**, of all which saw consumption decrease between 2000 and 2011.
- The weakest productivity gains were in metals and fossil energy, where extraction has remained linked to economic growth. This trend is not isolated to OECD countries; metal and fossil fuel extraction is increasing worldwide and is growing particularly rapidly in the BRIICS countries.[4] In the OECD area, the extraction of metal ores has grown at the same pace at the economy – each more than doubled between 1980 and 2010. Increased mining activity in Chile, Australia and Mexico is primarily driving this trend. But the fact that domestic consumption of metals in OECD countries is growing more slowly than extraction (66% vs. 103%) indicates that a large portion of extraction is being exported outside of the OECD area.

... but are due to the economic slowdown after the 2008 financial crisis

The impact of the global financial crisis must be taken into consideration when reviewing and interpreting these trends. In most OECD countries, the economic slowdown caused material extraction and consumption to flatten or decrease (in some cases significantly). On average, domestic material consumption in OECD countries dropped by nearly 11% between 2007 and 2011, while GDP remained virtually level. If productivity is measured relative to 2007 consumption levels, gains are reduced.

Box 5.1. **Decoupling**

The concept of "decoupling" refers to breaking the link between "environmental bads" and "economic goods." Using this concept helps analyse and assess the linkages between environmental degradation and economic development. In practice, the measurement of decoupling refers to the relative growth rates of a pressure on the environment and of an economically relevant variable to which it is causally linked.

Decoupling occurs when the growth rate of the environmental pressure (EP) is less than that of its economic driving force (DF) over a given period. One distinguishes between absolute and relative decoupling. Decoupling is said to be absolute when the environmental variable is stable or decreasing while the economic variable is growing. Decoupling is said to be relative when environmental variable is increasing, but at a lower rate than the economic variable.

The decoupling concept has however no automatic link to the environment's capacity to sustain, absorb or resist pressures of various kinds (deposition, discharges, harvests). A meaningful interpretation of the relationship of EP to economic DF will require additional information. Also, the relationship between economic DF and EP, more often than not, is complex. Most DF have multiple environmental effects, and most EP are generated by multiple DF, which, in turn, are affected by societal responses. Changes in decoupling may thus be decomposed in a number of intermediate steps. These may include changes in the scale of the economy, in consumption patterns, and in economic structure — including the extent to which demand is satisfied by domestic production or by imports. Other mechanisms in the causal chain include the adoption of cleaner technology, the use of higher quality inputs, and the post facto clean up of pollution and treatment of waste.

In the field of natural resource and materials use two modes of decoupling can be distinguished.

- **"Resource" decoupling** or "dematerialisation" involves reducing the rate at which primary resources are used per unit of economic output.
- **"Impact" decoupling**, on the other hand, seeks to increase economic activity whilst decreasing negative environmental impacts from pressures such as pollution, CO_2 emissions or the destruction of biodiversity.

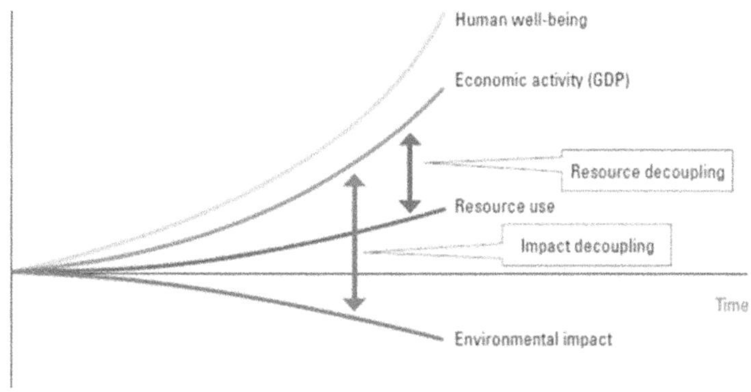

Decoupling and the rebound effect. Resource decoupling rests on the assumption that the same or greater output can be achieved with fewer inputs and that any innovation that results in better resource productivity will contribute to decoupling. In practice, however, this may not be true due to the rebound effect. If a commodity is made cheaper because it has been produced with less resources this may result in increased demand for this commodity. While the rebound effect has been well studied at the micro level and its effects were found to be limited (rebounds from 0 to 40%), questions remain in terms of its effects at the macro-economic level.

Source: Based on OECD (2002), UNEP (2011).

Figure 5.8. Domestic material productivity (GDP/DMC), OECD regions, 1980, 1990, 2000, 2005, 2011

(USD per kilogramme per year)

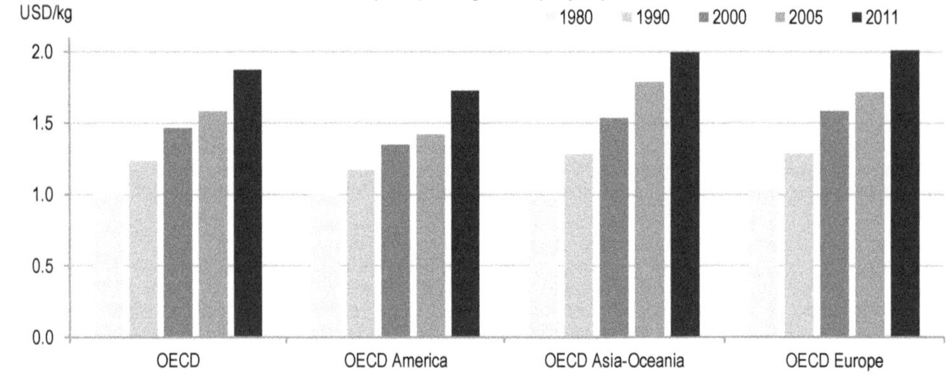

Source: OECD (2013), "Material resources", *OECD Environment Statistics* (database)

Figure 5.9. Material productivity, GDP/DMC, OECD Countries and BRIICS, 2011, 2000

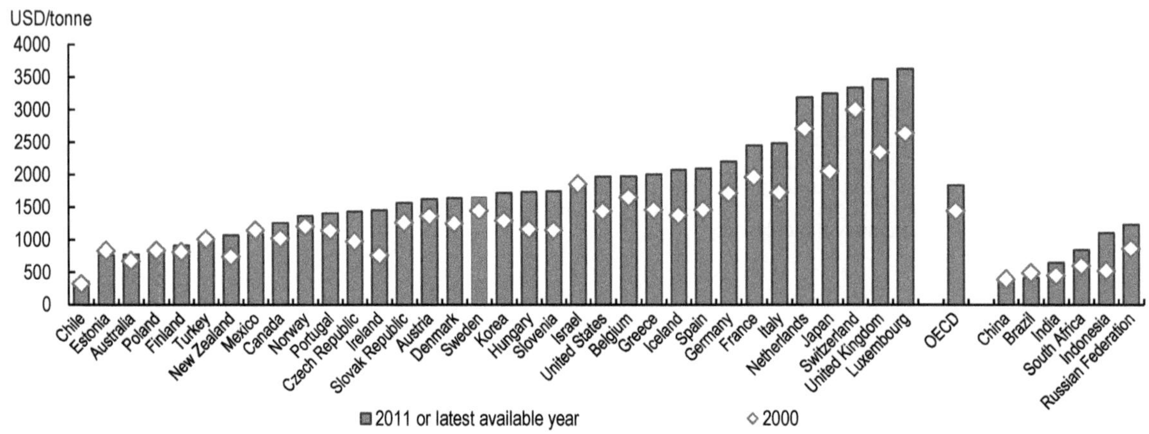

Source: OECD (2013), "Material resources", *OECD Environment Statistics* (database)

Figure 5.10. Change in domestic material consumption (DMC), OECD regions

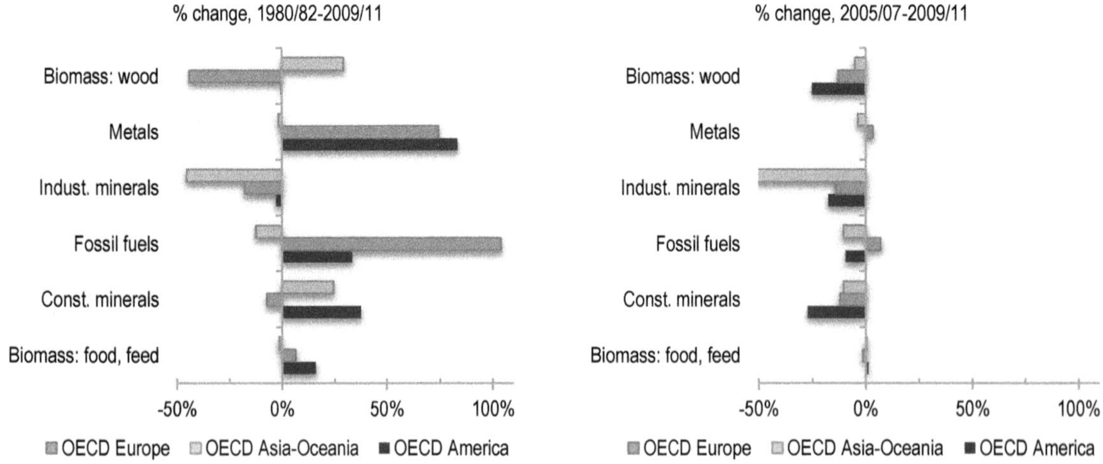

Source: OECD (2013), "Material resources", *OECD Environment Statistics (database).*

Figure 5.11. Non energy material consumption versus GDP, OECD countries, 1990-2010

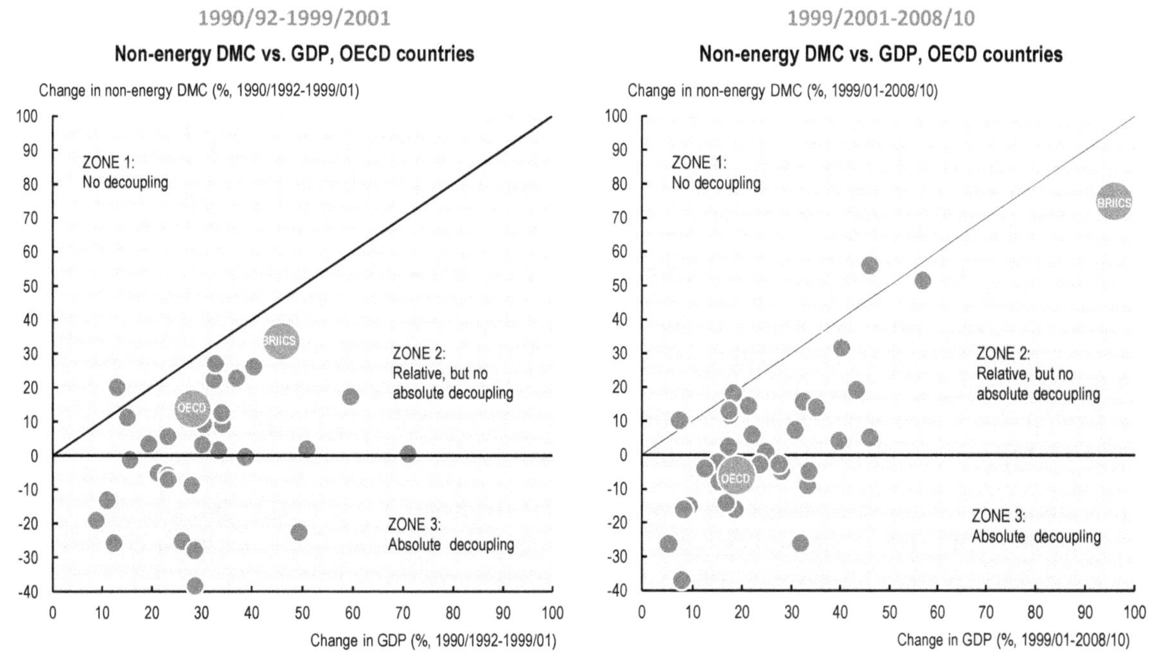

Source: OECD (2013), "Material resources", *OECD Environment Statistics* (database)

Figure 5.12. Decoupling trends: domestic material consumption versus GDP, OECD, 1990-2011

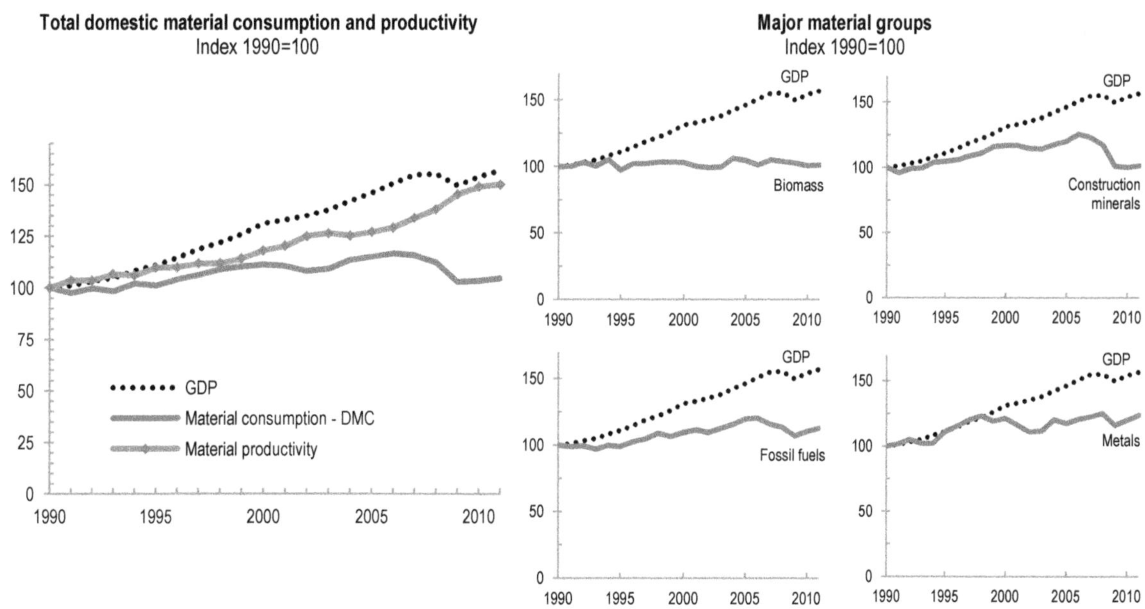

Source: OECD (2013), "Material resources", OECD Environment Statistics (database).

Per capita consumption is levelling-off, but remains high and the amounts vary widely across countries

Prior to 2008, per capita material consumption (DMC/person) in OECD countries had begun to stabilise around 19 tonnes per person per year. With the global financial crisis, per capita consumption dropped to under 18 tonnes, essentially returning to 1980 levels.

- The average person living in an OECD country consumed roughly 46 kg of materials per day in 2011, including 10 kg of biomass, 18 kg of construction and industrial minerals, 13 kg of fossil energy carriers, and 5 kg of metals.
- This is 60% more than the amount consumed on average around the world.

Within the OECD area, per capita consumption is highest in the Americas (over 20 tonnes per person), followed by the Asia-Oceania (15.5 t) and Europe (14 t). Though all regions have witnessed declining per capita consumption in recent years, OECD Europe is the only region where the decline has been consistent since 1980. The amount of material each person consumes on average varies widely across OECD countries, even for countries within the same region.

- In general per capita consumption tends to be **highest** in countries that are less densely populated and rich in natural resources (e.g. Australia, Canada, Chile, Ireland, New Zealand, Norway). In these countries per capita material consumption ranges between 25-45 tonnes per person per year.
- The **lowest** levels of per capita consumption tend to be found in countries that are densely populated and relatively natural resource-poor (e.g. Japan, United Kingdom, Italy, the Netherlands, Switzerland).
- In contrast, in 2010 per capita consumption in India and in Indonesia was around 4 to 5 tonnes per person (the lowest in the BRIICS countries) and 17 tonnes per person in China (the highest in the BRIICS countries, at a level close to that of the OECD region).

Figure 5.13. Material consumption intensities per capita (DMC per capita), OECD regions, 1980, 1990, 2000, 2005, 2011

(tonnes per person per year)

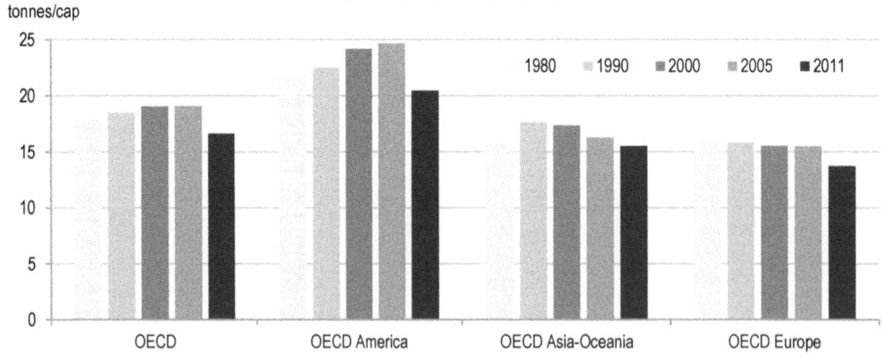

Source: OECD (2013), "Material resources", *OECD Environment Statistics* (database)

Figure 5.14. Material consumption intensities per capita (DMC per capita), OECD countries and BRIICS, 1980-2008, in tonnes per person

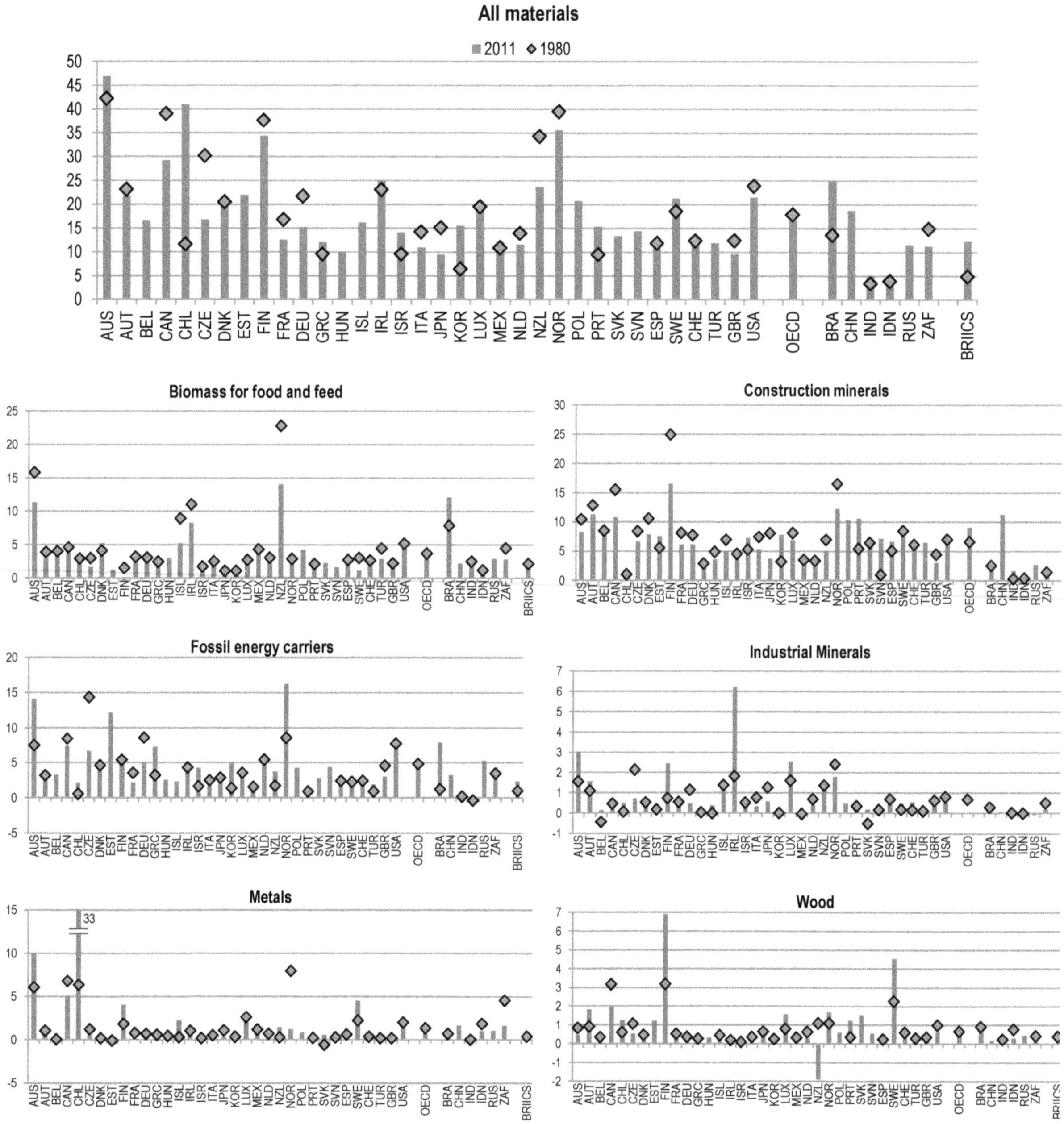

Note: OECD averages do not include Estonia, Ireland or Slovenia. Data refer to Domestic Material Consumption (DMC).

Source: OECD (2013), "Material resources", *OECD Environment Statistics* (database)

Overall reliance on imports is increasing

While the extraction of material resources domestically is stabilising, material imports are increasing and making up a growing share of material inputs in OECD economies. As a group, OECD countries have been net importers of raw materials for decades. This despite including resource-rich, export-oriented member countries such as Australia, Canada, Norway and, more recently, Chile. In 2010, more than half of the imports consisted of fossil energy.

OECD countries have a physical trade balance of 1.4 Gt (net imports).[5] They are net importers in all material groups except for biomass for food and feed (because of significant grain exports from North America). No OECD region is a net exporter of material resources overall though some regions are net exporters in specific material groups – e.g. OECD Americas in biomass (food, feed and wood) and OECD Asia-Oceania in metals.

Imports make up over 30% of material inputs in Europe and in Asia-Oceania, and less than 15% in the Americas

Direct material input (DMI) measures the direct input of materials for use in the economy that are of economic value and that are used in production and consumption activities, including the production of exports and services. DMI equals DEU plus imports.

What are indirect flows? Two types of material flows are embodied in goods – direct flows and indirect flows. Direct flows are the materials that make up the components of a product (e.g. plastic in cell phones). Indirect flows account for the upstream flows of materials required to make a product. They include both material inputs to production (used materials) and the associated outputs in the form of pollution and waste, and the materials that remain unused in the environment, such as mining overburden or harvest residues. These materials are not physically imported and usually remain in the producing country. Indirect flows are sometimes referred to as "ecological rucksacks" and together with unused domestic extraction make up the **hidden flows** associated with the production and consumption of materials.

See Glossary.

Even with the sharp retraction in trade by OECD countries in the wake of the financial crisis, which caused imports to drop in 2008, the physical trade balance of OECD countries has grown since 1995. During that period net imports into the OECD Americas and Europe regions grew, while decreasing in OECD Asia-Oceania.

In 1995 imports accounted for almost 20% of direct material input (DMI) on average in OECD countries, by 2010 this share had risen to 25%. Imports make up over 30% of DMI in OECD countries in Europe and the Asia-Oceania, and less than 15% in the Americas, whereas about 5 to 6% of material inputs into BRIICS economies are imported.

Progress on productivity is moderate once indirect flows are considered

Increasing imports of material resources are important in the context of measuring **resource productivity** because semi-finished or finished products weigh significantly less than the raw materials from which they are derived (e.g. iron ore versus steel). As a result, declining material consumption cannot be completely attributed to efficiency gains; some improvements are likely to be a reflection of increased **substitution** of domestic production by imports through a shifting of resource-intensive production from OECD economies to non-OECD economies.[6]

International trade has allowed the **physical redistribution of key material resources** that are unevenly distributed around the world, widening the distance between where goods are produced and where they are consumed. This dislocation between production and consumption has raised concerns over the distribution of the **environmental pressures** from material use. Importing countries enjoy the consumption of imported goods while the environmental costs of producing those goods remain in the exporting country (Dittrich *et al.*, 2012).

Indirect material flows associated with trade is a concept that is used to quantify the magnitude of material resources used indirectly to produce goods, but that are not embodied in those goods. They take into account upstream material flows associated with internationally traded products need to be compiled to understand to what extent global value chains influence a country's material use and resource efficiency.

- A country's direct physical trade balance (PTB) reveals to what extent it relies on foreign material resources or, conversely, it provides materials to other countries.
- Indirect PTB captures the *additional* material resources relied upon or being provided.

Figure 5.15. Physical trade balance (PTB), OECD, 1995-2010

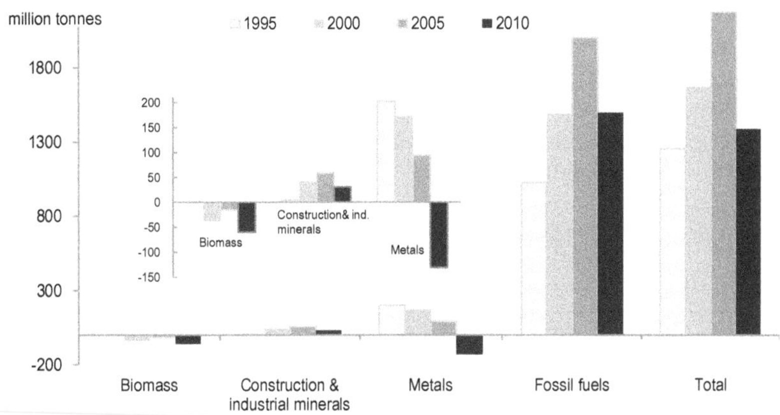

Note: Data include estimates.

Source: OECD (2013), "Material resources", *OECD Environment Statistics* (database)

Figure 5.16. Direct and indirect physical trade balance, OECD regions

(billion metric tonnes)

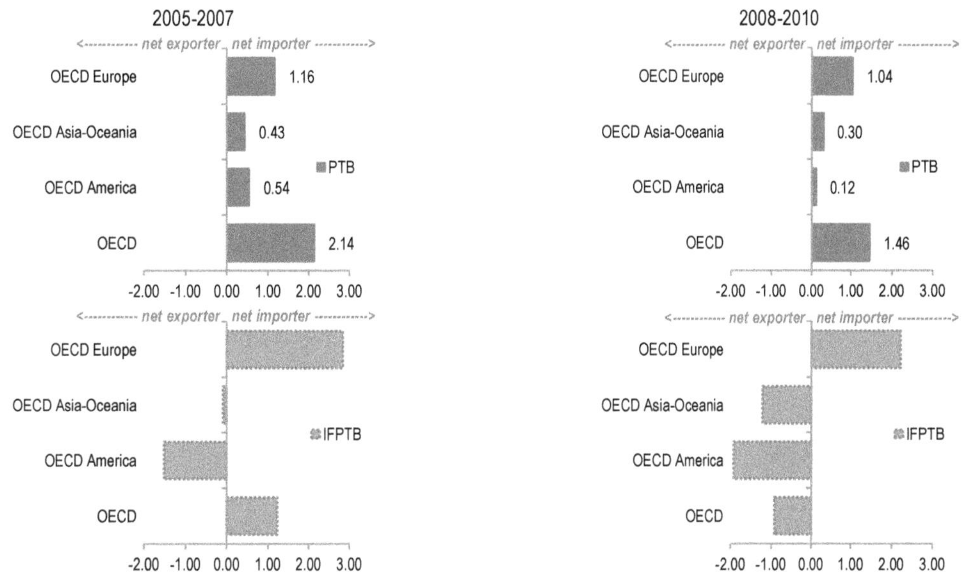

Note: Data include estimates.

Source: OECD (2013), "Material resources", *OECD Environment Statistics* (database)

Once the indirect flows associated with trade are taken into account, the material requirements of an economy can expand or shrink significantly, depending on whether a country is a net importer or a net exporter and the material intensity of their traded goods.

Estimates of indirect trade flows are available for only some OECD countries and for some years, but illustrate that these flows are significant, in particular those associated with fossil energy carriers and metals.

Accounting for hidden flows is important because they can reduce gains that have been made in reducing direct material consumption. For example, Japan is one of the leading countries in the OECD in terms of resource productivity and is one of only a handful of countries where the consumption of material resources had decoupled from economic growth in absolute terms even prior to the 2008 financial crisis. Between 1980 and 2010, Japanese domestic material consumption decreased by over 30% while the economy expanded by 90%. When including unused domestic extraction and estimated indirect flows from trade, the decrease in material consumption appears more modest - 21% between 1980 and 2010. Similarly, in Germany domestic material consumption decreased by 18% between 1995 and 2010, but accounting for unused extraction and indirect flows cuts this by 7 percentage points.[7]

Including hidden flows, OECD countries account for roughly half of global material requirements

Total material requirement (TMR) measures the material basis of an economy. It include all direct material inputs into an economy (DMI), unused domestic flows (UDE) and the indirect flows associated with imports. **Total material consumption (TMC)** quantifies the amount of materials used, both directly and indirectly, for *domestic* production and consumption activities. TMC is equal to TMR less exports and their indirect flows.

See Glossary.

Estimates of indirect material trade flows and unused domestic extraction that are currently available do not include excavated soil from construction, dredged sediment or erosion from agricultural land, which are important components that are required to estimate the total material requirement (TMR) or total material consumption (TMC) of OECD countries.

TMR and TMC are the most complete indicators from an environmental point of view because they account for hidden flows. But for this same reason they are the most difficult to estimate. Based on currently available information the total material requirement of OECD economies was likely around 80 Gt in 2010 and total material consumption around 45 Gt (excluding excavated soil, dredged sediment or soil lost though erosion). Based on these estimations the average person living in an OECD country consumes, directly and indirectly, about 40 tonnes of raw materials per year or over 100 kg per day.

Figure 5.17. Estimated per capita "total" material consumption, OECD regions, 2010/11

(tonnes per person per year)

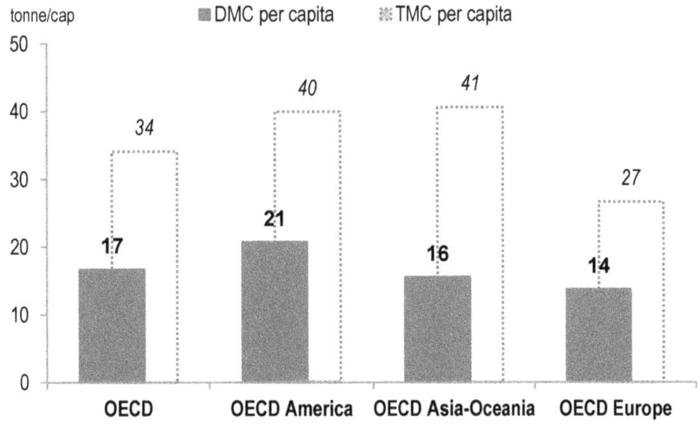

Notes: Figures for TMC are partial estimates and do not include excavated soil from construction, dredged sediment or erosion from agricultural land, nor do they include all indirect flows. Actual TMC figures would be higher.

Source: OECD (2013), "Material resources", *OECD Environment Statistics* (database)

TRENDS IN MATERIAL USE BY MATERIAL GROUP

The following sections describe major trends in the extraction, consumption and trade of different material groups in OECD countries. No attempt has been made here to assess the implications of these trends for environmental quality and resource productivity. This would require better information on environmentally weighted material flows, and further details on material flows that raise specific environmental challenges. The factsheets presented in Part II of this report provide insights into some of these flows.

CONSTRUCTION MINERALS

Construction minerals account for the largest share of material consumption in OECD countries

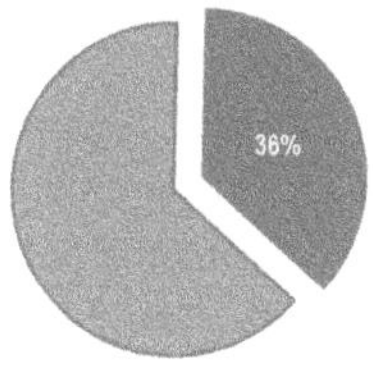

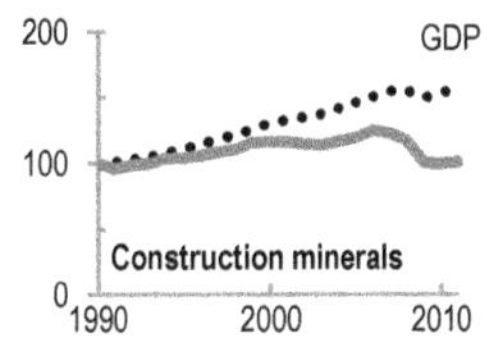

Construction minerals account for the largest share of direct material **extraction and consumption** in OECD countries (39% in 2010). This group of materials consist of minerals, such as sand, gravel and crushed stone, used in the construction of housing, buildings, bridges, roads and other infrastructure. Demand for construction minerals is widespread across OECD countries and around the world, but international trade is limited because suitable minerals are also widely available in most countries. They also have relatively **low economic value per unit of mass** and are bulky, making transportation across medium and long distances uneconomic. Construction minerals dominate the material mix in OECD countries, but their contribution to the overall physical trade balance of the OECD area is the smallest of all material groups even when indirect flows are considered.

The **low volume of indirect flows** associated with construction minerals is partly due to the relatively small amount of unused materials generated during mineral extraction. The ratio of unused to used material is less than 10% in OECD countries.

> Box 5.2. **Environmental impacts**
>
> Some of the **potential environmental impacts** associated with the extraction and consumption of construction minerals include the sealing of land area, soil compaction, loss of biodiversity, carbon emissions (particularly from the cement industry), land use change due to extraction. Construction and demolition waste make up the largest waste stream in many OECD countries although the recovery of demolition waste (especially concrete) for use as construction aggregate is increasing.

Given the **limited volume of physical trade**, per capita domestic extraction is virtually the same as per capita domestic consumption in OECD countries. And because of the low UDE/DEU ratio associated with construction minerals, total material consumption (TMC) is only slightly higher than DMC. This is true for any level of GDP per capita. In general, per capita consumption of construction minerals grows significantly when GDP per capita is below 20 000 dollars USD[8] but tends to stay between 5 and 15 t per capita per year once average income exceeds 20 000 USD.

Flows of construction minerals are considered non-toxic and their specific **environmental impacts** (i.e. impact per unit mass) are low relative to other materials, such as industrial minerals or metals. From an environmental point of view, the use of construction minerals remains important because the overall magnitude of their flows is high in terms of weight. Construction minerals account for over 20% of total material extraction (used and unused materials) in OECD countries. The cumulative environmental impacts of the use of these materials can be very high (OECD, 2008b). In many OECD countries, waste from construction and demolition is the largest waste stream.

Fossil energy carriers

Fossil energy carriers and fuels represent over a quarter of material consumption in OECD countries

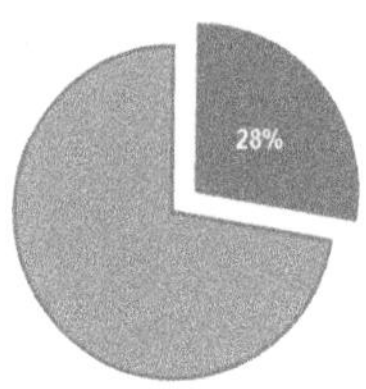

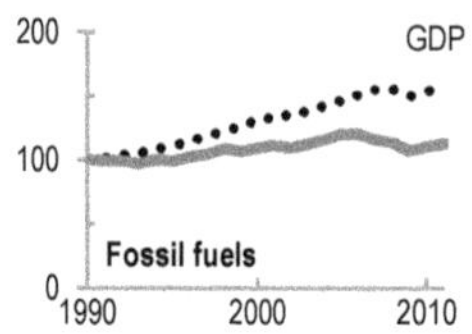

Fossil energy carriers account for one fifth of domestic material **extraction** and more than one quarter of domestic material **consumption** in OECD countries. Unlike construction minerals, international flows of fossil energy carriers are large. International trade in fossil energy carriers by OECD member countries has been increasing over time. In 2012, OECD countries produced 3.9 billion tonnes of oil equivalent (Gtoe) of primary energy while their total primary energy supply (TPES) was 5.3 Gtoe. As a consequence, 25% of the energy consumed by OECD countries in 2012 was imported from non-OECD countries. Fossil fuels account for over 80% of TPES in OECD countries and despite steps taken after the first oil supply shock in 1973 to reduce oil dependency, oil remains the largest component of TPES (36% in 2012) (IEA, 2013). Australia, Canada, Denmark, Mexico and Norway are the only countries within the OECD that meet their demand for fossil energy carriers wholly through domestic sources (i.e. their domestic material dependency, DEU/DMC, exceeds 1). All other OECD countries are net importers of fossil energy carriers.

Extraction

In 2010, 60% of all **extraction** (DEU) of fossil energy carriers in the OECD area took place in the Americas region with the United States alone accounting for 45%. OECD countries in Europe represent one fourth of extraction with the remaining 15% occurring in member countries in Asia-Oceania, although virtually all of this extraction is attributable to Australia. The highest levels of per capita domestic extraction tend to be in less densely populated countries with large fossil fuel-based energy sectors, such as Australia, Canada or Norway.

Consumption

In general the **consumption (DMC)** of fossil energy carriers in the OECD area follows the same pattern as extraction. OECD countries in the Americas account for the largest share of consumption (50%), followed by European countries (32%) and countries in Asia-Oceania (19%). The United States remains the largest single consumer of fossil energy carriers in the OECD area.

On average, a person living in an OECD country in 2010 consumed (DMC) 4.6 t of fossil energy carriers (compared to a global average of 1.9 t). But consumption levels vary from as high as 16 t per person in Norway to 1.5 t per person in Portugal. A number of factors influence per capita consumption of fossil energy carriers, including: differences in resource endowments, the proximity of supplies, the existence of transport infrastructure to deliver the fuel (especially important for natural gas), and different levels of taxation (likely to affect the characteristics of demand units through price signals). A country's energy mix is another important factor. Different types of fossil energy carriers have different net calorific values (i.e. energy per unit mass). Approximately 1.5 to 2 times more coal (by weight) is needed to deliver the same amount of energy as oil and 2-3 times more coal is required when compared to natural gas. As a result, coal-intensive countries tend to have higher values of DMC per capita, while countries relying predominantly on natural gas tend to have lower values of DMC per capita.

Hidden flows

From a material flow perspective, **hidden flows** are one of the biggest challenges associated with the use of fossil energy carriers. Unused domestic extraction (UDE) associated with fossil energy carriers makes up the largest share of total UDE in OECD countries (accounting for nearly 80%) and around the world (67%). The volume of unused materials extracted varies by type of fossil energy carrier. For coal, UDE is several times larger than DEU while for oil and gas the ratio of unused to used extraction is generally less than 20%. Because mining techniques can vary with the nature of the deposit, the origin of the coal being used is also important. Of the estimated 19.5 Gt of unused materials extracted with fossil energy carriers in OECD countries in 2010, the majority was associated with coal mining. Imports of fossil energy carriers are also associated with large indirect flows, which underlie the large indirect physical trade balance of several OECD countries.

Consequently, **total material consumption** (TMC) of fossil energy carriers is likely significantly greater than domestic material consumption (DMC), but its magnitude is heavily dependent on the fossil energy mix of a given country. In general, once indirect flows from trade and unused extraction are accounted for, per capita consumption increases the most in countries where coal dominates fossil fuel consumption and the least in countries that are primarily reliant on natural gas. For example, in Australia where coal accounts for over 70% of domestic material consumption of fossil energy carriers, TMC per capita is at least 25 times greater than DMC per capita and is estimated in excess of 300 t per person per year in 2010. In Switzerland, where around 1% of the DMC of fossil energy carriers is represented by coal, TMC per capita is 2 times greater than DMC per capita, estimated at around 3.9 t per person a year.

BIOMASS FOR FOOD AND FEED

Biomass for food and feed representone fifth of material consumption in OECD countries

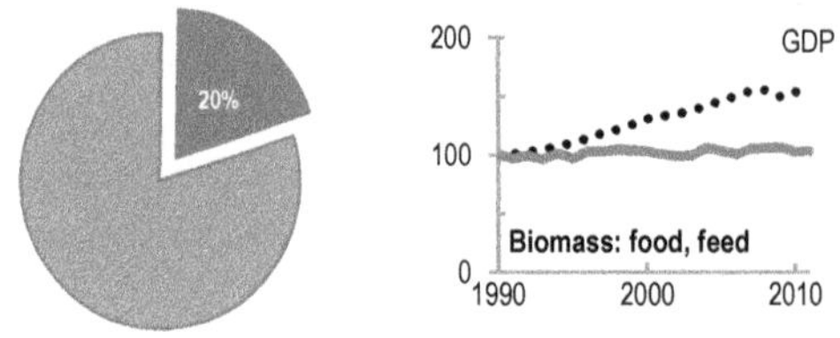

Agricultural biomass provides the food to sustain human populations and is one of the most fundamental of all material flows. It is the second largest component of global material extraction (used materials, i.e. DEU) and the second largest component in OECD countries after construction minerals. The share of biomass for food and feed harvested annually in OECD has been declining relative to non-renewable resource extraction, but the agricultural sector remains important to many OECD economies. About 36% of land in the OECD area is used for agriculture and OECD countries are major producers of world food supplies. Net exports reached 100 Mt in 2010. OECD countries are major producers and exports of the main traded agricultural commodities – cereals, meat and dairy products – excluding tropical products and rice (OECD, 2008e).

The amount of agricultural biomass that a country harvests and consumes depends on a number of factors, including population, climate, the amount of arable land, dietary habits (e.g. meat-based or vegetarian) and regulatory aspects (e.g. international trade and subsidies). The world's most populous countries and regions tend to harvest and consume the most agricultural biomass: Brazil, China, India, Europe, and the United States. But within the OECD area, countries with low population densities and a large share of agricultural land devoted to pasture land and grassland to support cattle and dairy industries (i.e. Australia, Ireland and New Zealand) have the highest rates of extraction on a per capita basis – in excess of 10 tonnes per person per year.

Consumption

Within the OECD area changes in the average level of wealth seem to have little influence on the per capita rate of biomass **consumption**; whereas in the BRIICS and other countries with similar levels of GDP per capita consumption rises rapidly with increases in income. In the latter group of countries, rising wealth likely leads to changes in dietary habits, including the increased consumption of meat and higher levels of food consumption overall. In the OECD area, where dietary habits are largely established, the changes in the level of individual wealth have limited effects on the rate of biomass extraction. Changes in biomass requirements in OECD countries most likely stem from changes in population, including the age distribution and the associated changes in food demand.

In general OECD countries where pastureland makes up the major part of agricultural land have the highest levels of DMC per capita (i.e. Australia, New Zealand and Ireland; Iceland is the exception). Otherwise, DMC per capita in OECD countries ranges between 1 to 7 tonnes per year (or 3 – 20 kg per day). Per capita consumption is generally lowest in OECD Asia, 1-1.5 tonnes per year, and highest in North America, around 4-5 t per year. Lower levels of biomass extraction and consumption per capita in Asian countries relative to Europe and North America are likely attributable to dietary habits. Countries with diets more focused on meat are amongst the largest consumers of biomass per capita. DEU per capita is very similar to the level of DMC per capita, revealing that international trade of biomass in physical terms is fairly limited when compared to the amount of domestic production.

Hidden flows

A relatively small amount of **unused materials** are generated from harvesting activities, but the consumption of biomass has other important environmental implications. It directly impacts on ecosystems, biodiversity and ecological services such as carbon sequestration and water purification. The use of land for agriculture competes directly with other land uses, including land use by nature. Consequently, the indirect flows associated with imports and exports of food and agricultural products are significant and once taken into account can flip countries from being a net exporter to a net importer of biomass for food and feed.

Total material consumption for food and feed is likely 15-20% greater than domestic material consumption for many OECD countries.

METALS AND METAL ORES

Metals and metal ores make up a small but growing share of material consumption in OECD countries

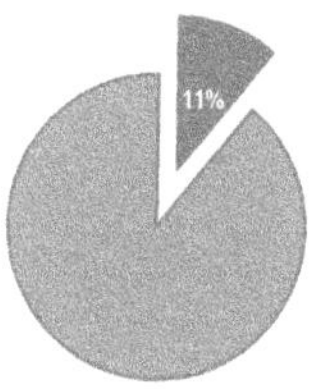

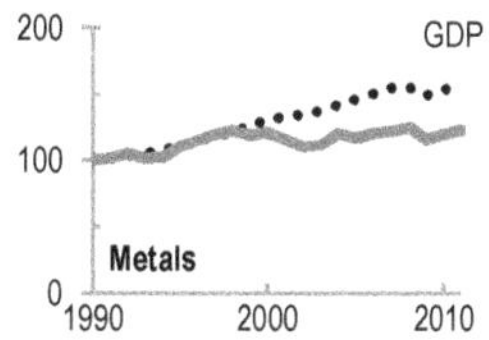

The strongest increase in domestic **extraction and consumption** in OECD countries has been in metals and metal ores. DEU has doubled and DMC has grown by 65% since 1980 to reach 2.2 Gt in 2011. In the OECD area, those countries rich in metallic mineral resources tend to be the largest producers and consumers of metals and metal ores. Australia, Canada, Chile, Mexico, Poland, Turkey and the United States accounted for 95% of metal ore extraction in OECD countries in 2010 and more than 80% of consumption. France, Germany, Italy, Japan, Korea and Spain are other important metal consumers within the OECD area.

The close parallel between producer and consumer countries is because the indicator DMC is based on mine output, meaning the volume of metal ore processed rather than volume of the metals obtained from them (i.e. metal output). Metals are characterised by low mass concentration in their ores, generally close to 30-50%. A large amount of other materials are also extracted with metal ores, which is included in DEU if it is part of the mine output that is processed (i.e. the metal ore) and otherwise is counted as unused domestic extraction. The metal content of a mine's total output, including **unused materials**, is typically around 1 to 5%. In comparison, the mass concentration of liquid and gaseous fossil energy carriers at the wellhead is generally close to 100% (excluding coal).

Australia appears to be the only OECD country where a significant portion of the metal ore extracted is exported to be refined and processed overseas. It exported 450 Mt of metal ores in 2010, most of which was iron ore and bauxite (aluminium ore). The energy-intensity of the aluminium smelting process makes it more economical to export bauxite for processing to countries with relatively cheap and abundant sources of energy. Iron ore is exported to fast-growing neighbouring Asian economies, such as China, who face much lower labour costs and have large domestic supplies of coal available to power the refining process.

With the exception of countries where metal ores have an important role in the economy (i.e. Australia, Canada, Chile, Mexico, Poland, Turkey and the United States), DMC per capita ranges between 100 kg and 4 tonnes per person a year in OECD countries. Some of this variation is due to differences in economic structure. Countries with large manufacturing sectors typically consume more metals. The type of metal ore being extracted also influences DMC, again because DMC is based on mine output rather than metal output. The amount of non-target materials (processed output and unused materials) generated as part of the ore extraction process is 3-4 times greater than metal content for iron ore, about 20-30 times larger for metals like nickel, lead and zinc, more than 200-300 times larger for precious metals like gold and platinum, and a few thousand times larger for uranium.

Box 5.3. **What drives international flows of metals?**

Like fossil energy carriers, reserves of metal ores are geographically concentrated in a handful of countries. But the cost of refining metal ore into metal is another important factor driving metal flows. In general the heavier the material, the more costly it is to transport. Unlike fossil energy carriers, metal ores become much lighter once upgraded to concentrates or processed into semi-finished products, making them more economical to transport long distances. Generally, metal ores are processed – at least partly – close to their extraction site. However, determining whether it is economical to co-locate extraction and processing activities also involves weighing transportation costs against the nature of refining process, energy costs and the price of the refined material. Other factors such as geopolitical risks or labour costs also come into play.

INDUSTRIAL MINERALS

Industrial minerals represent a very small share of material consumption in OECD countries

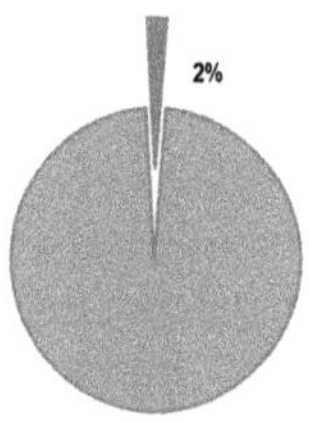

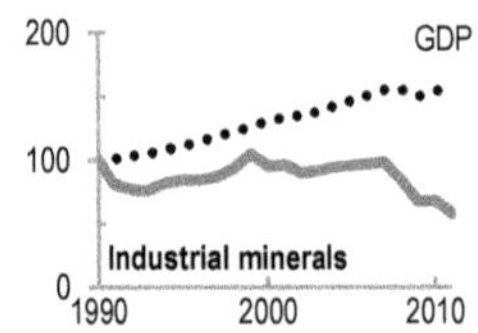

Alongside wood, industrial minerals account for the smallest share of material **extraction** both in OECD countries and around the world. Around 600 Mt were extracted in OECD countries in 2010, representing around 3% of all materials extracted (not including unused extraction). **Unused materials** and both direct and indirect trade flows are small in absolute terms.

The material flows of industrial minerals are relatively small, particularly in comparison to fossil energy carriers or construction minerals, but their specific **environmental impacts** can be very high. Industrial minerals include a wide variety of **high-value minerals**, ranging from diamonds to phosphate rock to asbestos. Flows of industrial minerals (and products derived from them such as chemical fertilizers and pesticides) can be toxic, accumulating in the environment and living species and presenting a danger to human and ecosystem health.

The minerals in this group have very different **physical and chemical properties** and many are used in highly specialised applications. Applying Material Flow Analysis at the material level, rather than the group level, would provide greater insight into the specific factors driving the production and consumption of each mineral. But data quality issues hamper a more detailed analysis of material flows of industrial minerals.[9] The factsheet on phosphorus in Part II of this report describes some of the economic and environmental issues related to the production and consumption of phosphate rock, the dominant material in this group by weight.

WOOD

Wood represents the smallest share of material consumption in OECD countries

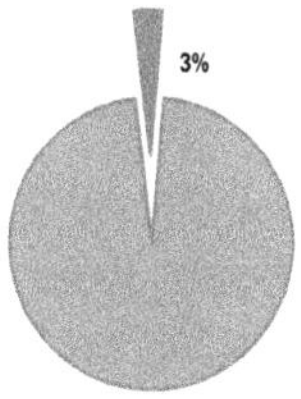

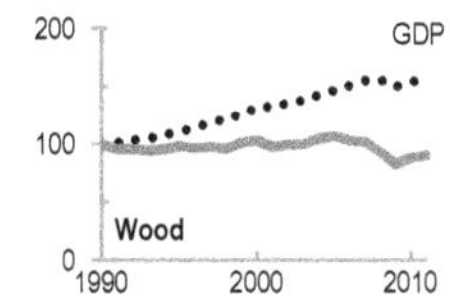

OECD countries hold over 25% of the world's forest land, roughly 10 million km^2 (FAO, 2010b). In 2010, the harvesting of wood materials in OECD countries totalled 630 Mt or around 3% of domestic material extraction. Canada has the largest amount of forest land in the OECD area and the United States is the single largest wood producer among member countries.

But in **per capita terms**, the largest producers are generally those countries with low population densities and significant amount of forest land: Canada, Estonia, Finland, New Zealand and Sweden. In these countries, DEU per capita exceeds two tonnes per person per year whereas in non-wood producing countries rates are generally less than half a tonne per person per year. With the exception of South Africa, all of the BRIICS countries are major global producers of wood. The BRIICS countries hold over 40% of the global forest land (FAO, 2010b) and harvested over almost 780 Mt of wood materials in 2010.

Countries that are the largest **producers** of wood (both in absolute and per capita terms) tend to also be the largest **consumers**, indicating that wood is largely being processed locally. Consumption is also influenced by differences in end uses for wood across OECD countries (i.e. residential and building construction, pulp and paper, wood fibre derivatives[10], biofuels and bioplastics). OECD countries as a group are net **importers** of wood materials. Canada is the largest global supplier of forest products both among OECD countries and globally, with net wood material exports reaching 11 Mt in 2010. Japan is the largest net importer of wood materials in the OECD. Imports are mainly of timber for use in the construction industry. See also the factsheet on paper in Part II of this report.

As with biomass from agriculture, the amount of **unused material** associated with the harvest of wood is relatively small.

Box 5.4. **Deforestation and climate change.**

Forests play a vital role in carbon sequestration. As they grow, plants and trees remove carbon from the atmosphere through photosynthesis. When soils are disturbed through ploughing or trees are cut down, the stored carbon oxidises and escapes back into the atmosphere as CO2. Annual emissions from deforestation are estimated to account for 18% of global greenhouse gas emissions, greater than produced by the whole of the global transport sector. The bulk of emissions from deforestation arise when the land is converted to agricultural production. Conversions to agricultural land through slash and burn techniques releases most of this as CO2 (Stern, 2005).

WASTE AND SECONDARY RAW MATERIALS

About one fifth of the materials extracted worldwide end up as waste

The amount of waste generated by economic activity globally is rising in line with growing consumption of raw materials. The increasing volume of waste raises concerns not only for the quality of the environment, but also in terms of supply security as many valuable materials are being disposed of as waste and are potentially lost to the economy.

Information gaps constrain a detailed analysis

Despite these concerns, there are important gaps in our knowledge of the magnitude and nature of global waste and waste flows. These gaps stem from a number of issues, including different definitions of waste across countries and inconsistent or non-existent tracking and reporting of waste streams. Moreover in developing countries, where waste collection often takes place on an informal basis, there is little information available.

For these reasons, calculating the amount of waste generated worldwide is challenging. Global annual waste generation is roughly estimated in excess of 12 billion metric tonnes (Gt) per year, including over 0.4 Gt of hazardous waste.[11] OECD countries produce around one third (4 Gt) of the world's waste, including over 0.085 Gt of hazardous waste. The BRIICS countries generate as much as 7 Gt of waste per year. Based on these estimates the equivalent of about one fifth of global material extraction (60 Gt) ends-up as waste each year, while the rest is emitted to the atmosphere (e.g. through the combustion of fossil fuel) or is added to man-made material stocks in the economy in the form of infrastructure, investment and consumer goods. [12]

Trends in waste generation vary significantly across OECD countries

Where data are available, they show diverse trends in **total waste generation** over the last decade across OECD member countries. Whereas total waste generation has decreased 10-20% in Germany and the United Kingdom, it has been flat in Japan while increasing by 30-60% in Chile, Italy and Korea.

There are also diverse trends in the **composition of waste** across and within OECD countries. In the OECD Europe region construction and demolition waste represents the lion's share of total waste (40%), followed by waste from manufacturing (15%), mining and quarrying (14%), and households (10%). In Japan manufacturing industries generate the largest share of waste (30%), followed by agriculture and forestry (20%), and sewage and refuse disposal and construction (16-17% each), while in Chile municipal waste (39%) is the largest share of total waste generated followed by construction (34%), and manufacturing industries (11%). (OECD Environmental data; and Eurostat Environmental Data Centre on Waste, 2011)

These developments reflect economic growth and structural changes, and waste and materials management practices. They may however also reflect changes in the statistical coverage of waste flows over time.

Box 5.5. **What's in our waste?**

The composition of solid waste varies across countries and is influenced by a number of factors. Income plays an important role in the composition of municipal solid waste. Generally waste in high-income countries tends to contain more packing materials and manufactured products/materials, and less organic waste. Conversely organic waste can make up 50-80% of municipal waste in lower income countries (Chalmin & Gaillochet, 2009). Other factors that have been observed to have an influence are seasons, education levels, age, housing type and location (rural/urban).

MUNICIPAL SOLID WASTE

Efforts by OECD countries to curb waste generation show first results

The best documented waste stream is municipal solid waste (MSW), which includes waste collected from households, and similar waste from small businesses, institutions, and office buildings. It accounts for roughly 10% of global waste generation. An estimated 1.3 – 1.9 Gt of municipal waste is produced every year worldwide, with OECD countries accounting for between one third to one half.

Over the last two decades, OECD member countries have invested significant efforts into curbing MSW generation and minimising the amounts that go to final disposal. The amounts being generated appear to have stabilised and per capita generation shows a downward trend. Between 2000 and 2012 per capita MSW generation decreased by 5.4% in the OECD area.

While some of the municipal waste reduction is likely attributable to the economic and financial crises, which has constrained household consumption, significant efforts on the part of OECD countries to better manage municipal waste over the past decades are largely responsible for this positive trend. This is visible in the share of material being recovered from municipal waste for recycling or composting, which has increased from 19% in 1995 to 34% in 2012 in OECD countries. It should be noted that the economic feasibility of recycling depends on population density, distance to markets and transportation costs of secondary materials. Countries where these factors are unfavourable, will therefore usually display lower levels of recycling.

Waste generated per capita remains high compared to other countries in the world

OECD countries, however, remain some of the world's biggest producers of municipal waste in per capita terms. On average a person living in an OECD generated 530 kg of MSW generation per year in 2012 compared to 500 kg in 1990. It is important to note that there is wide variation in waste generation intensities between OECD member countries, indicating that factors beyond income, such as the rate of urbanisation, consumption patterns, and lifestyles, also play an important role.

Per capita waste generation is increasing in some of the emerging economies, reaching on levels similar to OECD countries. In Russia an estimated 560 kg of municipal waste was generated per inhabitant in 2012, up from 290 kg/person in 1985. Rates are lower in China, between 200-300 kg per inhabitant (based on OECD, 2009 and Chalmin & Gaillochet, 2009), and in urban areas of development countries, around 150 kg/person (Chalmin & Gaillochet, 2009).

Figure 5.18. Trends in municipal waste, OECD

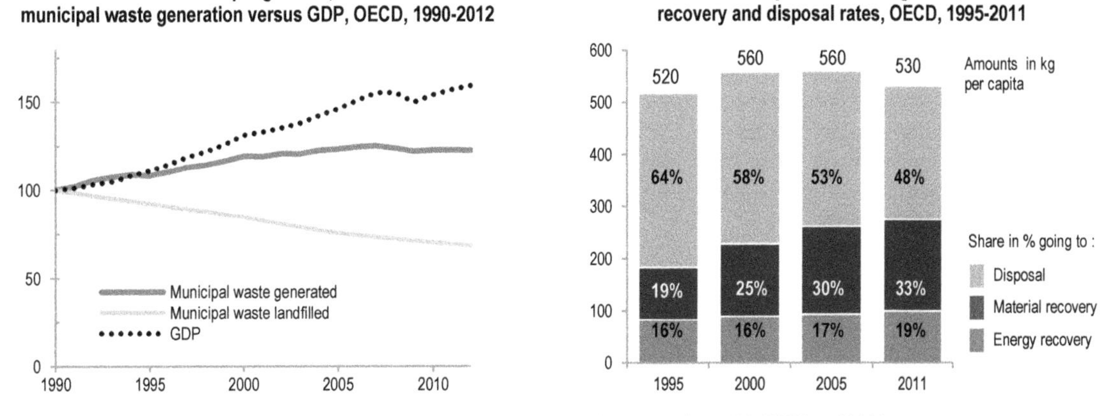

Source: OECD (2014b), "Municipal waste", *OECD Environment Statistics* (database). *http://dx.doi.org/10.1787/data-00601-en*

MATERIAL RECOVERY

Recycling rates have increased for a number of high volume materials, but remain low for many high value materials

In parallel, more and more materials are being diverted from disposal facilities and fed back into the economy through recycling or energy recovery. Virtually all OECD countries have developed ambitious recycling policies and programmes, resulting in recycling rates well above 50% for many **high-volume materials** and products (such as glass, paper, beverage cans and steel). In some countries and for some materials collection rates for recycling approach 95%, such as for glass in Belgium, the Netherlands and Switzerland where rates exceed 90%. In almost all OECD countries recycling rates have increased considerably over the last decade.

While recycling rates have reached very high levels for some of the ferrous and non-ferrous metals, there are a lot of **precious or specialty metals**[13] that are not recycled or for which recycling rates remain very low. The UNEP International Panel on Resources estimates that out of 60 surveyed metals, only 18 are currently recycled at rates above 50%, and 36 metals have recycling rates of less than 10%, leaving significant scope for further progress in this area (UNEP, 2011). Rates remain low for many of these metals because recycling is uneconomic or unfeasible with current technology and know-how. Increasing demand and rising prices for metals makes scrap recovery more attractive, leading to greater investment in recycling research and technologies (e.g. rare earth elements).

Trade in waste and recyclables has the potential to maximise economic and environmental efficiencies, but, despite legal safeguards, illegal shipments remain a problem

The globalisation of trade has made the transboundary movement of **non-hazardous** waste an attractive and cost-efficient recovery and disposal option for many countries. There is little harmonisation in import-export waste data making it difficult to assess the volume of waste that is being traded internationally. According to Basel Convention reports more than 8.5 Mt of waste was traded in 2001, but data are incomplete as not all countries report waste movements to the Basel Convention and radioactive waste is not included (UNEP, 2004).

While the trade in waste can maximise cost efficiencies and the use of specialised technologies, there is also the potential to mask trade in contaminated or hazardous wastes. A number of legal instruments have been put in place to control the transboundary movement of waste, in particular **hazardous wastes**, including the United Nations' *Basel Convention on the Control of Transboundary Movements of Hazardous Wastes and their Disposal*, the OECD *Decision of the Council* C(2001)107/FINAL *concerning the control of transboundary movements of waste destined for recovery operations*, and *Regulation (EC) No 1013/2006 on Shipments of Waste* of the European Commission. Despite these legal safeguards, the illegal shipment of waste remains a problem throughout the world and poses human health, environmental and financial risks to the countries involved.[14]

Distinguishing between waste and non-waste is increasingly difficult and raises new challenges for trade polices

Increased trade in non-hazardous recyclable materials could reduce the demand for raw materials and contribute to more efficient use of increasingly scarce resources. A study of the OECD's Joint Working Party on Environment and Trade found that one of the challenges to growth is the classification, and therefore regulation, of scrap as waste (OECD, 2009). End-of-life materials and products are defined differently in different countries: some countries consider them "hazardous waste," some see them as "non-hazardous waste"; others consider them to be "used products"; while still others control their movements, but without classifying them as hazardous waste. And as products become increasingly complex (e.g. consumer electronics, computers, end-of-life vehicles, ships) the line between "waste" and "resource" becomes less clear cut.

Markets for secondary raw materials are expanding, but have to cope with volatile commodity prices

The size of the global market for secondary materials is estimated at between 700 and 800 Mt and valued at over 200 billion USD (Chalmin, 2010; BIR). The main markets for secondary materials are for **recovered metals** (ferrous and non-ferrous), paper and plastics. Because of their economic value and recyclability, metals dominate the global recycling market with **ferrous** metals alone accounting for nearly half. In 2009 world steel production was over 1 200 Mt, including the use of 460 Mt of steel scrap (BIR, 2010). The market for recovered **non-ferrous** metal scrap is significantly smaller in terms of volume – around 24 Mt according to Chalmin & Lacoste (2006) – but its value per tonne value is higher than ferrous scrap. Recovered **paper** is estimated to make up half of the global paper market, which produced 371 Mt of paper and paperboard in 2009 (Magnaghi, 2009). For **plastics** there are little global data on the use of recovered plastics; however, in 2007 12.2 Mt of plastics were recovered in the EU countries, Switzerland and Norway, representing roughly half of production, of which approximately 5 Mt were recycled and the remainder used for energy recovery (OECD, 2010b).

One of the fastest growing waste streams in the world today is waste from electrical and electronic equipment (e-waste) such as personal computers, printers, televisions, mobile phones, refrigerators and air-conditioning units. E-waste is categorised as hazardous waste due to the presence of toxic materials such as mercury, lead and brominated flame retardants are considered as hazardous waste according to the Basel Convention. E-waste may also contain precious metals such as gold, copper and nickel and rare materials of strategic value such as indium and palladium. These precious and heavy metals could be recovered, recycled and used as valuable source of secondary raw materials.

INTERNATIONAL MATERIAL FLOWS

OECD countries are important importers and exporters of material resources, but remain net importers as group

Countries' differing economic structures and natural resource endowments – and their uneven distribution around the world – are an important factor behind international trade flows. In neoclassical trade theory, natural resource endowments provide a country with a source of comparative advantage. Countries and regions that are relatively well-endowed in natural resources tend to supply raw materials to those that are relatively poorly endowed.

The OECD material flow database estimates the weight of material imports and exports of OECD and BRIICS countries, but not bilateral trade flows. This limits the analysis that can be done. The text below builds on a prelimary analysis carried out in 2010-2011, on the basis of 2008 data. It does not reflect developments subsequent to the 2008 economic crisis.

- As a group, **OECD countries** are net importers of material resources. Only Australia, Canada and Norway are major net exporters of material resources.[15] In 2008 the net exports across all material groups from these three countries reached over 1.1 Gt. Exports from Canada and Norway mainly consist of fossil energy carriers. Australia's exports are equally divided between fossil energy carriers (coal) and metals. Other net exporters in the OECD include Mexico, Sweden, New Zealand and Estonia, but their export flows are relatively small (combined net exports of 23 Mt in 2008). With the exception of these seven countries, all other OECD member countries were net importers of materials in 2008. Japan, the United States, Korea, Germany, France, Italy, Spain and the United Kingdom are the leading importers in the OECD area and worldwide. In 2008 they accounted for over 80% (2.3 Gt) of total net material imports by OECD countries.

- Within the **BRIICS** group of countries, Russia, Brazil, Indonesia and South Africa are net exporters of raw materials, while China and India are net importers. Russia is the world's leading supplier of raw materials with net exports of 670 Mt in 2008, consisting mainly of fossil energy carriers. Brazil's net exports are made of mainly of metals and biomass. Indonesian exports are predominantly fossil energy carriers while South Africa's are evenly split between metals and fossil energy carriers. Over the last decade China has grown to become a major demander of raw materials. Net imports of over 650 Mt in 2008 placed China second only to Japan (665 Mt), the world's top importer of raw materials. Metals dominate China's imports, followed by fossil energy carriers. India's imports mainly comprise fossil energy carriers.

Exports have increased to meet growing demand from Asia and the United States

Over the last 30 years there has been **little change in the role of countries** vis-à-vis the supply and demand of material resources; countries that are suppliers have tended to remain suppliers and countries that are demanders have tended to remain demanders.[16] This finding is consistent with Dittrich and Bringezu's (2010) global study on physical trade flows using data from the UN Comtrade database.

Within the **OECD**, net exports from Australia, Canada and Norway quadrupled between 1980 and 2008. Of **BRIICS** countries, Indonesian exports saw a similar increase, while Brazil's increased by a factor of 9. Russia's net exports doubled between 1995 and 2008.

This surge in exports has been partly driven by **increased demand** from a few highly industrialised and emerging economies. China's net imports of material resources increased nearly 60-fold from 1985 to 2008. Net imports of the United States also increased, although less dramatically, growing by a factor of 4 over the same time period. European and Japanese net imports increased relatively modestly between 1985 and 2008.

Physical versus monetary trade balances

The dominance of manufactured goods in terms of the **value** of international trade and the reverse in terms of the **weight** of trade implies that the unit value, i.e. kilogram-for-kilogram value, of manufactured goods is greater than primary commodities. Consequently, being a net exporter in physical terms will not necessarily translate into a monetary trade surplus and vice-versa.

The composition of trade (i.e. the types of goods being traded) and the market value of traded goods are important determinants of a country's physical and monetary balance of trade. For example, Japan and Germany are longstanding and important net importers of raw materials, yet both countries run monetary trade surpluses because they process imported raw materials into high-value goods, many of which are exported.[17] Similarly, China has emerged as the 'world's factory', requiring large volumes of imported raw materials to manufacture goods primarily destined for global market. On the flip side, Australia and South Africa are important global suppliers of raw materials, but both countries run monetary trade deficits because the value of their exports (primary resources) is lower than their imports (manufactured products).

Table 5.1. Physical and monetary trade balances, top net importers and exporters, selected OECD countries and BRIICS, 1995-2008

Suppliers	Net exports (billion tonnes)	Trade surplus/deficit (billion USD)	Demanders	Net Imports (billion tonnes)	Trade surplus/deficit (billion USD)
Australia	6.2	-8.1	USA	9.4	-659.7
Canada	4.0	38.9	Japan	9.3	105.3
Norway	2.6	44.2	South Korea	3.6	18.5
			Germany	3.2	188.2
Russia	6.8	79.6	China	3.3	93.0
Brazil	2.9	17.2	India	0.9	-33.1
Indonesia	2.5	26.5			
South Africa	1.1	-2.7			

Source: OECD (2013), "Material resources", *OECD Environment Statistics* (database). OECD main economic indicators (MEI) on international trade (*http://dx.doi.org/10.1787/data-00045-en*)

Indirect flows and the physical dimension of trade

Global trade shifts resources and commodities between countries, as well as the associated depletion of resources and environmental burdens. As discussed in the previous section, the **indirect flows associated with trade** measure the amount of materials required upstream to produce a traded good. Although indirect flows do not measure a specific environmental impact, they reflect *potential* environmental pressures. When combined with direct trade flows, indirect flows can help identify the extent to which the environmental consequences of the production and consumption of material resources by a country or region extend beyond their borders, where the **environmental burden** is located and how it shifts between countries and regions (OECD, 2008b).

Some dematerialisation in industrialised countries goes on par with outsourcing of material intensive process abroad

A number of empirical studies have investigated direct material flows and **global trade patterns**, but due to data availability only a handful of studies focus on indirect flows (Giljum and Eisenmenger, 2004). Not surprisingly, these studies find in general that resources flow South-North, meaning from developing (non-OECD) to industrialised (OECD) countries. Accounting for indirect flows reveals that some of the **dematerialisation** taking place in industrialised countries has been achieved through the **outsourcing** of material and energy-intensive production processes abroad. Consequently, accounting for indirect flows generally increases the magnitude of a country's physical trade balance, but does not necessarily change its direction (i.e. surplus/deficit).

This is confirmed by a recent study by Dittrich *et al.* (2010, 2012). This study provides the most recent and comprehensive analysis of the evolution of indirect trade flows at the global level. It finds that over the last 30 years the indirect flows associated with international trade have increased more rapidly than direct trade flows, increasing from 9 Gt to 41 Gt between 1970 and 2005 – nearly 5 times compared to 3.5 times for direct flows. **Metals** (ores, semi-manufactured and manufactured goods) account for around half of all indirect flows stemming from international trade in goods while **biomass** is the second most important group. Although fossil energy carriers dominate direct international trade flows (mainly due to trade in petroleum), they accounted for less than 17% of indirect flows in 2005. Most of the indirect flows of fossil energy carriers stem from hard coal. In addition to hard coal, other materials associated with high shares of indirect flows include iron (ores, concentrates and steel), copper and tin. Since the 1970s iron's share of indirect flows has been decreasing while those of copper and hard coal have been increasing.

Although raw materials dwarf manufactured goods in terms of physical trade volumes (80% versus 20% in 2005), they contribute equally to indirect flows. Relative to their weight manufactured goods have higher **raw material equivalents** and their trade is therefore associated with larger indirect material flows compared to raw materials. The higher material requirement of manufactured goods is also consistent with the inevitable losses (energy and process wastes) associated with each step in the processing of primary materials.

Raw material equivalents is a term used in material flow analysis and accounting. It designates the used extraction of raw materials needed for the production of a good or service, including the mass of the product itself. It is used to convert products into their primary resource extraction equivalent (OECD, 2008a).

See Glossary.

Considering indirect flows does not change the global picture, but reveals important differences across countries

Taking indirect flows into account magnifies, but does not significantly alter the role of countries as global resource suppliers/demanders.

- In the **OECD** area European countries[18] and Japan remain significant net importers while Australia, Canada, Chile, New Zealand and Norway remain export-oriented. Chile's indirect physical trade balance, in particular, is strongly influenced by its growing exports of copper ore, extracted primarily from open pit mines. The situation in the United States and Mexico, however, does change with indirect flows. In the 1970s the U.S. was a net importer in direct terms, but a net exporter with indirect flows included (due to embedded biomass exports). In the decades following, American net imports (mainly oil) grew significantly and the U.S. is now one of the world's top net importers of materials including indirect flows.[19] Similarly, Mexico has been a long standing (although relatively minor) net exporter in direct terms, but due to the indirect flows associated with coal and agricultural imports, is a net importer in indirect terms.
- In the **BRIICS** group of countries, the rise of China and India as major resource demanders over the last 30 years and the emergence of Russia and South Africa as key global suppliers are even more pronounced in indirect terms. With indirect flows, Indonesia and Brazil remain strongly export-oriented.

Dittrich *et al.* (2012) find few other major resource demanders in the rest of the world. Most small islands and city states (e.g. Cayman Islands, Singapore) are net importers. The countries of the Middle East and North Africa are a mix of suppliers and demanders. Exports from the region are dominated by oil and gas, which generate relatively smaller indirect flows and are often insufficient to counterbalance imports of material-intensive manufactured goods. Most of the countries of Latin America are net exporters of raw materials.

The fact that three of the world's most important suppliers of raw materials are OECD member countries implies that income is not the sole factor determining whether a country is a physical net exporter or net importer of raw materials. Natural resource endowment and population density appear to have a stronger influence (Dittrich *et al.*, 2012).

RESOURCE STOCKS

Stocks of resources are found both in the natural environment and in the economy Understanding the relationship between natural and man-made stocks is important for industry and for government policies that aim at improving resource productivity

Rising consumption, volatile commodity prices and supply chain issues with some raw materials continue to fuel concerns over the long-term security of supply of non-renewable resources. In the case of metals, which can be infinitely recycled, answering the question "how much is there?" requires looking not only at the amount of metal available in mineral deposits that have been identified and those have not yet been discovered, but also the amount of metal being used by society.

Material flow analysis is a useful tool for understanding the relationship between these two stocks. Material flow analysis is based on the principle of mass balancing and founded on the first law of thermodynamic. It assumes that matter (mass, energy) is not created or destroyed by any physical process. Raw materials, water and air are extracted from the environment as inputs into the economy and transformed into products that are eventually returned to the environment as outputs in the form of waste and emissions. The *first part of this chapter* focused exclusively on the flows of materials into, through and out of the economy. But not everything that flows into the economy flows back out immediately; some materials accumulate over time in the economy in the form of buildings, transportation infrastructure or durable and semi-durable goods (e.g. automobiles, machinery and equipment, and household appliances). These materials are eventually released back to the environment in the form of construction and demolition waste, end of life vehicles, e-waste, and household waste.

Resource stocks can be broadly classified into two groups: natural (virgin) stocks and anthropogenic (man-made) stocks. Natural stocks are the untouched raw materials found in natural resources in the environment. Anthropogenic stocks are the amount of material in society that has been extracted, processed, put into use, currently providing service, or discarded or dissipated over time. Both types of stocks need to be taken into consideration when looking at the long term sustainability of supply.

See Glossary.

NATURAL STOCKS

Reserves of non-renewable resources are dynamic and tend to grow over time

The first step in assessing the availability of materials derived from non-renewable resources begins with **quantifying the finite amount available in nature**. Resource geologists have been estimating the amount of minerals and other deposits suitable for exploitation for years. These figures are dynamic and in practice tend to grow – rather than shrink – over time. For example, in 1970 world copper reserves were estimated at about 280 million metric tonnes (Mt). Since then, about 400 Mt of copper have been produced worldwide and today world copper reserves are estimated at 630 Mt, more than double those in 1970 (USGS, 2011).

Estimates of the magnitude of non-renewable resources stocks **change over time** with extraction, scientific knowledge, economic conditions, and technological developments. Increased scientific knowledge and understanding of the geology of minerals can lead to the discovery of new deposits or other natural occurrences. Reserves may be considered a working inventory of mining companies' supply of an economically extractable mineral commodity; as a consequence cost factors play a huge role in determining the amount of reserves at any given point in time (USGS, 2011).

Rising demand and market prices for minerals can encourage the extraction of formerly subeconomic reserves (e.g. oil sands). Other factors that alter costs such as taxes and input prices (i.e. energy costs) can also influence reserve estimates. Technology plays a dual role. Technical innovations can reduce the costs of extraction and production, transforming marginal or sub-economic reserves into reserves. Technology can also advance scientific knowledge, leading to new discoveries.

Terms and classifications

There are various terms to describe and classify mineral resources based on scientific, economic and technological constraints. In the classification system used by the U.S. Geological Survey (USGS), the main elements are resources and reserves.

- The **resource** is the broadest category. It is defined as "a concentration of material in such a form and amount that economic extraction is currently or potentially feasible" and includes both identified and undiscovered resources (USGS, 2011).
- The **reserve** base is a subset of the identified resource that meets specified minimum physical and chemical criteria related to current mining and production practices.[20] It includes resources that are currently economic (reserves), marginally economic (marginal reserves) and some of those that are subeconomic (subeconomic resources). The term reserves refers to only that part of the reserve base that is considered economically extractable with current technology.

Figure 5.19. U.S. Geological Survey Classification System for Mineral Resources

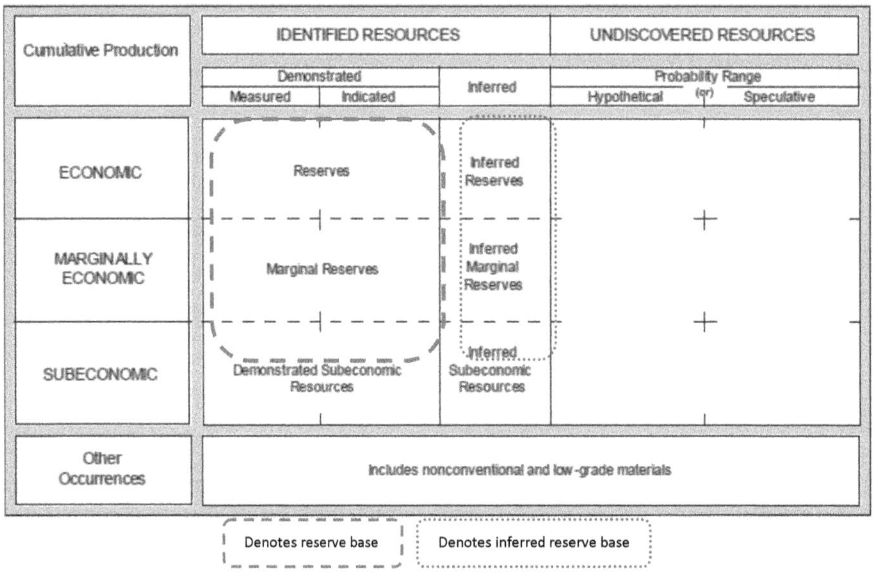

Source: Based on U.S. Geological Survey (2011).

Taking into account economic, scientific and technological boundaries, estimating how much of a non-renewable resource is in the natural environment remains just that – an estimate. The USGS does not directly measure reserves. Information comes from a variety of sources, mainly national governments, industry and academia, who may use different evaluation criteria.[21] Industry information is often proprietary and not publicly available.

Reserve estimates are based on **current technology and economic factors**. They provide a snapshot of the amount of a resource available today – not the amount that could potentially be worthy of extraction over the long term. A number of studies have focussed on estimating the amount of metal that could potentially be recovered in the long-run given anticipated movements in exploration and technology. One of the earliest estimates was made by Erickson (1974) who found that the potential recoverable resource (R) for most elements should approach $R = 2.45A \times 10^6$, where A = is the element's abundance in the earth's crust[22] in percent.[23] However, this estimate was based on currently recoverable resources and could only be applied to host, and not companion, metals. Erickson also proposed a simple method for estimating the recoverable resource potential assuming that R should approach 0.01% of the element's crustal abundance to a depth of 1 kilometre. A recent study by Graedel *et al.* (2011) found that for most elements estimates based on this simplified methodology did not provide "unreasonable upper limits" to the potentially recoverable resource and that, where available, USGS estimates of reserve base were not "unreasonable lower limits."

OECD countries are relatively poorly endowed in natural stocks of non-renewable resources

OECD countries account for the majority of consumption of the world's major **metallic minerals**, but as a group are themselves generally poorly naturally endowed. Some exceptions are copper ore, lithium, and silver where OECD countries hold over 50% of global reserves (based on 2011 USGS reserve data). OECD countries are particularly poorly endowed (5% or less of global reserves) in platinum group metals (platinum, palladium, rhodium, ruthenium, iridium, and osmium) and tin. Within the OECD area, **metal reserves** are heavily concentrated in a handful of mineral rich countries – Australia, Canada, Chile, Mexico and the United States. Australia in particular is a major global supplier of a very broad range of minerals. Member countries in Europe and Asia do not have large deposits of metallic minerals and few countries have internationally significant reserves, with the exception Greece (bauxite), Ireland (zinc, lead), Poland (silver, lead, copper), and Sweden (iron, lead).

The situation is similar for **agricultural minerals**, such as phosphate rock and potash. With the exception of Canada, with the world's largest potash reserves, OECD countries are relatively poor in natural occurrences of agricultural minerals. Australia, Canada, Israel and the United States have globally significant reserves of phosphate rock, but together these represent only 3% of the world's reserves. And absent Canada, OECD countries have less than 5% of the world's potash.

MAN-MADE STOCKS: URBAN MINES

The urban mine offers a potential future source of key materials

Anthropogenic stocks have been less well studied than geologic stocks, but are a growing area of interest particularly in industrialised economies where geologic stocks are limited, but man-made stocks are believed to be large. Much of the study of anthropogenic stocks focuses on metals because they can be infinitely recycled and unlike minerals, which dissipate with consumption (e.g. fossil fuels, salt for de-icing), metals retain their chemical and physical properties over time. Many of the potential negative environmental impacts associated with the production and consumption of metals can be reduced with recycling. At the same time pressure on virgin stocks could be reduced. As a result, there is greater recognition that the structures, building and products surrounding us in the economy today could be the urban mines of the future.

Terms and classifications

Like natural stocks, anthropogenic stocks can be classified and described in different ways (Kapur and Graedel, 2006; UNEP 2010):

- *Employed stock* is the amount of the resource in the economy. It is the amount that has been extracted from nature, but has not been discarded.
  - *In-use stock* is the largest component of employed stock. It is the amount of the resource that is currently being actively used in the economy, locked in infrastructure, buildings and various durable products (e.g. computers, automobiles, and household appliances).
  - *Hibernating stock* is stock that is no longer being used, but has not been discarded. Abandoned infrastructure and obsolete consumer electronics stored in drawers and shelves are examples of hibernating stock.
  - *Stockpiles* held by governments and in metal processing and manufacturing facilities are neither actively in use nor hibernating. Although information is incomplete, these amounts are believed to be fairly small. Processing and manufacturing stockpiles turnover quickly and only three governments – the United States, China and Japan – are known to maintain stockpiles of selected metals (UNEP, 2010).
- *Expended stock* is the amount of the resource that has been used by society and returns to the environment.
  - *Deposited stock* is that part of the expended stock that has been discarded as waste and been deposited in landfills and mining containment ponds.
  - *Dissipated stock* is the amount of the resource that has been used by the economy and lost due to human wear or natural dissipation (e.g. corrosion).

Figure 5.20. Generalised typology of natural and anthropogenic stocks

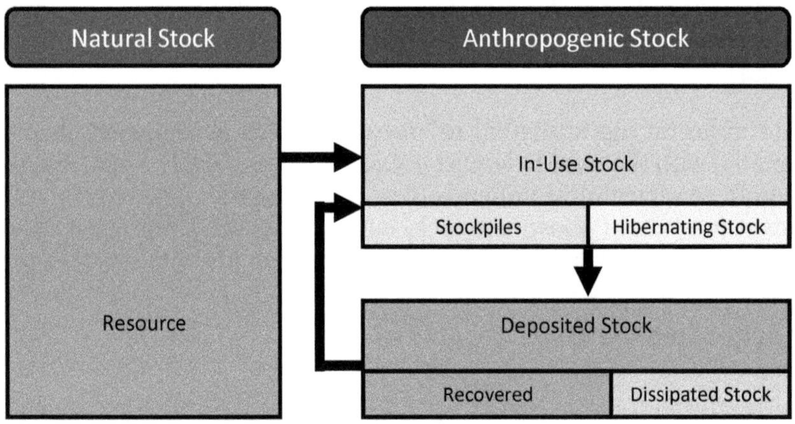

Source: Adapted from UNEP (2010b) and Kapur and Graedel (2006).

But estimating the magnitude of the urban mine is a challenge

Anthropogenic stocks are usually estimated using either a top-down or a bottom-up approach. The **top-down** approach infers the amount of metal employed in society by calculating the cumulative differences between their inflows and outflows. The **bottom-up** approach starts with individual product groups, estimating their average metal content, then summing across the number of products in use taking into account the behaviour of their flows (UNEP, 2010; Gerst & Graedel, 2008; Graedel *et al.* 2006).

Both methodologies have their own challenges and depend heavily on the availability and reliability of data. Top-down approaches generally rely on national level input-output data that are usually only available on an annual basis. Because the estimate of stock is "derived", the top-down method could be viewed as less precise than bottom-up estimates (UNEP, 2010). On the other hand, the bottom-up approach is constrained by the ability to count all relevant products and determine their metal content. Information on the metal content of goods like cars, computers and appliances can be obtained from manufacturers, but homes and building are more difficult because they are less uniform. For products with long service times, the material mix can evolve over time.

The UNEP **International Resource Panel** (2010) conducted a comprehensive scientific review of the literature available to date on anthropogenic metal stocks. They found a total of 54 studies published between 1932 and 2007 covering 24 different metals, resulting in 124 estimates. Seventy percent of these studies were published since 2000, a sign of burgeoning interest in this area.

Over 70% of the studies focussed on five metals: copper, lead, zinc, iron and aluminium. Not surprisingly the most common metal in use in society is iron, followed by aluminium and copper. The studies reviewed also reveal strong differences in the per capita stock found in advanced industrialised economies versus less industrialised countries, highlighting the importance of metals in supporting economic development. In absolute terms, most anthropogenic metal stocks are found in industrialised countries. As a result, it is estimated that the average person living in a more developed country uses 10-15 metric tonnes of anthropogenic metal stocks, compared to a figure likely around 2-3 metric tonnes for a person living in a less developed country.[24]

Table 5.2.Summary of Anthropogenic Metal Stock Estimations Reviewed by the UNEP Resource Panel

Metal	Number of estimates	Percent of all estimates (%)	Global per capita stock (kg/person)	MDC per capita stock (kg/person)	LDC per capita stock (kg/person)
Aluminium	9	7.4	80	350 - 500	35
Antimony	1	0.8		1	
Cadmium*	3	2.5	40	80	
Chromium	3	2.5		7 - 50	
Cobalt	1	0.8		1	
Copper	34	27	35 - 55	140 - 300	30 - 40
Gold*	2	1.6		35 - 90	
Iron	13	10.7	2 200	7 000 - 14 000	2000
Lead	20	16.4	8	20 - 150	1 - 4
Magnesium	1	0.8		5	
Manganese	1	0.8		100	
Mercury*	1	0.8		10	
Molybdenum	1	0.8		3	
Nickel	3	2.5		2 - 4	
Palladium*	2	1.6		1 - 4	
Platinum*	2	1.6		1 - 3	
Rhodium*	1	0.8		0.2	
Silver*	2	1.6	110	13	
Tin	2	1.6		3	
Titanium	1	0.8		13	
Tungsten	1	0.8		1	
Zinc	14	11.5		80 - 200	20 - 40

Note: MDC = More Developed Countries and includes Australia, Canada, the European Union EU15, Norway, Switzerland, Japan, New Zealand, and the United States. LDC = Less Developed Countries includes all countries except those defined as MDC.

* denotes data in grams per person.

Source: UNEP (2010b).

There are only a few metals for which there are sufficient estimates to form a reliable picture of the magnitude of anthropogenic stocks, namely copper, iron, aluminium and lead. For these metals, man-make stocks are significant and their flows could provide an important source of metal in the future. Anthropogenic stocks of iron are estimated between 12 and 18 billion tonnes, about 15-20%

of iron ore reserves in 2011 based on iron content. Anthropogenic copper stocks could represent up to 60% of reserves and for lead up to 65% of reserves.

Estimates of anthropogenic metal stocks quantify the amount that could one day be available for recycling and reuse. Scientific, economic and technological constraints are not considered (with the exception of dissipated stocks). Unlike natural stocks, the availability (flow) of anthropogenic stocks is first and foremost constrained by their use. The service lives of products determine when the materials from which products are made become available. Compared to stocks, the flows of man-made materials out of the economy and into obsolescence are relatively small although they vary over time and across countries depending on their level of development and consumption patterns (see for example Müller *et al.*, 2006). The largest flows of metal scrap come from more industrialised economies, where man-made stocks are largest. Emerging and developing economies, particular those in Asia, are in the process of accumulating man-made stocks, building infrastructure and buying more durable goods. It is expected scrap flows from those countries will increase significantly in coming decades as stocks are discarded and replaced.

Tracking anthropogenic stocks can be used as a planning tool, not only for estimating the future availability of scrap, but also for understanding consumption patterns and barriers to recovery and recycling. As such, increasing our knowledge about anthropogenic stocks is an integral to improving resource productivity. Anthropogenic stock estimation is a growing area of study. But much work still needs to be done, particularly to close gaps with regards to less developed countries and specialty metals.

ENDNOTES

1 Figures do not include Slovenia or Estonia as historical data on the material flows of these countries prior to the early 1990s is limited.

2 Precious metals include gold, silver and the six platinum group metals (iridium, osmium, palladium, platinum, rhodium, and ruthenium).

3 Jackson, T. (2009). Prosperity without Growth: The Transition to a Sustainable Economy. United Kingdom: Sustainable Development Commission. 48-49.

4 Several studies have suggested that the intensity of use of a mineral (the use of a mineral commodity divided by GDP) depends on the level of economic development as measured by GDP per capita, and that the pattern of intensity of use follows an inverse U-shape as economies develop). As development takes place, countries focus on building infrastructure (such as rails, roads, and bridges, housing and other buildings and water supply and electricity transmission) and people buy more durable goods, which rapidly increases the demand for mineral commodities. As economies mature, all other things being equal, they move to a less materials-intensive phase, spending more on education and other services, which reduces the intensity of minerals use (Malenbaum, W. 1975; Altenpohl, D.G. 1980; Tilton, J.E. 1990).

5 Figures include all OECD member countries, including Slovenia and Estonia. Excluding Slovenia and Estonia leaves the physical trade balance largely unchanged.

6 See Rothman (1998), Giljum, S. and N. Eisenmenger (2003) and Dittrich (2012).

7 See note about data limitations, especially for the calculation of unused extraction and indirect flows in the « Reader's Guide ». Data on indirect flows was calculated based on methodologies outlined in Dittrich *et al.* (2012).

8 USD in constant 2005 USD and purchasing power parities (PPPs).

9 Available material flow data does not always allow the distinction to be made between construction and industrial minerals. Figures for OECD countries that are EU members plus Norway and Switzerland include estimates.

10 Examples of wood fibre derivatives include: micro crystalline cellulose, nitrocellulose, carboxymethylcellulose, lignosulphonates.

11 This global estimate is consistent with the *2009 World Waste Survey*, which estimated that between 3.4 and 4 billion tonnes of municipal and industrial manufacturing waste alone was produced worldwide in 2006 and that some 1 Gt of construction and demolition waste and 6.4 Gt of waste from the mining, electricity and waste industries based on data available for a selection of countries (Chalmin & Gaillochet, 2009).

12 It is important to note that some process residuals may be totally benign while others may be a concern for the environment or human health. Equally, some residuals may have economic value and could theoretically be recovered.

13 Ferrous metals are: Fe, Cr, Mn, V, Ni, Nb, Mo; Non-ferrous metals: Mg, Al, Ti, Co, Cu, Zn, Sn, Pb; Precious metals: Ru, Rh, Pd, Ag, Os, Ir, Pt, Au; Specialty metals: Li, Be, B, Sc, Ga, Ge, As, Se, Sr, Y, Zr, Cd, In, Sb, Te, Cs, Ba, La, Ce, Pr, Nd, Sm, Eu, Gd, Tb, Dy, Ho, Er, Tm, Yb, Lu, Hf, Ta, W, Re, Hg, Tl

14 An international inspection exercise found that of the 72 total targeted inspections conducted over a one month period from June-July 2010, 39 cases (54%) involved infringements (INECE, 2010). The illegal waste streams most often encountered during the inspection exercise were: e-waste wrongly declared as second hand goods, waste batteries wrongly described as plastic or mixed metal scrap, cathode ray tubes from television and computer monitors wrongly described as plastic or metal scrap, and refrigerators containing chlorofluorocarbons. However, the reasons for mislabeling the waste can be either deliberate or unintentional and not all 39 of the cases of infringement can be interpreted as intentional illegal acts.

15 Although the United States is an important global supplier of biomass for food and agriculture, it is has been a long-standing net importer of all other material groups (particularly fossil energy carriers) and is, as a result, a net importer of raw materials overall.

16 Within the OECD an exception is Chile, which was a net exporter in the early 1980s but by 2008 had become a net importer due to growing fossil energy carrier imports. Although there has been little evolution in the roles of countries, two trends are notable.

17 It is important to note that monetary trade balances are calculated as imports minus exports while physical trade balances are the reverse.

18 The only exception is Turkey, whose indirect physical trade balance was close to zero in the 1970s and in 2005 was comparable to that of other major European countries.

19 In 2008, however, the U.S. was a net exporter in indirect terms – the first time in nearly a decade – as imports of petroleum decreased while coal and biomass (food & feed) exports rose. In direct terms the U.S. remained a net importer of raw materials although the U.S. physical trade balance was roughly equivalent to the indirect trade balance resulting in a negligible overall trade balance.

20 Although the U.S. Geological survey stopped publishing reserve base figures in 2009, conceptually it remains part of the classification system for mineral resources.

21 Estimating reserves of minerals that occur or are mined as by-products is particularly challenging because their demand is driven by demand for their parent metal (e.g. gallium and aluminium).

22 It is estimated based on the average composition of major rock types. "Oxygen (O) constitutes almost 50% of the Earth's crust by weight and is the most abundant element. Other major elements include: silicon (Si), which is the second most abundant, constituting 27.72% of the crust by weight; aluminium (Al) third; sodium (Na); magnesium (Mg); calcium (Ca); and iron (Fe). Other elements, including such desired metals as gold (Au), silver (Ag), and platinum (Pt), are rare in the crust."(Dictionary of Earth Sciences)

23 Erickson's estimates were based on the McKelvery (1960) reserve-abundance relationship. McKelvey found that the amount of reserves in the United States of the metals most commonly explored was roughly equal to their crustal abundance (in percent) multiplied by one billion: $r = A \times 10^9$.

24 In their review of literature on anthropogenic stocks, the UNEP Resource Panel defines more developed countries (MDC) as Australia, Canada, the European Union EU15, Norway, Switzerland, Japan, New Zealand, and the United States and less developed countries (LDC) as all other countries.

REFERENCES

- Arrow, Kenneth *et al.* (2004), "Are we consuming too much?" Journal of Economic Perspectives, 18(3), summer, pages 147-172.
- Behrens, A. *et al.* (2007), "The material basis of the global economy: Worldwide patterns of natural resource extraction and their implications for sustainable resource use policies," Ecological Economics, Volume 64, Issue 2, Pages 444-453.
- BIR (Bureau of International Recycling), Bureau of International Recycling website, *www.bir.org*
- BIR (2010), World Steel Recycling in Figures 2005-2009, BIR, Brussels.
- Chalmin, P. (2010), World Markets for Recycled and Recovered Commodities: Time to Smile Again? Bureau of International Recycling, Brussels.
- Chalmin, P. and C. Gaillochet (2009), From Waste to Resource: An Abstract of World Waste Survey 2009, Veolia Environmental Services and CyclOpe, Paris.
- Davis, G. (2010), "Trade in Mineral Resources," Economic Research and Statistics Division, Staff Working Paper ERSD-2010-01, World Trade Organisation, Geneva.
- Dittrich, M. (2010), Physische Handelsbilanzen. Verlagert der Norden Umweltbelastungen in den Süden? Kölner Geographische Arbeiten 91, Köln.
- Dittrich, M. and S. Bringezu (2010), "The physical dimension of international trade, Part 1: Direct global flows between 1962 and 2005," Ecological Economics, Vol. 69, pages 1838-1847.
- Dittrich. M., S. Bringezu and H. Schütz (2012), "The Physical Dimension of International Trade, Part 2: Indirect Global Resource Flows between 1962 and 2005", Ecological Economics.
- European Commission, Resource Efficiency, Resource Efficiency Scoreboard, *http://ec.europa.eu/environment/resource_efficiency/targets_indicators/scoreboard/index_en.htm*
- EEA (European Environment Agency) (2011), Key messages on material resource use and material resource efficiency for the Roadmap to a resource efficient Europe, EEA, Copenhagen.
- EEA (2010), "Material Resources and Waste," The European Environment: State and Outlook 2010, EEA, Copenhagen.
- Erickson, Ralph (1973), "Crustal Abundance of Elements, and Mineral Reserves and Resources," in D.A. Brobst and W.P. Martin (eds.), United States mineral resources, Geological Survey professional paper 820, U.S. Government print office, Washington, D.C.
- Eurostat, Environmental Data Centre on Waste (2011), *http://epp.eurostat.ec.europa.eu/portal/page/portal/waste/data/main_tables* [accessed 10 May 2011]
- FAO (United Nations Food and Agriculture Organisation) (2011), State of the World's Forests 2011, FAO, Rome.
- FAO (2010a), State of the World Fisheries and Aquaculture 2010, FAO Fisheries and Aquaculture Department, FAO, Rome.
- FAO (2010b), Forest Resources Assessment 2010, FAO, Rome.
- Gerst, M. and Graedel, T.E. (2008), "In-Use Stocks of Metals: Status and Implications," Environmental Science & Technology, Vol. 42, No. 19, pp. 7038-7045.
- Giljum, S., *et al.* (2008), "Global dimension of European natural resource use. Results from the Global resource Accounting Model (GRAM)", SERI Working paper No. 7.
- Giljum, S. and N. Eisenmenger (2003), "North-South Trade and the Distribution of Environmental Goods and Burdens: A Biophysical Perspective," SERI Working paper, No. 2, SERI, Vienna.
- Graedel, T.E. *et al.*, (2011), "Estimating Long-Run Geological Stocks of Metals," Working paper, Working Group on Geological Stocks of Metals, UNEP International Panel on Sustainable Resource Management, UNEP, Paris.

- G8 Environment Ministers Meeting (2008), Kobe 3R Action Plan, Ministry of the Environment of Japan, Tokyo.
- IEA (2013), *Energy Balances of OECD Countries 2013*, OECD Publishing, Paris, *http://dx.doi.org/10.1787/energy_bal_oecd-2013-en.*
- IEA (2010), *Energy Balances of OECD Countries 2010*, OECD Publishing, Paris, *http://dx.doi.org/10.1787/energy_bal_oecd-2010-en-fr.*
- IEA (International Energy Agency) (2008), Worldwide Trends in Energy Use and Efficiency: Key Insights from IEA Indicator Analysis, IEA, Paris.
- INECE (International Network for Environmental Compliance and Enforcement) (2010), International Hazardous Waste Inspection Project at Seaports: Results and Recommendations, INECE Seaport Environmental Security Network, INECE, Washington, D.C.
- Joardar, S.D. (2000), "Urban Residential Solid Waste Management in India: Issues related to Institutional Arrangements," Public Works Management & Policy, Vol. 4, No. 4, p. 319-330.
- Krausmann, F. *et al.* (2009), "Growth in global material use, GDP and population during the 20th century," Ecological Economics, Vol. 68, pages 2696-2705.
- Kapur, A. and Graedel, T.E. (2006), "Copper Mines Above and Below the Ground," Environmental Science & Technology, 15 May 2006, pp. 3135-3141.
- Lacoste, E. and P. Chalmin (2006), From Waste to Resource: An Abstract of World Waste Survey 2006, Veolia Environmental Services and CyclOpe, Paris.
- Love, Patrick (2010), Fishers: While Stocks Last?, OECD Insights, OECD, Paris.
- McKelvey, V.E. (1960), "Relation of reserves of the elements to their crustal abundance," American Journal of Science, Vol. 258A, pp. 234-241.
- Millennium Ecosystem Assessment (2005). Ecosystems and Human Well-being: Synthesis, Island Press, Washington, DC.
- Müller, D., *et al.* (2006), "Exploring the engine of anthropogenic iron cycles," PNAS, Vol. 104, No. 33, pp. 16111-16116, doi:10.1073/pnas.0603375103.
- NRCan (Natural Resources Canada) (2010), State of the Canada's Forests 2010, Government of Canada, Ottawa.
- NRCan (1997), Sustainable Development of Minerals and Metals, Monograph, No. 4, NRCan, Ottawa.
- OECD (2014), *OECD Economic Outlook: Statistics and Projections* (database), *http://dx.doi.org/10.1787/eo-data-en.*
- OECD (2014b), *Green Growth Indicators 2014*, OECD Green Growth Studies, OECD Publishing, Paris, *http://dx.doi.org/10.1787/9789264202030-en.*
- OECD (2014c), "Municipal waste", *OECD Environment Statistics* (database), *http://dx.doi.org/10.1787/data-00601-en.*
- OECD (2013), "Material resources", *OECD Environment Statistics* (database), *http:*//dx.doi.org/*10.1787/data-00695-en.*
- OECD (2012), *Sustainable Materials Management: Making Better Use of Resources*, OECD Publishing, Paris, *http://dx.doi.org/10.1787/9789264174269-en.*
- OECD (2012), *OECD Environmental Outlook to 2050: The Consequences of Inaction*, OECD Publishing, Paris, *http://dx.doi.org/10.1787/9789264122246-en.*
- OECD (2011a), "Resource Productivity in the G8 and the OECD: A Report in the Framework of the Kobe 3R Action Plan", OECD, Paris, *http://www.oecd.org/env/waste/47944428.pdf.*
- OECD (2011b),*Towards Green Growth*, OECD Green Growth Studies, OECD Publishing, Paris, *http://dx.doi.org/10.1787/9789264111318-en .*
- OECD (2011c), *Towards Green Growth: Monitoring Progress: OECD Indicators*, OECD Green Growth Studies, OECD Publishing, Paris, *http://dx.doi.org/10.1787/9789264111356-en.*
- OECD (2011b), Sustainable materials management: Case studies, *http://www.oecd.org/env/waste/smm-casestudies.htm*
- OECD (2010b), *The Economic Impact of Export Restrictions on Raw Materials*, OECD Trade Policy Studies, OECD Publishing, Paris, *http://dx.doi.org/10.1787/9789264096448-en.*
- OECD (2009), "Reducing barriers to international trade in non-hazardous recyclable materials: exploring the environmental and economic benefits, Part 1: A synthesis report," Joint Working Party on Environment and Trade, OECD, Paris.
- OECD (2008a), Measuring Materials Flows and Resource Productivity: Synthesis Report, OECD, Paris.

- OECD (2008b), Measuring Materials Flows and Resource Productivity, Volume 1: The OECD Guide, OECD, Paris.
- OECD (2008d), *OECD Environmental Outlook to 2030*, OECD Publishing, Paris, *http://dx.doi.org/9789264040519-en.*
- OECD (2008e), *Environmental Performance of Agriculture in OECD Countries Since 1990*, OECD Publishing, Paris, *http://dx.doi.org/10.1787/9789264040854-en.*
- OECD (2007), *OECD Environmental Performance Reviews: China 2007*, OECD Publishing, Paris, *http://dx.doi.org/10.1787/9789264031166-en.*
- OECD (2002), *Aggregated Environmental Indices: Review of Aggregation Methodologies in Use*, OECD Publishing, Paris. *http://www.oecd.org/officialdocuments/displaydocument/?cote=env/epoc/se(2001)2/final&doclanguage=en.*
- OECD (n.d.), *National Accounts Statistics* (database), *http://dx.doi.org/10.1787/na-data-en.*
- OECD (n.d.), "International trade", *Main Economic Indicators* (database) , *http://dx.doi.org/10.1787/data-00045-en.*
- Rothman, D. S. (1998). "Environmental Kuznets curves—Real progress or passing the buck? A case for consumption-based approaches." Ecological Economics, 25(2), 177-194.
- SERI (Sustainable Europe Research Institute) (2011), Factsheet Measuring Resource Extraction, SERI, Vienna.
- SERI *et al.* (2009), Overconsumption? Our Use of the World's Natural Resources, SERI, GLOBAL 2000 and Friends of the Earth Europe, Vienna.
- SERI/WU (Sustainable Europe Resource Institute/Vienna University) (2014), *Global Material Flow Database.* 2014 Version. Available at *www.materialflows.net.*
- Stern, Nicolas (2005), Stern Review: The Economics of Climate Change, HM Treasury, UK Government, London.
- Thornton, Iain (1995), Metals in the Global Environment: Facts and Misconceptions, International Council on Metals and the Environment, Ottawa.
- UNEP (United National Environment Programme) (2014) Decoupling 2: technologies, opportunities and policy options. A Report of the Working Group on Decoupling to the International Resource Panel. von Weizsäcker, E.U., de Larderel, J, Hargroves, K., Hudson, C., Smith, M., Rodrigues, M.
- UNEP (2011a), Decoupling and Sustainable Resource Management: Scoping Challenges, A Report of the Working Group on Decoupling to the International Resource Panel, M. Swilling and M. Fischer-Kowalski, UNEP, Paris.
- UNEP (2011b), Recycling Rates of Metals – A Status Report," A Report of the Working Group on Global Metal Flows to the International Resource Panel, Graedel, T.E., Allwood, J., Birat, J.P., Buchert, M., Hageluken, C., Reck, B.K., Sibley, S.F., Sonnemann, G., UNEP, Paris.
- UNEP (2011c) Decoupling natural resource use and environmental impacts from economic growth, A Report of the Working Group on Decoupling to the International Resource Panel. Fischer-Kowalski, M., Swilling, M., von Weizsäcker, E.U., Ren, Y., Moriguchi, Y., Crane, W., Krausmann, F., Eisenmenger, N., Giljum, S., Hennicke, P., Romero Lankao, P., Siriban Manalang, A., Sewerin, S
- UNEP (2010a), Assessing the Environmental Impacts of Consumption and Production: Priority Products and Materials, A Report of the Working Group on the Environmental Impacts of Products and Materials to the International Panel for Sustainable Resource Management. Hertwich, E., van der Voet, E., Suh, S., Tukker, A., Huijbregts M., Kazmierczyk, P., Lenzen, M., McNeely, J., Moriguchi, Y., UNEP, Paris.
- UNEP (2010b), Metal Stocks in Society: Scientific Synthesis, A Report of the Working Group on the Global Metal Flows to the International Panel for Sustainable Resource Management, UNEP, Paris.
- UNEP (2004), Vital Waste Statistics, UNEP, Nairobi.
- USGS (U.S. Geological Survey) (2014), Mineral Commodity Summaries 2011, U.S. Geological Survey, Reston, Virginia.
- USGS (2011), Mineral Commodity Summaries 2011, U.S. Geological Survey, Reston, Virginia.
- USGS (1998), Metal Prices in the United States through 1998, U.S. Geological Survey, Reston, Virginia.
- Wagner, L. A. (2002), Materials in the Economy – Material Flows, Scarcity, and the Environment, U.S. Geological Survey Circular 1221, U.S. Geological Survey, Denver.
- World Bank, World Development Indicators, *http://data.worldbank.org/data-catalog/world-development-indicators*
- WTO (World Trade Organisation) (2011), "Trade growth to ease in 2011 but despite 2010 record surge, crisis hangover persists," Press release 628, April 7, WTO, Geneva
- WTO (2010), World Trade Report 2010: Trade in Natural Resources, WTO Secretariat, Geneva.
- WTO (2008), International Trade Statistics 2008, WTO Secretariat, Geneva.
- Wuppertal Institute for Climate, Energy and the Environment, www.wupperinst.org

Part II: Key material resources factsheets

ALUMINIUM FACTSHEET

Within a relatively short time, aluminium has become one of the most widely used metals in the world today and a metal of choice in the transportation industry where fuel efficiency has become of paramount importance in the face of growing concerns over climate change. However, the production of primary aluminium is itself extremely energy intensive and an important contributor to global greenhouse gas emissions. With aluminium consumption increasing, particularly in the high-growth emerging economies, the challenge ahead will be to reduce the industry's overall energy consumption, including through maximising opportunities to recycle scrap.

See the Reader's guide for information about the selection of key material resources.

Overview

Characteristics and uses

Aluminium is the second most abundant metallic element and the third most abundant element in the earth's crust after oxygen and silicon. Aluminium is lightweight, malleable yet strong, durable, corrosion resistant, impermeable and a good conductor of heat and electricity. These unique properties combined with its relative cost-effectiveness have led to aluminium's widespread use in a variety of applications across the economy. Owing to aluminium's versatility, global annual production of primary aluminium has expanded rapidly since the Second World War and totalled an estimated 41 million metric tonnes (Mt) in 2010 (USGS, 2011).

The largest market for finished aluminium is the transportation sector where the metal is used in the manufacture of motor vehicles, airplanes, railway and subway cars, and trailers. Aluminium's favourable strength to weight ratio has helped manufacturers increase fuel efficiency to meet fuel economy standards. Other major applications for aluminium include building and construction (doors, windows, siding), electrical engineering (transmission lines, electronics), and packaging (cans, foil). Aluminium is also used to a lesser extent to manufacture cookware and in water treatment and medical applications.

Table 1. End-uses of finished aluminium products, Worldwide, 2007

End-use	Share
Transportation	27%
Building and construction	24%
Electrical	21%
Packaging	13%
Other	15%

Source: International Aluminium Association (2009a).

Figure 1. Aluminium production, Worldwide, 1948-2010

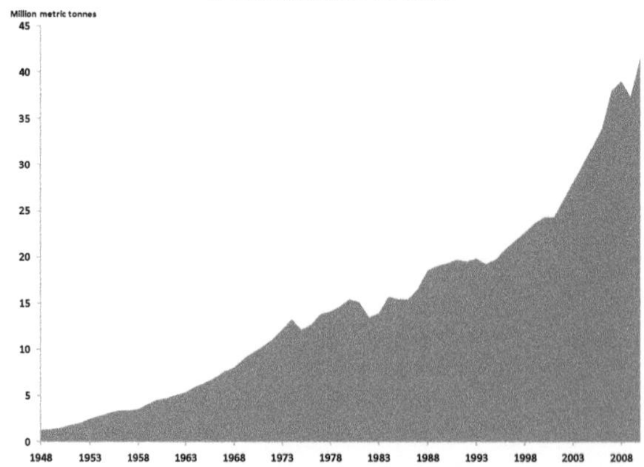

Source: U.S. Geological Survey (2010a, 2010, 2011).

Production, recycling and substitution

The production of aluminium from primary sources is a multistep process that begins with mining aluminium ore, most commonly bauxite. The mined bauxite is treated, if required, then transported to a refinery where it is processed into alumina (aluminium oxide). The alumina is then smelted into aluminium metal through an energy intensive electrolytic process. In 2010, 211 Mt of bauxite and around 82 Mt of alumina were extracted produced worldwide (USGS, 2010b). It is estimated that 85-90% of all mined bauxite is used by the aluminium industry. Bauxite is also used in the production abrasives, cement and chemicals.

Secondary (or recycled) aluminium can be produced from new scrap or old (or post-consumer) scrap. New scrap is scrap recovered from primary aluminium production. It can be generated at all three stages of the production process: metal production (i.e. smelting), the fabrication of alloys and semi-finished aluminium products and the manufacture of finished aluminium products. Old scrap is scrap recovered from applications once they have reached the end of their life (e.g. wire and cable, used beverage cans, packaging, car parts). As a result, the quality of new scrap is typically known while old scrap is of variable quality and must be separated, sorted and treated before being melted down. Because of the additional effort required to produce secondary aluminium from post-consumer scrap, old scrap sells at a discount. However, in terms of quality, there is no difference between a finished product made from new scrap and one made from old scrap. Similarly, products made from primary sources are no different than ones made from recycled aluminium.

Recycled aluminium (new scrap plus post-consumer scrap) accounts for a significant and growing portion of overall aluminium supply. In 2006 the secondary production of aluminium accounted for one quarter to one third of world aluminium production or 12 -16 Mt compared to 5 Mt in 1980 (the International Aluminium Institute's estimate of 33% (16 Mt) is significantly higher than the figure of 11.8 Mt (25%) estimated by the U.S. Geological Service therefore both figures are presented here). There are varying estimates of the post-consumer or old scrap content in secondary aluminium. The International Aluminium Institute (IAI) (2009) estimates that 50% of secondary aluminium comes from post-consumer sources, but end-of-life sources only accounted for 40% of secondary aluminium production in the U.S., the world's top producer of recycled aluminium, in 2008 according to data from the U.S. Geological Survey (USGS).

A number of factors make aluminium a highly desirable metal for recycling. Aluminium retains its properties and quality regardless of the number of the times it has been recycled because melting does not change its atomic structure. It also has relatively few disparate end-uses, which facilitates recovery and recycling. However, energy cost savings provide by far the greatest incentive to recycle aluminium. Producing recycled aluminium uses only 5% of the energy required to produce new aluminium because melting scrap requires only a fraction of the energy needed to refine alumina into aluminium metal.

Despite aluminium's unique qualities and pervasive use economy-wide it is not irreplaceable. Substitute commodities are readily available for virtually all applications, but usually with some loss of efficiency. Composites, although heavier, can substitute for aluminium in aircraft fuselages and wings. Magnesium, titanium and steel can be used in ground transportation and structural engineering. In construction, aluminium can be replaced by composites, steel, wood and vinyl and by copper in electrical applications although aluminium can conduct twice as much electricity. Glass, paper, plastic, and steel are common alternatives for aluminium in packaging.

Supply and demand

World bauxite resources are estimated between 55 and 75 billion metric tonnes (Gt), with 32% located in Africa, 23% in Oceania, 21% in South America and the Caribbean, 18% in Asia, and 6% in the rest of the world (USGS, 2011). Reserves are defined by U.S. Geological Survey as the estimated amount of the material in such a form or amount of concentration that economic extraction is currently or potentially feasible. Global reserves, meaning the portion of the resource that is currently considered economically extractable, are estimated at 28 Gt. The geographic distribution of reserves is reflective of bauxite's tendency to form in tropical and sub-tropical regions. The largest bauxite reserves are found in Guinea (7.4 Gt), followed by Australia (5.4 Gt), Brazil (3.4 Gt), Vietnam (2.1 Gt), Jamaica (2.0 Gt). Other significant reserves are found in India, Guyana, China, Greece, and Suriname (each with reserves of between 500 Mt and 1 Gt). Aside from Australia and Greece, there are no other major bauxite reserves found in the OECD area.

Countries with the largest reserves of bauxite are also the main **bauxite** producers. Australia is the world's top producer, accounting for a third of global production and virtually all of the production within the OECD area (figures for the production, import and export of bauxite, alumina and aluminium from 1992 to 2009 have been provided by the British Geological Survey). However, most bauxite extraction takes place outside of the OECD area (65% of global extraction in 2009). Non-OECD production is dominated by the BRIICS countries, which produced close to 47% of the world's bauxite in 2009. After Australia, China (15%), Brazil (13%), Indonesia (8%) and Guinea (7%) are the world's top bauxite producers.

Global **alumina** production is heavily concentrated in OECD and BRIICS countries. OECD countries accounted for nearly 40% global alumina production in 2009 while the share of BRIICS countries was close to 50%. China is the world's top alumina producer, supplying 30% of the global supply, followed by Australia (26%), Brazil (11%), the United States (4%) and India (4%).

Although the production of **primary aluminium** takes place in a larger number of countries relative to alumina production, production volume remains dominated by BRIICS and OECD countries. In 2009 BRIICS countries accounted for 56% of the aluminium produced worldwide. China, the world's single largest producer, accounted for 35% of production while Russia was second with 10%. OECD countries produced 30% of global aluminium. Production in concentrated in a handful of member countries: Canada (8% of global production), the United States (5%), Australia (5%) and Norway (3%).

A large stock of aluminium scrap is required for a fully developed aluminium recycling industry. Consequently, **secondary aluminium** production is dominated by more developed regions of the world (North America, Japan and Europe). OECD countries accounted for over 70% of global secondary aluminium production in 2006, with the United States (30% of world production) and Japan (9%) as the top producers within the region. The BRIICS countries accounted for nearly all of the production by non-OECD countries, with China producing 20% of global recycled aluminium and Russia producing nearly 5% (Menzie *et al.*, 2010).

Along with production, the global trade in bauxite, alumina and aluminium has also expanded rapidly. Estimates by Moriguchi and Hashimoto (2006) find that trade flows by weight of these three commodities grew by 110% between 1983 and 2003, driven primarily by strong growth in aluminium metal trade (258%). Russia, Canada, Australia, Norway and Iceland are the top exporters of primary aluminium (unwrought and unwrought alloys). Together these five countries exported 11 Mt of primary aluminium, representing over 60% of total exports and 30% of total production worldwide in 2009. Top aluminium importers consist of the world's largest industrialised countries: the United States, Japan, China, Germany and South Korea. Aluminium imports by these countries reached over 9.5 Mt in 2009.

Today China is the world's largest consumer of primary aluminium, having overtaken Japan, Germany and the United States in the last 15 years. Unlike those countries, China meets most of its demand through domestic production, which has grown by a factor of 12 since 1992. Imports make up only 12% of Chinese consumption.

Figure 2. Regional shares of bauxite, alumina, primary and secondary aluminium production and top producers, 2009

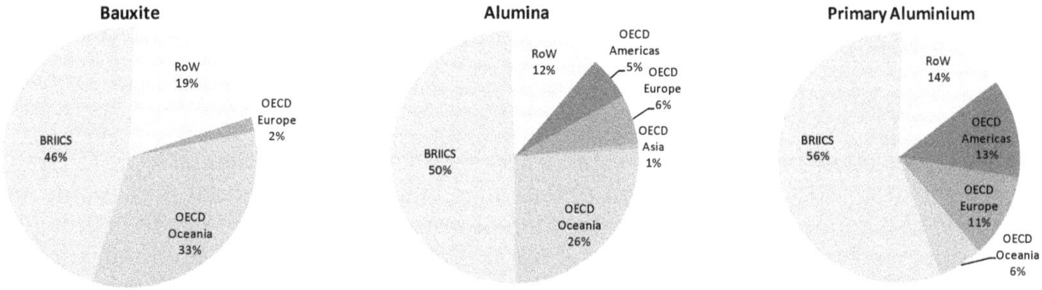

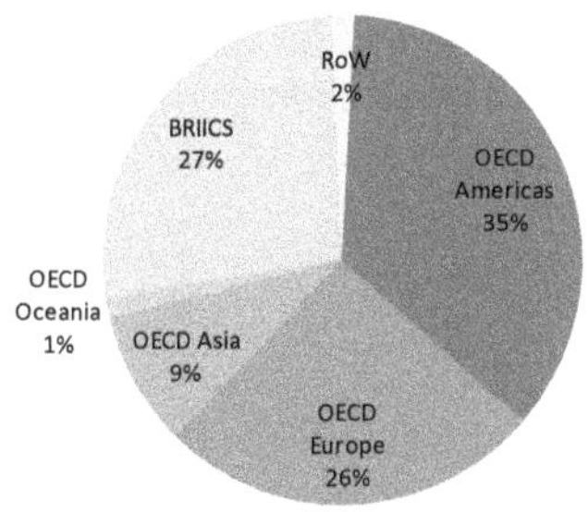

Top 5 Producers and Shares of Global Production, 2009

Bauxite	Alumina	Primary Aluminium	Secondary Aluminium
Australia (33%)	China (31%)	China (35%)	United States (30%)
China (15%)	Australia (26%)	Russia (10%)	China (20%)
Brazil (13%)	Brazil (11%)	Canada (8%)	Japan (9%)
Indonesia (8%)	United States (4%)	Australia (5%)	Germany (7%)
Guinea (7%)	India (4%)	United States (5%)	Italy (6%)

Notes: Secondary aluminium production figures refer to 2006.

Source: Bauxite, alumina and primary aluminium production data from the British Geological Survey (2010); secondary aluminium production data from Menzie *et al.* (2010) based on the U.S. Geological Survey figures.

Environmental and economic sustainability

Prior to the 2008 financial crisis, surging demand had been driving an unprecedented boom in global mining. Between 2000 and 2007 global aluminium production grew by over 57% or 5% annually compared to 26% over the 1990s or 2.3% annually (USGS, 2010a). Similarly, the real price of aluminium rose 45% between 2000 and 2007 (5.5% annually), compared to a 3% decrease over the 1990s. Although the recent increase in the real price of aluminium has more modest in comparison to other industrial metals (e.g. iron ore and copper), finite resources coupled with rapid growth in the overall use of metals and their prices has raised general concerns regarding long term metal supplies as well as the environmental impact of accelerating metal production.

Figure 3. Real prices of industrial metals, 1960-2010

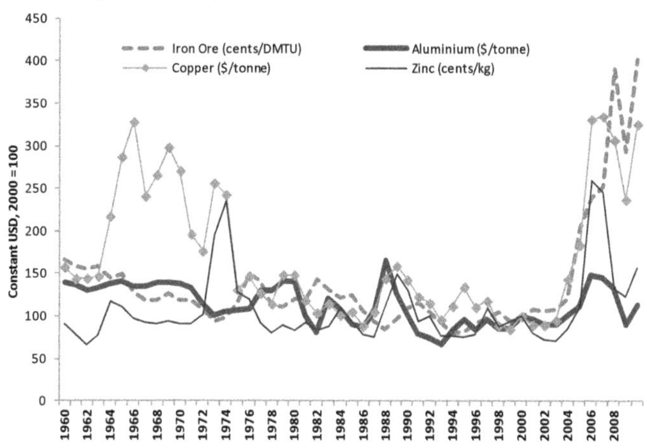

Source: World Bank Global Economic Monitor (GEM) Commodities database.

Environmental implications

The production of aluminium takes place in stages with each stage associated with its own environmental implications.

Bauxite production

Beyond the depletion of the resource, the most significant environmental impact from bauxite mining is the destruction and alteration of the immediate land and habitat at the mine site due to the removal of overburden and the construction of infrastructure to support the mining operation (e.g. housing, medical facilities, energy and water distribution systems, communications systems, equipment and vehicle repair facilities, and transportation infrastructure). Mining regulations vary by country but typically require that lands be rehabilitated following the termination of mining operations, but the lengthy lifespan of a bauxite mine (sometimes 100 years or more) entails a significant disruption to the surrounding ecosystem. The most significant wastes produced from bauxite extraction are tailings and waste water from cleaning and grinding the ore, as well as air emissions from diesel-powered mining equipment.

Alumina production

The main waste resulting from the production of alumina is a residual of the clarification stage of the Bayer chemical process called "red mud." As its name would imply, red mud is a mixture of water and small-sized minerals and elements that is reddish in colour. While its exact chemical composition depends on the bauxite ore from which it originated, red mud often contains silica, aluminium, iron, calcium, and titanium as well as trace amounts of barium, boron, cadmium, chromium, cobalt, gallium, vanadium, scandium, lead and radio nuclides (EPA, 1990). The International Aluminium Institute (IAI) (2003) estimated that for every metric tonne of alumina, approximately two metric tonnes of red mud were produced in 2000, while in Menzie *et al.* (2010) the European Aluminium Association estimated a figure in the range of 0.8 to 1.2 tonnes of red mud per tonne of alumina using 2005 data. The volume of red mud produced depends on a number of plant and process specific factors, including the grade of bauxite ore used. Higher grade bauxite produces less red mud, but as the grade of aluminium ore expected to decrease over time the incremental volume of red mud would be expected to increase absent other measures. Overall 93 Mt of red mud was produced from alumina processing in 2008 of which 90% was attributable to aluminium production (Menzie *et al.*, 2010).

The disposal of red mud poses a significant challenge. Red mud is chemically complex and highly alkaline and if not disposed of soundly can be harmful to the environment and human health. The most common method of disposal is the use of lined containment ponds reinforced by dams or dykes. Once in the ponds, the red mud settles at the bottom and the waste water is removed, treated and then reused or disposed of, or it simply evaporates. The remaining sediment is allowed to dry naturally and is typically disposed of in situ as part of land reclamation activities. Red mud is also disposed of at sea once neutralised or in landfills though both of these methods are less common.

The U.S. Environmental Protection Agency (1990) does not deem red mud a hazardous material; however elevated levels of some constituents, such as chromium, arsenic and radium-266, found at some disposal sites can pose a risk to human health. Breaches in containment ponds also pose a threat. On October 6, 2010 a breach at a Hungarian red mud disposal site caused approximately 750 million litres of red mud to flood nearby villages contaminating soil and surface water, killing ten people and causing burns and skin and eye irritations. The spill reached the Raba River (a tributary of the Danube) temporarily elevating the pH of the river to levels dangerous for plant and animal life. If not properly cleaned up, agricultural production in the area could be affected as the highly alkaline nature of red mud inhibits plant growth. Similarly, once reclaimed, red mud containment ponds are unsuitable for agricultural use. However, efforts are being made to find ways to recycle or reuse red mud, including in bricks, cement, asphalt, and roofing and flooring tiles.

Primary aluminium production

By far the most significant environmental concern related to the production of aluminium is greenhouse gas (GHG) emissions. According to the IAI, the production of (new) primary aluminium is responsible for approximately 1% of global man-made GHG emissions.

Sixty percent of emissions are related energy production to power the smelting process. Producing one tonne of aluminium requires an estimated 15,000 kilowatts of electricity (Menzie *et al.*, 2010), which in most cases is generated through the combustion of fossil fuels. The amount of GHG emissions produced from energy consumption varies by region and energy fuel mix; China, the world's top aluminium producer, relies heavily on coal-fired electricity generation while Russia and Canada use mainly hydroelectricity.

Figure 4. GHG Emissions from Aluminium Production by Region, 1990-2005

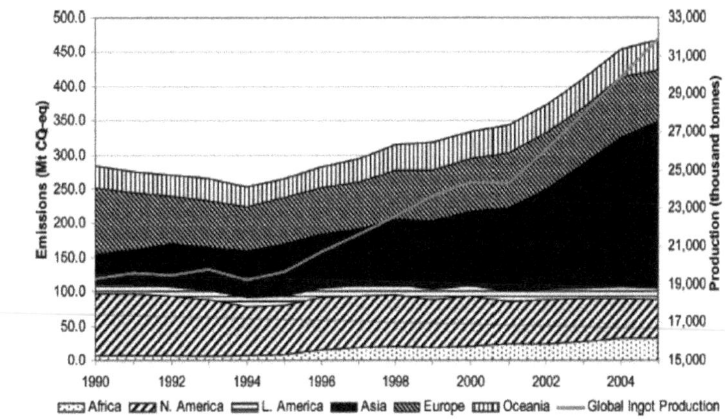

Source: McMillan and Keoleian (2009).

The remaining 40% of GHG emissions are produced as a result of the industrial production process itself (mining, refining, smelting and casting). Carbon dioxide (CO_2) gas forms as a by-product of the smelting process when carbon in the anode combines with oxygen in aluminium oxide (alumina). The per fluorocarbons (PCFs) tetrafluoromethane (CF_4) and hexaflurethane (C_2F_6) form when the normal smelting process is disturbed. These instances, called "anode events", occur when the level of the dissolved alumina in the cell drops too low. PFCs are particularly potent global warming gases because they take a long time to break down once in the atmosphere and they have high global warming potential (1 kg of PFC is equivalent to 6,500 kg of CO_2). According to the IAI, the smelting process produces 1.6 tonnes of CO_2 per tonne of aluminium on average and the equivalent of one tonne of CO_2 in PFC emissions. In 2005 industrial processes produced 140 million tonnes of CO_2 equivalents, including 30 Mt of PFCs.[1]

Global GHG emissions intensity from new aluminium production has remained fairly stable. Between 1990 and 2005 GHG emissions essentially grew in step with aluminium production – both increased by approximately 65% or 3.4% annually (McMillan and Keoleian, 2009; USGS, 2009a). Asia's share of emissions grew significantly driven by a sharp increase Chinese aluminium production, while emissions in Europe and the United States decreased. However, as McMillan and Keoleian (2009) note, this decrease cannot be completely attributed to improvements in GHG emission intensity as U.S. aluminium production also decreased during this period. PFCs made up a declining share of GHG emissions; in 1990 24% of emissions were due to PFCs and by 2005 this had been reduced to 15% with the largest decreases occurring in North America and Oceania.

Secondary aluminium production

In addition to using only 5% of the energy required to produce new aluminium, the production of recycled (secondary) aluminium does not produce any PFCs. A model of 15 European Union members estimated that the production of one tonne of recycled aluminium metal alloy in 2002 required 1.4 kilowatts of energy, 936 kg of scrap, 81 kg of turnings, 33 kg of alloys, 33 t of dross,[2] 16 t of oxide, and 2 t of salt and produced 6 kg of dust, 15 kg of water and oil and 90 kg of non-metallic residue (Menzie *et al.*, 2010). However, it is unclear whether production was modelled on new scrap or old scrap. Recycling old scrap takes more time and produces more air emissions because the composition of old scrap must be analysed after it is melted and adjusted by adding primary aluminium or alloys to obtain the desired composition. Old scrap also contains other materials, such as plastic, paint, and oil, which produce air pollutants when smelted, requiring that appropriate emissions control systems are in place.

The aluminium industry has voluntarily taken steps to reduce its impact on the environment, particularly with regard to reducing its greenhouse gas emissions. According to the IAI, whose members represent 80% of global aluminium production, by 2006 the aluminium industry had reduced its PFC emissions by 80% per tonne of primary aluminium produced relative to a 1990 baseline and has set a new target of a 50% reduction by 2020 relative to 2006 levels (IAI, 2009b). Absolute GHG emissions directly resulting from primary aluminium production and upstream production processes (i.e. not including emission resulting from energy consumption) have held steady at 1990 levels even though production doubled over the same time period. The industry has also made inroads in reducing energy consumption in both the aluminium smelting and alumina production processes and is seeking to reduce fresh water consumption intensity and increase the proportion of land rehabilitated annually.

Security of supply

Given bauxite's crustal abundance, the U.S. Geological Survey views reserves as sufficient to meet aluminium demand well into the future. However, if bauxite production continues to grow at an average rate of 5% per year and no new reserves or technologies are discovered, today's reserves of 28 Gt are expected to be exhausted in less than 50 years under current production and consumption patterns based on OECD estimates (2008a). Reserves would be exhausted in approximately 80 years under a 2% production growth scenario and in 200 years under a zero growth scenario. If bauxite deposits were exhausted past economic limits aluminium could be produced from other mineral deposits (e.g. nepheline, anothite), which experts estimate could extend the upper limit of global extractable aluminium resources to 20 petatonnes (20×10^{15} tonnes) (UNEP, 2011).

In terms of short-term supply, although bauxite mining and alumina production are geographically concentrated in a handful of countries supply disruptions have been rare. Any disruptions that have occurred have tended be at the aluminium production stage due to energy supply issues because large amounts of energy are needed to power the smelting process. Consequently, a growing share of global aluminium production is taking place in countries that have no bauxite reserves of their own, but that do have access to stable, cheap and plentiful energy sources (e.g. hydroelectricity in Canada and Norway; natural gas in Bahrain, and Dubai; and hydro and geothermal in Iceland). The trend towards outsourcing aluminium production is expected to continue as producers seek to lower their energy costs. Menzie *et al.* (2010) forecast that the Middle East and Africa, led by South Africa's plentiful coal reserves, are the regions that will experience the strongest growth in aluminium production capacity between 2011 and 2015.

As incomes rise in emerging and developing economies, demand for aluminium is expected to grow. Whether the world's aluminium resources will be adequate to meet future demand requires not only an examination of the amount of aluminium in geological reserves, but also the amount of aluminium that is currently in use in the economy (anthropogenic stocks) in products and applications and that is potentially available for recycling. A literature review by the United Nations Environment Programme's International Panel for Sustainable Resource Management (2010) found several studies that have measured anthropogenic aluminium stocks at different levels (i.e. global, national, sub-national) and points in time. The trends illustrated by the studies are consistent with general aluminium production and consumption patterns. Global per capita man-made stocks have risen dramatically over the last 50 years – from 2.2 kilogram per capita in 1947 to 82 kg per capita in 2003. As expected Europe, the U.S. and Japan have high levels of in-use stocks per capita (in the 200-480 kg per capita range in studies since 2000) while levels in China are relatively low (less than 40 kg per capita in 2005).

End-use patterns are a significant factor in determining anthropogenic aluminium stocks and the volume of post-consumer scrap available for recycling. The IAI (2009a) estimates that 612 Mt or three quarters of the 800 Mt of aluminium that has been produced since the late 1800s remains in use today with 32% found in buildings, 28% in electrical applications, 28% in transportation (with 16% in automotive) and 1% in packaging.

The share of aluminium in infrastructure (electrical cables, building and construction) is large because of the long in-service lifetimes of those applications (30-50 years) compared to transportation (10-15 years for automobiles, but up to 40 years for railway equipment and airplanes) and packaging (less than 1 year). Consequently, transportation and packaging provide the largest share of post-consumer scrap for recycling – 42% and 28% respectively of the 8 Mt of old scrap recycled in 2007 (IAI, 2009a). However, the share of infrastructure scrap is beginning to grow as many of those applications reach the end of their life in developed countries.

Figure 5. Recycled Aluminium Scrap by End-Use Source

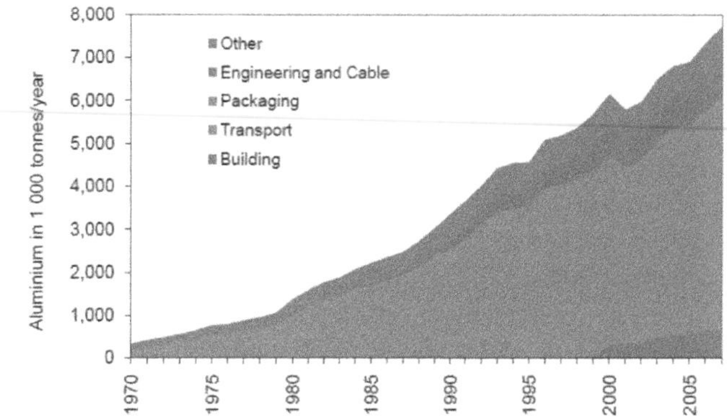

Source: International Aluminium Institute (2009a).

Decoupling

Although aluminium consumption levels are rising rapidly in China, India, and Brazil, per capita consumption remains well below that of OECD countries. The top aluminium importing countries are also some of the highest per capita consumers; Japan averaged 27 kg of aluminium per capita, the United States 31 kg per capita and Germany 32 kg according to an analysis of 2006 apparent consumption data by Menzie *et al.* (2010). For the BRIICS countries, per capita consumption ranged between 1-7 kg per capita with India having the lowest per capita consumption of the group and China and Russia the highest. It is estimated that global primary aluminium consumption averaged over 5 kg per person in 2008.

Figure 6. Apparent aluminium consumption per capita and GDP per capita, selected countries, 2006

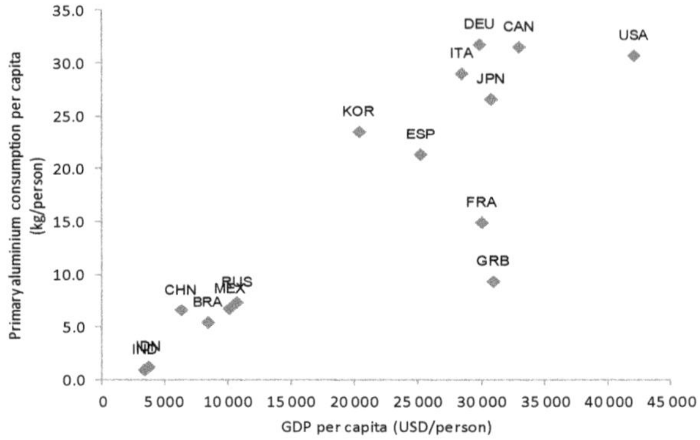

Source: Menzie *et al.* (2010).

Between 1983 and 2003, the apparent consumption of primary aluminium by OECD countries grew by 94% while GDP grew 79%, indicating that aluminium consumption was strongly linked to economic growth in the OECD area (OECD, 2008c). Over the same time period per capita aluminium consumption by OECD countries grew by 67% and per capita income grew by 54%. However, growth in per capita aluminium consumption does appear to stabilise in the late 1990s (at income around 22 000 constant USD) signalling that there may be a threshold income level beyond which aluminium consumption per person stops increasing. Menzie *et al.* (2010) found similar evidence in their analysis of the apparent aluminium consumption per capita in the world's 20 most populous countries. This finding is also consistent with studies of the industrial consumption of metals that found that consumption is low at very low income levels, but grows rapidly as income rises before levelling off. It is unclear whether this potential decoupling from economic growth in higher income countries is completely due to resource productivity gains. Patterns of aluminium consumption appear to change with rising income and material or product substitution may also be a contributing factor.

Income is also an important factor in determining the supply of post-consumer scrap potentially available for recycling. There is evidence suggesting that consumption for electrical end-uses decreases and consumption for transportation uses increases as incomes rise (Menzie *et al.*, 2010). This would imply that higher income countries are likely to have a larger supply of post-consumer scrap available for recycling in the near future. Demand for automobiles is growing exponentially in China and India, but substantial volumes of aluminium vehicle scrap will likely not materialise for at least a decade.

Outlook

- Given the significant environmental implications from aluminium production, in particular GHG emissions, managing global aluminium resources efficiently will be critical to green growth and sustainable development. But in the absence of significant efficiency gains at the plant level, including switching to non-GHG emitting fuel sources, absolute global emissions from aluminium production are expected to continue to rise. Although aluminium has played an important role in increasing fuel efficiency and reducing emissions in the transportation sector, rapidly increasing vehicle sales in emerging economies are contributing to greater aluminium demand and production-related GHG emissions.

- Maximising secondary aluminium's share of consumption will help in reducing the industry's overall GHG emissions, but recycling is not without its own challenges. A large portion of recycled aluminium comes from new scrap, which depends on primary aluminium production, while the volume of post-consumer scrap is heavily dependent on end-use patterns. In the emerging economies, where aluminium consumption is rising fastest, the volume of post-consumer scrap is limited and not expected to grow significantly for at least a decade. Opportunities for increased trade in aluminium scrap will have to be weighed against the environmental implications of transportation between countries. At the same time, in considering measures to increase post-consumer content in secondary aluminium it will be important to take into account the potential impacts on prices and costs of production.
- Whether there will be adequate aluminium reserves to meet long term future demand remains an ongoing debate. Current in situ reserves will be exhausted within 50 years at today's rate of consumption, but new technologies will likely lead to the discovery of new deposits, applications, production techniques, and substitutes, which will alter consumption patterns.
- In the short term, global demand for aluminium is expected to continue to increase driven by increasing consumption in low- and middle-income countries, notably China, Russia and Brazil. By 2025, global aluminium consumption could be more than triple today's level (OECD, 2010).

ENDNOTES

1 See *www.world-aluminium.org/Sustainability/Environmental+Issues/Greenhouse+gases.*

2 Dross is a waste product (scum) that forms on liquid metal during the smelting process. Dross often results due to the presence of dirt or other non-aluminium materials in old scrap.

REFERENCES

- BGS (British Geological Survey) (2010), *World Mineral Production 2004-2008,* British Geological Survey, Keyworth, Nottingham.
- BRGM (2008), *Annuaire Statistique Mondiale des Minerais et Métaux,* Société de l'Industrie Minérale, Paris.
- Environmental Protection Agency (1990), *Report to Congress on Special Wastes from Mineral Processing,* Chapter 3: Alumina Production, U.S. Environmental Protection Agency, Washington, D.C.
- Gordon, R.B., Bertram, M. and Graedel, T.E. (2006), "Metal Stocks and Sustainability", Proceedings of the National Science Academy, Vol. 103, no. 5, pages 1209-1214.
- IAI (International Aluminium Institute) (2010), Global Aluminium Industry Sustainability Scorecard 2009, International Aluminium Institute, London.
- IAI (2009a), Global Aluminium Recycling: A Cornerstone of Sustainable Development, International Aluminium Institute, London.
- IAI (2009b), *Aluminium for Future Generations: 2009 Update,* International Aluminium Institute, London.

- IAI (2003), Life Cycle Assessment of Aluminium: Inventory Data for the Worldwide Primary Aluminium Industry, International Aluminium Institute, London.
- IAI (n.d.), International Aluminium Institute website, *www.world-aluminium.org*
- International Monetary Fund (2006), *World Economic Outlook*, IMF, Washington, D.C.
- McMillan Colin A., and Keolian, Gregory A. (2009), "Not All Primary Aluminium is Created Equal: Greenhouse Gas Emissions from 1990-2005", *Environmental Science and Technology*, Volume 43, No. 5, pages 1571-1577.
- Menzie, W.D. *et al.* (2010), The global flow of aluminum from 2006 through 2025: U.S. Geological Survey Open-File Report 2010–1256, 73 p.
- Moriguichi, Y. and Hashimoto, S. (2003), *Material Flow Data Book: World Resource Flows around Japan*, National Institute for Environmental Studies, Tokyo.
- OECD (2011b), Sustainable materials management: Case studies, *http://www.oecd.org/env/waste/smm-casestudies.htm* .
- OECD (2008a), Measuring Resource Flows and Resource Productivity: Synthesis Report, OECD, Paris. http://www.oecd.org/env/indicators-modelling-outlooks/MFA-Synthesis.pdf
- OECD (2008b), Measuring Resource Flows and Resource Productivity, Volume 1: The OECD guide, OECD, Paris. http://www.oecd.org/environment/indicators-modelling-outlooks/MFA-Guide.pdf
- UNEP (United Nations Environment Programme) (2011a), "Estimating Long-Run Geological Stocks of Metals," A Working Paper by the Working Group on Geological Stocks of Metals to the UNEP International Panel on Sustainable Resource Management, 6 April 2011, Paris.
- UNEP (2011b), *Recycling Rates of Metals – A Status Report,"* A Report of the Working Group on Global Metal Flows to the International Resource Panel, Graedel, T.E., Allwood, J., Birat, J.P., Buchert, M., Hageluken, C., Reck, B.K., Sibley, S.F., Sonnemann, G., UNEP, Paris.
- UNEP (2010), *Metal Stocks in Society: Scientific Synthesis*, A Report of the Working Group on the Global Metal Flows to the International Panel for Sustainable Resource Management, UNEP, Paris.
- USGS (U.S. Geological Survey) (2011), *Mineral Commodity Summaries 2011*, U.S. Geological Survey, Reston, Virginia.
- USGS (2010a), Aluminium statistics, in Kelly, T.D., and Matos, G.R., comps., Historical statistics for mineral and material commodities in the United States: USGS Data Series 140 [Accessed 8 August 2011].
- USGS (2010b), Bauxite and alumina statistics, in Kelly, T.D., and Matos, G.R., comps., Historical statistics for mineral and material commodities in the United States: USGS Data Series 140 [Accessed 8 August 2011].
- USGS (2010c), *Mineral Commodity Summaries 2010*, U.S. Geological Survey, Reston, Virginia.
- The World Bank (2010), Global Commodity Prices: Review and Price Forecast, World Bank, Washington, D.C.

COPPER FACTSHEET

One of the first metals ever extracted by humans, copper has a long history of industrial use and is one of the most widely used metals in the economy today. An excellent conductor, copper plays a critical role in powering everything from homes, cars, and consumer electric and electronic devices to telecommunications and commuter rail networks. Strong demand and capacity constraints have led to an ongoing supply crunch and record level prices, renewing interest worldwide in copper recycling. Secondary copper markets are already well-developed and copper scrap is commonly traded internationally. The challenge ahead will be to increase stock of scrap through increased recovery and collection, particularly from fast growing waste streams, such as consumer electronics. Virgin copper resources will continue to be the world's primary source of copper, making continued improvements in extraction and production efficiency important. Managing the environmental impacts of extraction is also important, particularly water usage in arid areas.

See the Reader's guide for information about the selection of key material resources.

Overview

Characteristics and uses

Copper is a non-ferrous metal identifiable by its characteristic reddish brown colour. It is easily stretched, moulded, and shaped; is resistant to corrosion; and an efficient conductor of heat and electricity. When alloyed with other metals (such as tin to form bronze and zinc to form brass) copper gains increased strength, hardness and corrosion resistance.

Copper was first used by humans over 10 000 years ago to make coins and ornaments. Later it was used in tools and alloyed with tin to form bronze, which was stronger, harder and easier to cast, giving rise to the age bearing its name. Today copper is a major industrial metal, ranking third after iron and aluminium in terms of volumes consumed worldwide. Copper's versatility has led to its pervasive use in a wide range of applications. Copper and copper alloys are used in building construction (roofing, wiring, plumbing), power generation and transmission (cables, transformers), electronic product manufacturing (computers, cell phones, microwaves), and the production of industrial machinery (gears, turbine blades, heat exchange equipment) and transportation (vehicles, high speed trains, vessel hulls). Copper is also used in other consumer and general products such as cookware, musical instruments, and sculptures; and continues to be used in the coins of many countries. Within these end-use sectors, electrical applications copper, including power transmission and generation, building wiring, telecommunication, and electrical and electronic products, account for about three quarters of total copper use.

New applications for copper continue to be developed. The health and medical field is taking advantage of copper's natural antibacterial properties to help prevent the transfer of disease and microbes in hospitals and areas that lack access to clean water. Semiconductor manufacturers have also begun using copper for circuitry in silicon chips to increasing operating speed and use less energy.

Copper is found in the earth's crust in many forms. Some 160 copper minerals have been identified although only a small number are of economic importance (USGS, 2004; BGS, 2007). They are commonly divided into three groups: primary copper sulphides, copper oxides, and secondary copper sulphides. The most abundant and economically significant is the primary sulphide chalcopyrite ($CuFeS_2$), containing a maximum 34.6% copper content by weight.

In general copper deposits are formed through hydrothermal activity and are commonly found in areas of the world where tectonic plates have converged or diverged. Deposits are classified according to how they were formed. Porphyry copper deposits, the most common, are formed through igneous intrusions. Porphyry deposits are found in the mountainous regions of North America and South America, and around the western side of the Pacific Basin in the Philippines, Indonesia and Papua New Guinea; and they contain two-thirds of the world's copper resources (USGS, 2009). Sedimentary deposits, which are found in the Central African copper belt and parts of Eastern Europe, account for one fourth of copper resources, while sulphide deposits in volcanic rocks hold about 5 percent (USGS, 2004).

Figure 1. Copper end-uses by sector, United States, 1975 and 2010

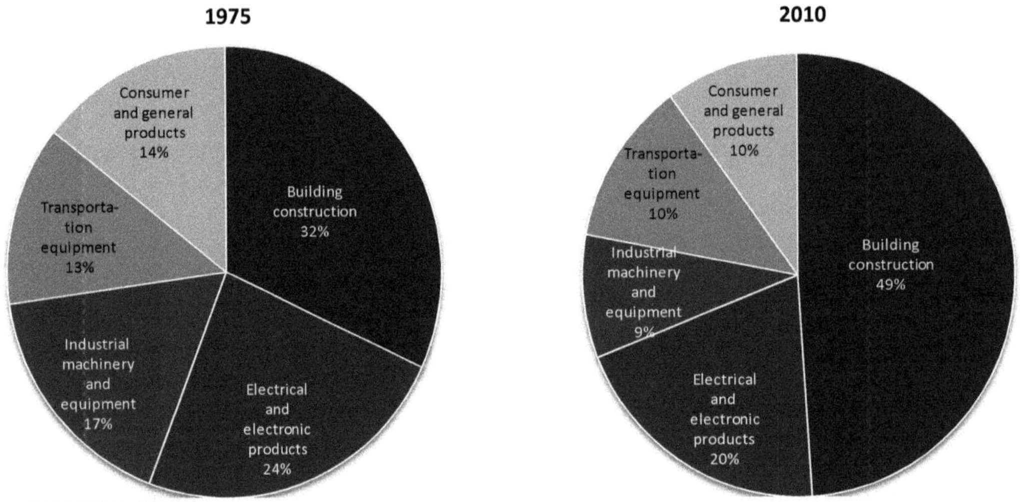

Source: USGS (2005), (2011a).

Production and processing

The production of copper from primary sources begins with mining copper ore. Depending on the characteristics of the mineral deposit and its geographic location, the ore is mined using one of three techniques: open-pit mining, underground mining or in-situ leaching. Open-pit mining is the most common approach. It is generally used when deposits are relatively near to the surface, low-grade, and/or very large. The ore is extracted by digging or blasting with explosives. It is then loaded onto trucks or conveyors and transported for further processing. Underground mining was the most common approach before the turn of the 20th century, but is less common today due to higher costs and safety concerns. Underground mining is better suited to small, high grade, deep deposits. In-situ leaching involves pumping a weak sulphuric acid leach solution into a deposit via an injection well. Copper dissolves in the solution, which is then pumped out through surrounding recovery wells. This approach is appropriate for deposits that are relatively deep and low grade. The deposit must be permeable and surrounded by impervious rock.

Mined ores generally contain between 0.5% and 3% copper and must undergo a concentration process to increase the copper content to 25-35% before it can be smelted (BGS, 2009). This process usually takes place close to the extraction site. It involves crushing and grinding the ore, followed by chemical and/or physical processing and separation stages (i.e. leaching or froth floatation). To become pure copper metal the concentration either undergoes a pyrometallurgical (smelting) or a hydrometallurgical (leaching) process. Pyrometallurgical treatment is used for copper sulphides while the hydrometallurgical process generally is used for copper oxides. Both processes produce high purity copper cathodes (99.99% Cu content), which are then shipped to mills and foundries where they are cast into copper rod (for wires), billets (tubes, rods, bar stocks), cakes (plate, sheets, foil), or ingots (alloying, casting).

Recycling and substitution

Copper can be infinitely recycled without loss of its properties and the secondary production of copper requires one-sixth of the energy required to produce primary copper. Recycled copper accounts for an estimated 35% of copper consumption (ICSG, 2010). It is estimated that approximately 80% of the copper that has ever been mined remains in use today (BGS, 2007). Copper can be recycled from new or old scrap. New scrap is generated and collected throughout the copper processing and manufacturing stages. It includes slag, drosses, borings and cuttings that are reused by the plant, foundry or mill where they originated. Old scrap is post-consumer scrap derived from copper products that have reached the end of their life (e.g. end-of-life vehicles, electrical appliances, roofing and wiring). Post-consumer scrap is more difficult to collect and its copper purity and content is highly variable. In 2010, old scrap provided 160 000 tonnes of copper in the U.S., equivalent to 9% of U.S. apparent consumption (USGS, 2011a).

A number of substitutes are available for copper in virtually all of its applications. Silver is a superior conductor of electricity, but considerably more expensive than copper for use in electrical wiring. Aluminium is a cheaper alternative, but less effective. Fibre optic cables can replace copper wire in some telecommunications applications. For water pipe and plumbing fixtures, copper can be replaced by aluminium or plastic. Other metals such as stainless steel, titanium and aluminium can substitute for copper in heat exchangers. Aluminium is also commonly replacing copper in automotive radiators.

Supply and demand

Figure 2. Shares of global copper reserves by country, 2010

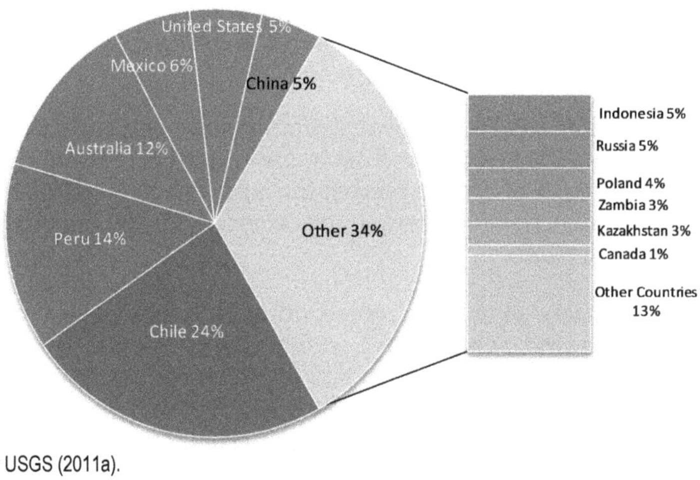

Source: USGS (2011a).

Preliminary assessments by the U.S. Geological survey have estimated global land-based copper resources in excess of 3 billion tonnes (Gt), with 550 million tonnes (Mt) in the United States and undiscovered deposits of 1.3 Gt in the Andes Mountains in South America (USGS, 2011a; Cunningham *et al.*, 2008).[1] In addition to land-based resources, significant volumes of copper are potentially found in deep sea environments. The estimate of resources includes volumes that are only surmised to exist. The UNEP Resource Panel's Working Group on the Geological Stocks of

Metal estimates that the lower limit of extractable global copper resources (i.e. the amount that is actually considered extractable over the long term) is around 1 Gt (UNEP, 2011b).

Global copper reserves are currently estimated at 630 Mt. The largest reserves are found in Chile (150 Mt), followed by Peru (90 Mt), Australia (80 Mt), Mexico (38 Mt) and the United States (35 Mt) (USGS, 2011a).

Global production of mined copper reached 16.2 Mt in 2010, a 30-fold increase from the beginning of the 20th century when less than half a million tonnes of copper was extracted worldwide. As with other major metals, the production of copper expanded rapidly after the Second World War. Unlike iron, aluminium and zinc, which witnessed a further acceleration in mine production beginning in the early 2000s, the rate of copper extraction was slower over the last ten years relative to the previous decade.

The extraction of copper takes place in over 50 countries around the world. Since overtaking the United States in the early 1990s, Chile has been the world's leading producer of mined copper. In 2010 Chilean production represented over a third of global production (5.5 Mt). Peru was second, producing 9% of global supplies, followed by China (7%) and the United States (7%). In addition to Chile and the United States, Australia, Canada and Poland are other OECD countries that are leading copper producers.

World smelter production reached 14.5 Mt in 2009. Smelter production has been lower than mine production since the mid-1990s due to the increasing use of hydrometallurgical techniques (which do not require smelting) (BGS, 2007). Almost half of smelting production takes place in OECD countries, mostly in the OECD Americas region. However, China is the single largest producer of smelter copper in the world. Chinese production represented nearly a quarter of global production in 2009. Chile is the world's second leading producer, followed by Japan.

Copper refining takes place in over 40 countries around the world. In 2009 global production of refined copper totalled 18.4 Mt, including 2.9 Mt of secondary production. Production patterns of refined copper are similar to those of smelter production. OECD countries account for over 50% of global production, most of which is in the OECD Americas region. Again China is the world's single largest copper refiner, producing 4.2 Mt (a 23% share) in 2009, followed by Chile (3.3 Mt, an 18% share) and Japan (1.4 Mt, an 8% share).

Secondary copper production has been growing rapidly since the early 2000s. Global secondary production of refined copper reached over 2.8 Mt in 2009 (16% of total refined copper production). China accounts for nearly half of global production and virtually all of the production by the BRIICS countries. OECD countries represent a 40% share, with the majority of production taking place in the OECD Europe region.

Copper is traded in a variety of forms, representing different stages of the production and manufacturing chain. Ores and concentrates, refined copper and copper scrap are the most important flows, together accounting for over 95% of global copper imports in 2009. These trade flows have shifted over the last decade with the relocation of global manufacturing capacity towards the rapidly industrialising economies of Asia, China in particular. Chinese imports of copper began to increase in the late 1990s and quickly surpassed Japan, which had formerly been the largest copper importer. Chinese import growth has been fairly dramatic; in 1992 China's share of world imports was 8%, by 2009 its share was almost 40%. China is the top importer of all three forms of traded copper – ores and concentrates, refined copper and copper scrap.

Copper imports have stayed relatively stable in OECD countries, growing modestly in the OECD Europe and Asia regions while declining slightly in the OECD Americas over the last 20 years. But OECD countries continue to be some of the leading importers of copper. Japan remains the world's second largest importer of copper, with a 14% global share in 2009, followed by Germany (7%) and

Korea (7%). Although they still remain well below China's, India's imports grew twice as fast between 1992 and 2009. India overtook the United States in 2004-2005 and is now the world's fifth largest copper importer.

Chile is the world's top copper exporter and has been for some time. Chilean exports represented almost a third of global exports in 2009. Many of the world's largest industrial economies are reliant on copper from Chile. In 2005 40% of China's copper concentrate imports came from Chile (BGS, 2011). Over the last two decades exports from Peru have also expanded quickly and Peru is now the second largest copper exporter, with a 12% global share. Indonesia, Australia and the United States are the next largest exporters. Contrary to imports, copper exports of OECD countries have been growing steadily since the early 1990s, mainly driven by increased exports from Chile. Overall, OECD countries are important suppliers of copper, accounting for approximately two-thirds of global copper exports.

China has also overtaken the United States to become the world's largest consumer of refined copper. Apparent consumption in 2009 was close to 8 Mt. The United States is the second largest consumer (1.7 Mt in 2009), followed by Germany, Japan and Korea. However, as a whole OECD countries produce more refined copper than they consume. Apparent consumption by OECD countries represented 40% of global usage, while OECD production made up for than 50% of refined copper production worldwide.

Figure 3. Global production of copper

Global copper mine, smelter and refinery production since 1980

Secondary copper production and copper prices, 1980-2009

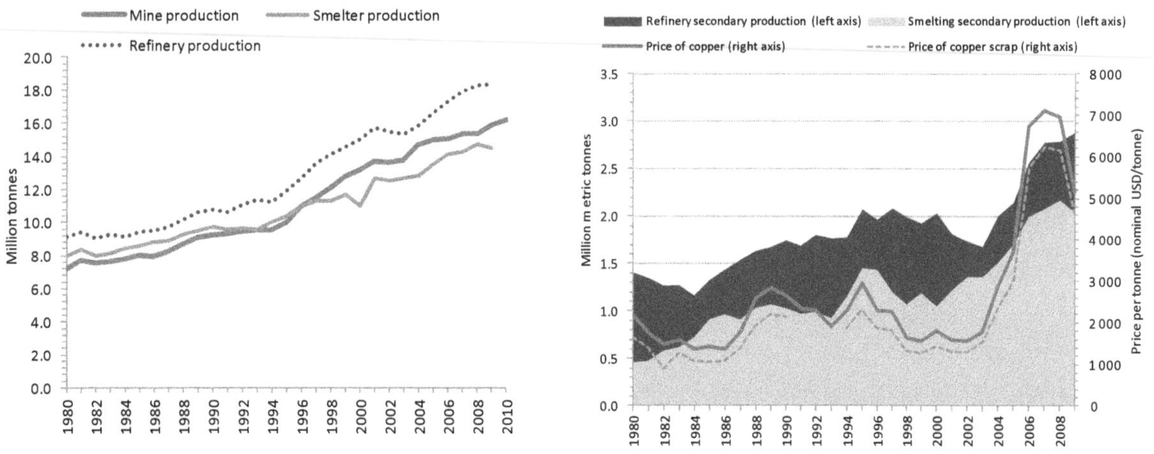

Notes: smelter and refinery production include secondary production.
Source: USGS (2011a).

Source: USGS and World Bank Global Economic Monitor (Commodities) database (*http://data.worldbank.org/data-catalog/global-economic-monitor*).

Regional shares of global copper production, 2009

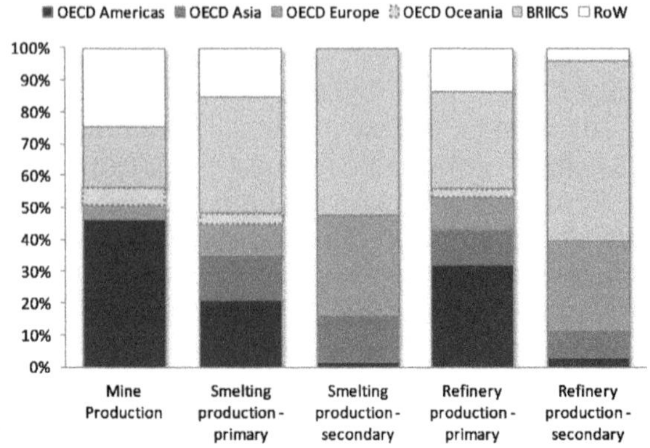

Top copper producers and global shares of production, 2009

Mine Production (2010)	Smelting production - primary	Smelting production - secondary	Refinery production - primary	Refinery production - secondary
Chile (34%)	China (21%)	China (39%)	Chile (21%)	China (49%)
Peru (8%)	Chile (12%)	Germany (14%)	China (18%)	Germany (13%)
China (7%)	Japan (10%)	Japan (12%)	Japan (8%)	Russia (8%)
USA (7%)	India (6%)	Russia (11%)	USA (7%)	Japan (7%)
Australia (6%)	USA (5%)	Belgium (6%)	India (5%)	Belgium (5%)

Notes: Smelting production (primary) includes undifferentiated production; secondary production includes estimates.
Source: BGS (2007) and USGS (2010).

Figure 4. Global shares of copper imports and exports by region, 2009

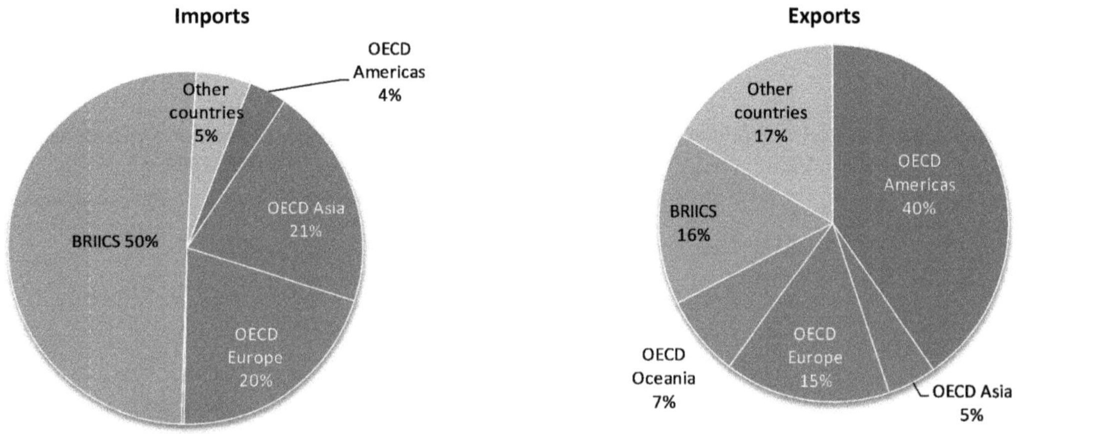

Source: British Geological Survey (2010)

Economic and environmental sustainability

Environmental implications

Primary copper production requires extraction and processing of very large amounts of ore. Porphyry deposits (the most common type of deposit) have copper grades that are relatively low, ranging between 0.2% - 1%, and are usually extracted using surface mining techniques (BGS, 2007). As a result, it is often necessary to move several hundred tonnes of copper ore, overburden and waste rock in order to produce one tonne of refined copper. [2] The impact on the environment from the alteration and destruction of the surrounding land and habitat can be significant.[3] Although their design, size and shape depend on a number of geological factors, surface mines tend to occupy a sizable portion of land. For example, the Bingham copper mine in the United States, visible from space, is 4 kilometres wide and 800 metres deep (USGS, 2009). It is only the 10th largest copper mine in the world by capacity, but has been in operation for 100 years (ICSG, 2010).

The process of mining copper ore and transforming it into metal generates many types of waste outflows – solid, liquid and gaseous. Solid residues and liquid effluent, such as tailings, waste water and slag must be disposed of according to the operating regulations. Tailings are usually deposited in large reservoirs to allow the solid particles to settle and the water to evaporate or be extracted for treatment or reuse. Tailings are sometimes disposed in the seabed (Alvarado *et al.*, 1999). A study by the U.S. Geological Survey found that 113 kilograms of tailings were generated per kilogram of copper (Goonan, 2004). Slag, a waste material from the smelting process, is usually re-used immediately within the plant, sold or disposed of. Approximately two kilograms of slag are generated for each kilogram of copper (Goonan, 2004).

The majority of copper is refined using the pyrometallurgical process, which produces emissions of carbon dioxide (CO_2), sulphur dioxide (SO_2), arsenic and other pollutants. Copper production is energy-intensive, in terms of both fuel and electricity requirements, and is a relevant source of energy-related CO_2 emissions. With each kilogram of copper produced, approximately 0.5 kg of CO2 is released (Goonan, 2004). SO_2 is produced during the pyrometallurgical smelting process when oxygen reacts with the sulphur in the copper sulphide ore. In the past copper smelters emitted large amounts of SO_2 into the air, but today most SO_2 emissions are captured and the sulphur recovered to make sulphuric acid or other useful products such as gypsum (Goonan, 2004). The hydrometallurgical process of refining copper, which requires large amounts of sulphuric acid for leaching, is one potential use for the sulphuric acid produced via the pyrometallurgical process. It is estimated that roughly 2 kg of sulphur dioxide are produced for each kg of copper (Alavarado *et al.*, 2002). The rate of SO_2 capture varies significantly between plants and countries, but the world's largest smelters capture an estimated 95% of the sulphur dioxide generated (Goonan, 2004).

Water usage is another important issue, particularly for copper mines located in located in arid zones such as Arizona or northern Chile. All mining operations require water. Water is used at nearly every stage of the copper production chain: concentration, smelting and electro refining or, in the hydro-metallurgical process, leaching, solvent extraction and electro winning.[4] The greatest volume of water is used in the concentration process, where water is used for floatation and the transportation of concentrates and tailings. In Chile average water usage by concentration plants was and 0.79 cubic metres per second (m^3/s) per tonne of mineral in 2006 (COCHILCO, 2008). The hydrometallurgical process also requires significant amounts of water, typically 2.5 – 3.0 m^3/s per ton of refined copper (Alvarado *et al.*, 1999). In both processes, hydrometallurgical and pyrometallurgical, water recirculation is a common practice and along with other efficiency measures (evaporation reduction, leak prevention) can reduce fresh water requirements by up to 50%.

Security of supply

Prior to the financial crisis, strong demand had been driving an unprecedented boom in global mining. The nominal prices of many industrial metals began to reach record levels. In May 2006 the London Metals Exchange (LME) spot price of copper reached 8 780 USD per metric tonne (current dollars) – an all-time high. Strong demand, coupled with tight production capacity and a draw-down of inventories resulted in a supply-demand imbalance that saw the average annual price of copper (current USD) nearly quadruple from 2003 to 2006. Even in real terms, the rise in copper prices has been historically significant. The tight supply situation caused more producers to turn toward secondary (recycled) copper. Global scrap use increased 23% from 2003 to 2006 according to data from the International Copper Study Group (ICSG). Over the same period the prices of copper scrap, which have always moved in close parallel to primary copper prices, rose over 250%. With the onset of the 2008 financial crisis, primary and secondary copper prices fell, but by 2010 had returned to historically elevated levels.

Although the recent tightness in global copper supplies and the resulting high copper prices were primarily due to insufficient production capacity, it raised concern over whether there will be enough copper in the long-term to meet our economic needs. Predicting future demand and supply of copper is a complicated affair with a number of technological, economic and societal factors at play. But experts largely agree that there are sufficient copper resources in the earth's crust to meet future demand (Gordon *et al.,* 2006; ICGS, 2006). Large deposits of copper have been discovered on all continents and new deposits continue to be discovered, increasing reserves over time. In 1950 copper reserves were estimated around 100 Mt (ICSG, 2006) and today are over 630 Mt. Remaining copper resources are large relative to current demand; it is it estimated that only roughly a quarter of global copper resources have been extracted to date (Gordon *et al.,* 2006). However, the rate of discovery of new copper resources has been significantly slower than the rate of copper extraction (Gordon *et al.,* 2006) and copper grades are decreasing in mature deposits (e.g. United States and Chile).

At the same time the stock of copper in use in the economy, and potentially available for recycling, continues to grow. The global per capita in-use stock of copper was estimated at 17 kg/person in 1929 and (in a separate study) at 35-50 kg/person today (UNEP, 2010). However, the rate at which in-use stocks become potentially available for recycling depends on the lifespan of their applications. Many copper applications have relatively long lives - 25-40 years for construction and building, 50 years for telecommunications and electrical power infrastructure. Although some applications have much shorter lives, such as consumer electronics, metal recovery is often challenging. Personal computers, mobile phones and other consumer electronics use much smaller quantities of copper per unit and in the absence of end-of-life (EOL) collection systems it is difficult to obtain a critical mass of units that makes the recovery of copper and other metals economic. In Europe, it is estimated that 60% of EOL electronics are not recycled and that 20-50 million tonnes of e-waste are generated worldwide each year (Hagelüken and Buchert, 2008; UNEP, 2005). If the price of copper and its scrap remain high, it may help drive greater recycling of EOL consumer electronics overall. It is estimated that 20% of e-waste is composed of copper and copper is the largest metallic component (by weight) in many personal electronic devices, much as mobile phones.

Figure 5. Average annual copper price, 1960-2010

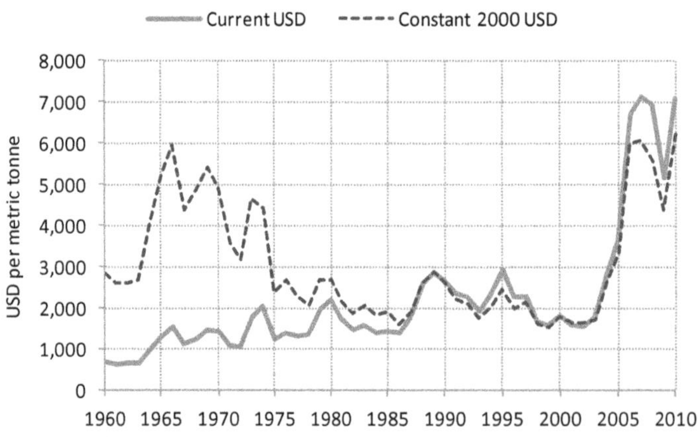

Source: World Bank Global Economic Monitor (GEM) Commodities database, *http://data.worldbank.org/data-catalog/global-economic-monitor*

Decoupling

Over the decade the production and apparent consumption of refined copper have become decoupled from economic growth in OECD countries overall, but this has been largely achieved through greater exports out of the OECD area. It coincides directly with the beginning of the period of rapid economic expansion of the large emerging economies around 2000, which saw a significant increase in refined copper exports from Chile to China. Prior to the onset of the 2008 financial crisis, decoupling had been uneven across OECD regions; strong decoupling in the OECD Americas and Oceania regions, a levelling-off in Europe, and continued growth in OECD Asia. Production and consumption of refined copper declined across all OECD regions in 2008 and 2009. Per capita consumption of refined copper has also decreased in OECD countries, from 7.4 kg/person in 1992 to 6.4 kg in 2009. Per capita consumption decreased across all OECD regions except Asia.

Conversely in the BRIICS economies, the production and consumption of refined copper continues to expand rapidly, growing at a rate well in excess of GDP. Although on a per capita basis apparent consumption of refined copper in BRIICS countries remains well below that of OECD countries (2.9 kg/person in 2009), it has increased 400% since 1992. Continued growth in per capita copper consumption in the world's most populous countries may be cause for concern. Experts have noted that if per capita consumption in BRIICS countries reaches the level of OECD countries then all of the copper resources in the earth's crust would be required to meet this demand (Gordon *et al.*, 2006). Per capita consumption in other countries is also growing, but at a slower rate. As a result, global per capita refined copper consumption grew from 2.0 kg/person in 1992 to 2.8 kg/person in 2009.

Figure 6. Production and consumption of refined copper, GDP and population growth, 1992-2009 (1992=100)

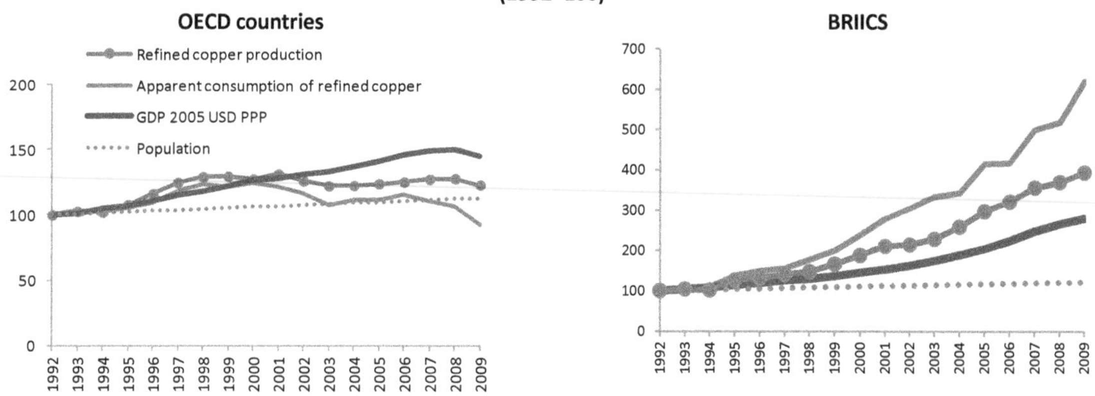

Source: British Geological Survey, OECD, World Bank.

Outlook

- After stalling briefly in 2009 in the aftermath of the global financial crisis, demand for copper rebounded in 2010 and growth is expected continue in 2011 and 2012. Copper prices have also resumed their upward trajectory, surpassing records levels reached in 2006. But it is expected that growth in mine and refinery production will not be sufficient to meet increasing demand and refined copper supplies are forecasted to remain tight in 2011-2012.
- Rising copper prices will provide greater incentive and opportunities for recycling. But copper is already one of the most commonly recycled metals with well-established scrap markets. Increasing the rate of recycling will require maximising the amount of old scrap available for recycling by increasing collection rates and reducing the amount being disposed of as waste. It is estimated that the amount of copper has already been disposed of in waste repositories is roughly equal to the amount current in use in the economy (Kapur and Graedel, 2006). This will be particularly challenging for copper from consumer waste streams (i.e. e-waste), where products are increasingly complex, highly mobile and in service for a relatively short time. Changes in product design to facilitate material recovery, end-of-life product management programs, and altering consumer behaviour (e.g. hoarding) will be important.

Increasing secondary production will help to reduce some of the pressure on virgin copper resources and the adverse environmental impacts associated with their extraction and consumption. But secondary production will only put a small dent in global copper demand. The world will still be reliant on primary copper sources. As a result focus should remain on improving the efficiency of primary copper extraction and production, both on the input side (e.g. water) and output side (e.g. SO_2 emissions).

ENDNOTES

1 The U.S. Geological Survey defines the term *resource* as "A concentration of naturally occurring solid, liquid, or gaseous material in or on the Earth's crust in such form and amount that economic extraction of a commodity from the concentration is currently or potentially feasible." This is much broader than the *reserve base*, which is defined as "that part of an identified resource that meets specified minimum physical and chemical criteria related to current mining and production practices, including those for grade, quality, thickness, and depth." It includes those resources that are currently economic (reserves), marginally economic (marginal reserves), and some of those that are currently sub-economic (sub-economic resources). The U.S. Geological Survey stopped publishing figures for reserve base after 2009 due to difficulties in estimating the non-reserve component. Reserve and resource estimates continue to be published.

See *Chapter 5* or *http://minerals.usgs.gov/minerals/pubs/mcs/2011/mcsapp2011.pdf* for more information.

2 Waste rock is poorly mineralised or very low-grade soil and rock, which are within the ore body or surrounding it.

3 While sometimes labeled as a waste, overburden is usually set aside in storage piles and later (re)used for land reclamation activities once the deposit has been exhausted.

4 Water is also used for dust control on mine roads and for drinking, cooking and bathing water for the mine camp though volumes for the latter are quite small.

REFERENCES

- Alvarado, S. *et al.* (2002), "Long term energy-related environmental issues of copper production," *Energy*, 27, pages 183-196.
- Alvarado, S., Maldonado, P. and Jaques, I. (1999), "Energy and environmental implications of copper production," *Energy*, Vol. 24, pages 307-316.
- BGS (British Geological Survey) (2007), *Commodity Profile: Copper*, Natural Environment Research Council, Keyworth, Nottingham.
- BGS (2010), *World Mineral Production 2004-2008,* British Geological Survey, Keyworth, Nottingham.
- COCHILCO (Chilean Copper Commission) (2008), *Best Practices and the Efficient Use of Water in the Mining Industry,* Chilean Copper Commission, Santiago.

- Edelstein, Daniel (2004), "Mineral Resource of the Month: Copper," Geotimes, June, American Geological Institute, Alexandra, VA.
- EPA (U.S. Environmental Protection Agency) (1994), "The Extraction and Benefication of Ores and Minerals: Copper", *Technical Resource Document*, EPA 530-R-94-031, Vol. 4, EPA, Washington, D.C.
- Goonan, T. (2005), *Flows of Selected Materials Associated with World Copper Smelting*, U.S. Geological Survey Open-File Report 2004-1395, U.S. Geological Survey, Reston, Virginia.
- Gomez, F., Ignacio Guzmán, J., and Tilton, J. E. (2007), "Copper recycling and scrap availability," *Resources Policy,* 32 (2007), pages 183-190.
- Gordon, R.B, Bertram, M. and Graedel, T.E. (2006), "Metal Stocks and Sustainability," *PNAS*, volume 103, number 5, pages 1209-14.
- Hagelüken, C. and Buchert, M. (2008), "The mine above ground: Opportunities and challenges to recover scarce and valuable metals from EOL electronic devices," presentation at IERC, 17 January 2008, Salzburg.
- ICSG (International Copper Study Group) (2010), The World Copper Factbook 2010, ICSG, Lisbon.
- ICSG (2006), "Copper on the move: Where it comes from, where it goes," *ICSG Insight*, Number 1, December 2006.
- Kapur, A. and Graedel, T.E. (2006), "Copper Mines Above and Below the Ground," *Environmental Science & Technology*, 15 may 2006, pages 3135-3141.
- Singh, M. (2010), *Water Consumption at Copper Mines in Arizona*, Special Report 29, State of Arizona Department of Mines & Mineral Resources, Phoenix.
- UNEP (United Nations Environment Programme) (2011a), *Recycling Rates of Metals – A Status Report,"* A Report of the Working Group on Global Metal Flows to the International Resource Panel, Graedel, T.E., Allwood, J., Birat, J.P., Buchert, M., Hageluken, C., Reck, B.K., Sibley, S.F., Sonnemann, G., UNEP, Paris.
- UNEP (2011b), "Estimating Long-Run Geological Stocks of Metals," A Working Paper by the Working Group on Geological Stocks of Metals to the UNEP International Panel on Sustainable Resource Management, 6 April 2011, Paris.
- UNEP (2010), *Metal Stocks in Society: Scientific Synthesis*, A Report of the Working Group on the Global Metal Flows to the International Panel for Sustainable Resource Management, UNEP, Paris.
- UNEP (2005), "E-waste, the hidden side of IT equipment's manufacturing and use," *Environment Alert Bulletin,* Number 5, UNEP/GRID-Europe, Geneva.
- USGS (United States Geological Survey) (2010) – *Mineral Commodity Summaries 2010*, U.S. Geological Survey, Reston, Virginia.
- USGS (United States Geological Survey) (2011a), *Mineral Commodity Summaries 2011*, U.S. Geological Survey, Reston, Virginia.
- USGS (2011b), *2009 Minerals Year Book: Copper [Advance Release]*, U.S. Geological Survey, Reston, Virginia.
- USGS (2010), Copper statistics, in Kelly, T.D., and Matos, G.R., comps., Historical statistics for mineral and material commodities in the United States: U.S. Geological Survey Data Series 140 [Accessed 16 August 2011].
- USGS (2009), *Copper – A Metal for the Ages*, Factsheet 2009-3031, USGS, Reston, VA.
- USGS (2005), Copper statistics, in Kelly, T.D., and Matos, G.R., comps., Historical statistics for mineral and material commodities in the United States: U.S. Geological Survey Data Series 140 [Accessed 16 August 2011].
- World Bank (n.d.), Global Economic Monitor (Commodities) database, *http://data.worldbank.org/data-catalog/global-economic-monitor*

IRON AND STEEL FACTSHEET

The backbone of industrialised economies, iron (in the form of steel) is by far the most important metal in the world today. Strong when alloyed, abundant and relatively inexpensive in comparison to other metals, iron is used extensively in the construction of buildings, bridges and railways and in the manufacture of motor vehicles, machinery and equipment, and appliances. The rapid pace of industrialisation in the large emerging economies of Asia, China and India in particular, has lead to an unprecedented increase in the demand for steel and rising prices for steelmaking materials (i.e. iron ore and ferrous scrap). Although resources are abundant improving resource productivity remains a priority because of climate change concerns stemming from the energy intensity of the steelmaking process. Increased use of ferrous scrap offers limited opportunities for energy and raw material savings in the near term, but there is potential to achieve a circular iron economy as global in-use stocks stabilise in the long term.

See the Reader's guide for information about the selection of key material resources.

Overview

Characteristics and uses

Iron is a metallic element that makes up 5% of the earth's crust. It is rarely found alone, but combined with other elements in rock-forming minerals. The most common iron ores are the iron oxides hematite (Fe_2O_3), magnetite (Fe_3O_4), which typically contain over 70% iron. Taconite, an iron-bearing sedimentary rock, is considered a low grade iron ore (20-30% iron content). Iron is highly reactive, oxidises easily and is naturally magnetic. It is also malleable and ductile, but when alloyed with carbon it becomes extremely strong.

Steel is the most common alloy of iron and carbon, containing less than 2% carbon and 1% manganese and small amounts of other elements, such as silicon, phosphorus, sulphur and oxygen. Crude steel is the first solid state of the metal after melting and before further processing (e.g. ingots, steel castings, and strand or pressure cast steel). There are thousands of grades of steel that have been developed for their different physical, chemical and environmental properties. The three major categories of steel are: carbon steel, steel alloys and heat-resisting steels. Steels that derive their properties mainly from carbon are called carbon steels. Alloy steels are steel that contain additional alloying elements (up to 4 percent), such as chromium, copper, molybdenum, nickel, titanium, tungsten and vanadium, to develop specific properties (e.g. strength, friction resistance). As their name indicates, heat-resisting steels have been alloyed with metals to improve their properties at high temperatures. Stainless steel is included in this category. The addition of chromium and nickel give stainless steel its corrosion resistance.

Iron is by far the most used metal in the world, accounting for 95% of the metal produced worldwide in terms of weight. Almost all iron produced is used to make pig iron, the predecessor material to steel. In 2010, 1 billion metric tonnes (Gt) of pig iron and 1.4 Gt of raw steel were produced worldwide (USGS, 2011a). There are thousands of applications for steel. As a result steel is found throughout the economy. Carbon steels are mainly used in building construction, cars and trucks, shipbuilding, transportation infrastructure, containers and packaging, and machinery and equipment. Alloy steels are used to manufacture specialty machine parts and tools, particularly those that operate at high-speeds. Stainless steels' corrosion resistance has led to their use in a broad range of products from medical instruments to car parts.

New grades of steel have been developed with improved strength to weight ratios. Called Advanced and Ultra High-Strength steels, these new light weight steels are being used in aircraft, spacecraft and automobiles to increase fuel efficiency while retaining strength and durability.

Production and processing

The production of primary iron and steel begins with mining iron ore from the earth's crust. The most common approach is surface (or open pit) mining, which requires removing overburden and waste rock to expose the iron ore deposit. Explosive charges are then used to break up the ore. Lump ore can be fed directly into blast furnaces for smelting. Low grade iron ores, such as taconite, must undergo a beneficiation process to increase the iron concentration before smelting. As with other metal ores this process involves the use of physical and chemical separation techniques (i.e. crushing, grinding, and froth floatation), but because of iron's magnetic properties, magnetic techniques are also used.

Iron is produced from iron ore using one of two methods. The majority of the world's iron is produced using blast furnaces, where iron ore is smelted with a high-carbon fuel (usually coke) to produce pig iron or hot metal. The molten pig iron is either delivered directly to a steelmaking plant or cast into pigs (ingots) for later use. Alternatively, iron ore can also be directly reduced to solid iron in the form of lumps, pellets or briquettes (called Direct Reduced Iron or DRI) using natural gas. In 2009 6% of the world's iron was produced via DRI processes while 94% was produced by blast furnace operations (pig iron) (USGS, 2011b).

The three most common methods of primary steelmaking are the basic oxygen furnace (BOF), the open hearth furnace (OHF) and the electric arc furnace (EAF) process. Basic oxygen and open hearth furnaces are used with iron that has been produced in a blast furnace (i.e. pig iron). The OHF process is relatively energy inefficient and its use has been declining steadily since the 1960s. Today around 3% of primary steel is made using OHF technology (World Steel Association, 2008). The predominant steelmaking technology is the BOF, which produced 66% of the world's primary steel (World Steel Association, 2008). In this process oxygen is injected into the molten pig iron to remove excess carbon, silicon and other impurities such as phosphorus and sulphur. Iron and steel scrap is usually added to help keep the melting point below 1 700°C. The EAF process smelts DRI and ferrous scrap into steel using heat generated with electricity. The DRI-EAF production route supplies 6% of the world's primary steel (World Steel Association, 2008). Because EAF technology can operate with a cold charge as opposed to molten metal, it is actually most commonly used to recycle ferrous scrap rather than to produce steel from DRI. A quarter of the world's steel is produced from scrap recycled in EAFs (World Steel Association, 2008).

Ferrous scrap is an integral input into the steelmaking process. Scrap is broadly divided into three categories: home scrap, new scrap and old scrap. Home scrap is generated within the steel mills and foundries as a by-product of their operations (e.g. trimmings and defective products), is collected and quickly recycled back into the steel furnace. New scrap is produced when steel is cut, machined, extruded, or drawn in steel product manufacturing plants. The casting process also produces scrap as excess metal. Old scrap or post-consumer scrap is generated when iron- and steel-bearing products reach the end of their service (e.g. junked automobiles, demolished steel structures, worn out railroad cars and tracks, obsolete appliances and machinery). Home and new scrap are physically clean with known chemical compositions while there is wide variation in old scrap. Old scrap must be carefully sorted before it can be used. But relative to other commonly recycled materials (i.e. paper, aluminium, copper) this process is facilitated by iron's magnetic properties. Scrap consumers generally prefer new scrap to old scrap (Fenton, 2005).

Once produced by one of the three methods, the hot steel is cast and shaped into semi finished products. Today the most common practice is to pour the steel into continuous casting machines to produce slabs, billets and blooms, which are subsequently rolled into semi-finished steel products such as plates, sheets, bars and other flat-rolled products.

Figure 1. Illustration of the steelmaking process

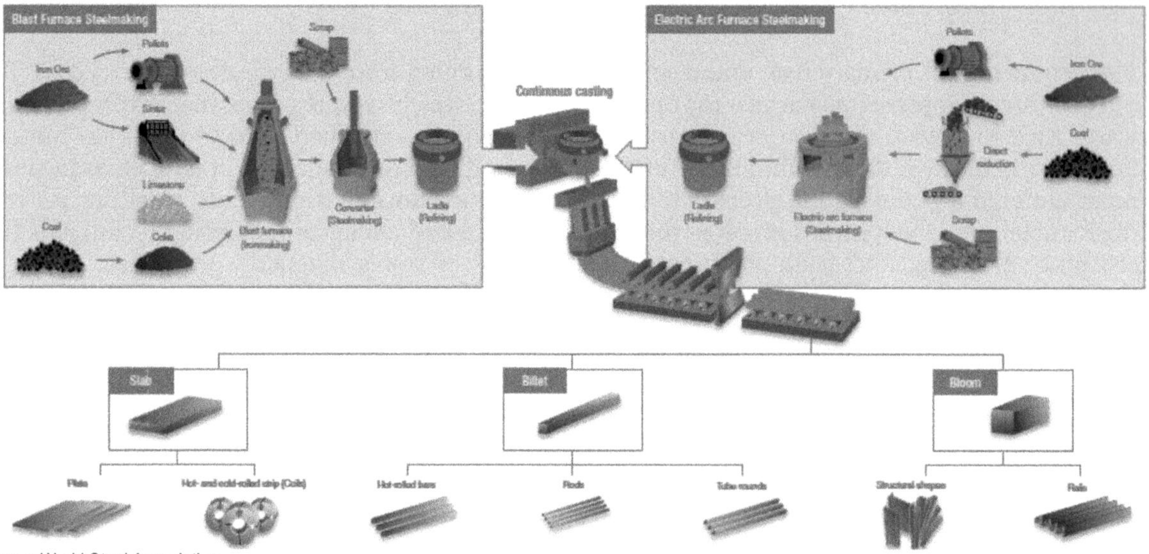

Source: World Steel Association

Recycling and substitutes

Steel is the most recycled material in the world. According to the World Steel Association over 475 million tonnes (Mt) of steel scrap was recovered worldwide in 2008 – more than paper, plastic, glass, copper, lead, and aluminium combined – and the recycling rate for the major steel products is estimated at over 80%. In the United States, the recycling rate of steel has exceeded 100%, meaning that more scrap is being recovered from obsolete steel products than is being used to produce new products (USGS, 2011b). The ferrous scrap market is well-established and efficient, and ferrous scrap is a vital raw material for the production of new steel and cast-iron products.

Ferrous scrap recycling conserves energy, landfill space, and raw materials. The melting of scrap requires significantly less energy than does the primary production of iron and steel thereby reducing the CO_2 emission produced by the industry. The World Steel Association estimates that over 1 400 kg of iron ore, 400 kg of coal, and 55 kg of limestone are saved for a tonne of steel scrap used.

Substitutes are available for most applications of iron and steel, but are usually higher cost of materials. Direct substitution is not necessarily straightforward as iron and steel can be alloyed, heat treated, and processed to obtain a wide variety of characteristics, such as strength, hardness, or corrosion resistance needed for particular applications. Aluminium is a common substitute for iron and steel when light weight is desired (e.g. automobiles, buildings, cookware, beverage cans). Plastics are also relatively light weight and can be easily moulded, and are often used in place of steel in mechanical parts, consumer products (toys) and food and beverage packaging. Plastics, along with concrete and wood also compete with iron and steel in construction applications.

Supply and demand

It is estimated that the world's iron ore resources are in excess of 800 Gt, with an estimated iron content of over 230 Gt (USGS, 2011a).[1] Iron ore reserves, that portion of the identified resource that is considered economically extractable today, were reported by the U.S. Geological Survey at

180 Gt in 2010, with an iron content of 87 Gt. In terms of iron content, Brazil holds the largest share of the world's iron reserves (18% or 16 Gt), followed by Australia (17% or 15 Gt), Russia (16% or 14 Gt), the Ukraine (10% or 9.0 Gt), China (8% or 7.2 Gt) and India (5% or 4.5 Gt). Other countries with important reserves include: Kazakhstan, the United States, Canada, Venezuela, Sweden and Iran.

Figure 2. Shares of global iron reserves, by country, 2010

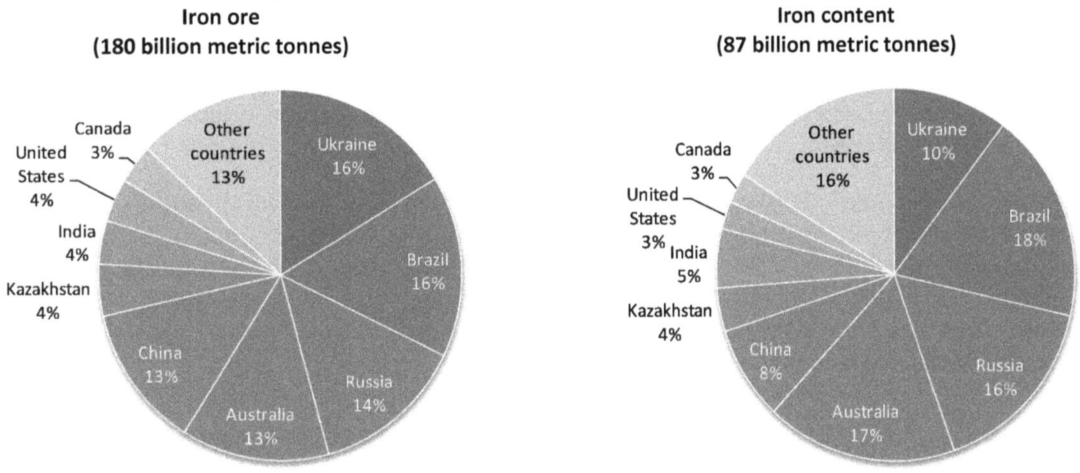

Source: USGS (2011a).

It is estimated that global mine production of iron ore in 2010 reached over 2.4 Gt, representing an 8% increase from the previous year (USGS, 2011a). China is the world's leading producer of iron ore. It extracted an estimated 900 million tonnes (Mt) of iron in 2010, roughly 38% of the iron extracted worldwide. Aside from Australia, the world's second largest producer with an estimated 420 Mt produced in 2010 (a 17% global share), global iron ore production is dominated by non-OECD countries with five countries (China, Brazil, India, Russia and the Ukraine) together accounting for over 70% of global extraction on 2010. Absent Australia, OECD countries represented less than 5% of global iron ore production.

Virtually all of the iron ore extracted in China is consumed domestically. Chinese exports of iron ore are negligible while imports have increased 6-fold in the last decade. In 2009 Chinese imports reached 640 Mt, around two-thirds of global imports (World Steel Association, 2011a). After China, the main importers of iron ore are primarily OECD member countries in Asia and Europe: Japan, South Korea, Germany, the Netherlands, France, and Italy. Australia, Brazil and India are the top exporters of iron ore; together these three countries represented almost 80% of global exports in 2009. Strong growth in Australian exports has been in key factor in transforming the OECD area from a net importer into a net exporter of iron ore over the last decade.

The BRIICS countries also dominate global production of crude steel, lead by China which alone accounted for 45% (630 Mt) of worldwide production in 2010 (USGS, 2011a). Japan was surpassed by China in the early 1990s, but remains the world's second leading steel producer, with an 8% global share (110 Mt). The United States, India and Russia are other major producers of crude steel. After a sharp drop in 2009, U.S. production rebounded in 2010; exports reached 90 Mt. Indian steel production has expanded rapidly over the last two decades, overtaking Russia and South Korea to become the world's fourth largest producer.

Exports of crude steel are dominated by a handful of countries. Russia, the Ukraine, Brazil, Japan and Turkey are the top five exporting countries, together accounting for over two-thirds of total world exports in 2010 (World Steel Association, 2011). Russian exports (15.3 Mt in 2010) alone represent a quarter of the world's exports. Crude steel imports are much less concentrated. In 2010 South Korea was the single largest importer of crude steel (6.2 Mt, 11% share), but followed closely by China, the United States, Thailand, and Germany. Although member countries are among the world's largest exporters, overall OECD countries are physical net importers of crude steel.

Scrap is an important raw material for the steel and foundry industries. Because scrap comes from obsolete automobiles and appliances, industrial machinery, manufacturing operations, and old buildings, relatively mature industrialised economies tend to be the main exporters of scrap. In 2010, the United States exported the most ferrous scrap in the world – over 20.5 Mt (World Steel Association, 2011a). Germany, the United Kingdom, France and Japan are other major scrap exporters. Turkey (which produces most of its steel by EAF) was the world's leading importer of scrap in 2010, followed by China, the United States, South Korea and Belgium-Luxembourg.

Together BRIICS and OECD countries consumed nearly 89% of the world's finished steel products in 2010 (World Steel Association, 2011a). China was the single largest consumer; Chinese apparent consumption reached 596 Mt, a 46% global share. The United States was the second largest consumer of finished steel although its global share has been declining steadily. India's consumption has more than doubled over the last decade and the country is now the third largest consumer, followed by Japan and South Korea.

Figure 3. Physical trade balances in iron and steel by region, 2001 and 2010 (or most recent year available)

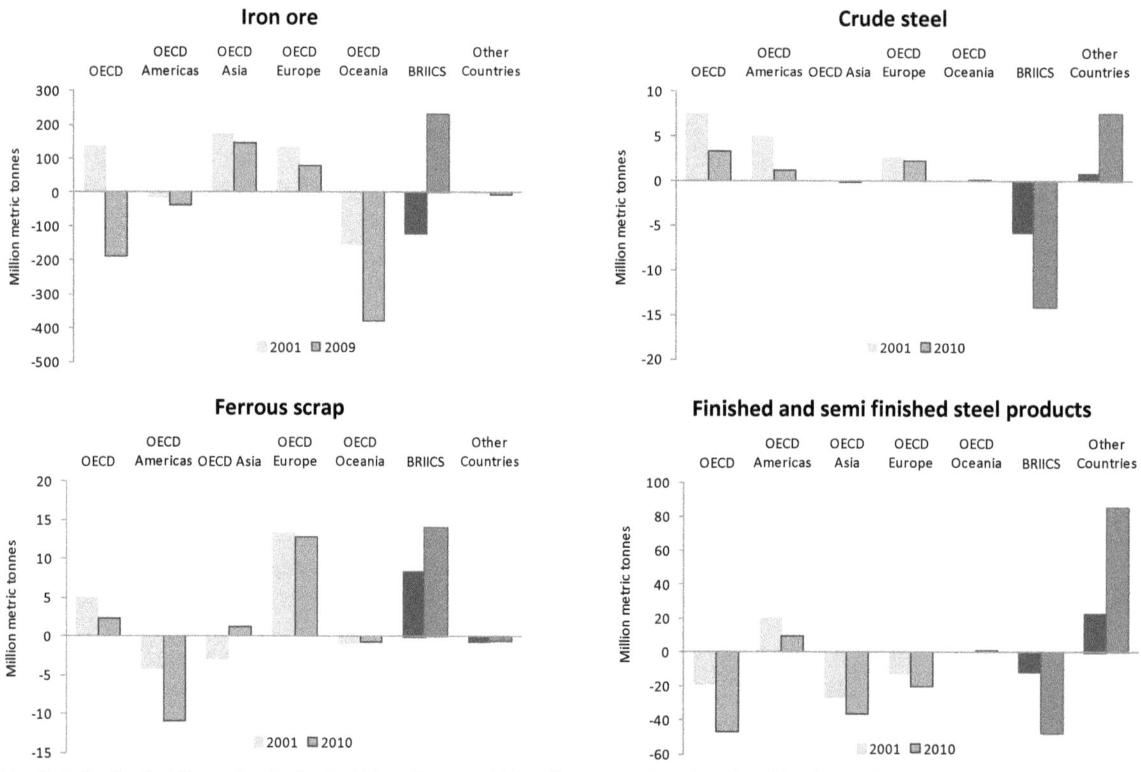

Note: Data for South Africa refers to South African Customs Union (Botswana, Lesotho, Namibia, South Africa, and Swaziland).
Source: World Steel Association.

Economic and environmental sustainability

Environmental implications

As with other metals, there are a variety of potential environmental impacts associated with the extraction of iron and the production of iron and steel. Many of these impacts can occur locally in the environment surrounding the mine site or production facility, such as habitat destruction, soil erosion, and soil and water contamination; while others can be more global in nature, such as climate change and loss of biodiversity.

One of the main environmental concerns associated with the production of iron and steel is the use of energy. The primary steelmaking process is energy intensive and in general fossil fuels, mainly coal, provide the main source of energy. Energy requirements are high because energy is an integral direct input to the iron reduction process, both as a chemical agent and as a source of heat. Coke (carburized coal) is the most common reducing agent in the blast furnace iron making process although other fuel sources can substitute for a portion of the coke. In 2010, over 720 million tonnes of coking coal was used in the production of steel. In addition, energy is also consumed indirectly during the mining, processing and transportation stages.

The use of large amounts of fossil fuels can have important implications for climate change. The International Energy Agency estimates the iron and steel industry produces for 4-5% of global CO_2 emissions and 90% of the steel industry's CO_2 emissions come from nine countries or regions: Brazil, China, the European Union, India, Japan, South Korea, Russia, the Ukraine and the United States. On average 1.7 tonnes of CO_2 are emitted for each tonne of steel produced (World Steel Association, 2009). Most of these emissions are produced from during the blast furnace iron-reduction process.

Because energy costs can represent 20-40% of the cost of producing steel, the industry has made significant efforts to improve energy efficiency and continues to actively manage energy use today. Over the last twenty years the industry has reduced its energy use significantly, largely through investments in new technology and increased production of secondary steel, which needs a quarter of the energy required to produce primary steel (OECD, 2008; Fenton, 2005). Between 1975 and 2004 the average energy required to produce a tonne of steel in North America, the EU-15 and Japan was cut in half (World Steel Association, 2008). Because of the inherent requirements for carbon in making iron and steel there are limits of the energy reductions that can be achieved through investment in new technology (Fenton, 2005).

In addition to being energy-intensive, steelmaking is also resource intensive. Approximately 0.4 tonnes of recycled steel and 1.6 tonnes of raw materials (e.g. iron ore, coal, limestone) needed on average to make one tonne of steel (World Steel Association, 2009). Large amounts of water are also used, mainly for cooling. Most of the by-products from the steelmaking reprocessed are reused or recycled. Iron and steel slag is processed and most commonly sold as a construction material.[1] The majority of water is recovered and re-circulated and a portion of by-product gas from coke ovens, blast furnace or BOF is recovered and reused.

Security of supply

Prior to the financial crisis, strong demand had been driving an unprecedented boom in global mining activity. The prices of many industrial metals began to reach record levels. Prior to 2000, the real price of iron ore had actually been decreasing. But strong demand for steel, particularly in China where steelmaking is heavily iron-ore dependent, saw iron ore extraction increase 124% between 2000 and 2010 and real prices rise over 300%. Although the economic downturn resulted in a steep decrease in world iron ore prices in 2009, prices have since recovered and in 2010 remained near record levels.

Even at the current rate of extraction global iron ore reserves are expected to last almost a hundred years. Regardless of iron ore's relative abundance, resource productivity remains a priority. Iron ore grades are decreasing. In the United States, ores grades have decreased from 50-60% to 25%-30% since the Second World War (Müller *et al.*, 2006). Extracting and processing lower grade ores, such as taconite, generally requires more water and energy and generates more waste than higher grade ores. Moreover, steelmaking remains very energy intensive and the iron and steel industry continues its efforts to reduce energy consumption, particularly of fossil fuels.

Steel production is also dependent on the availability of ferrous scrap. Along with the prices of other steelmaking materials (i.e. iron ore and energy), the price of steel scrap also increased significantly in recent years owing to the rising demand for steel. The U.S. composite price of No. 1 Heavy Melting steel scrap nearly quadrupled between 2000 and 2010, after declining by 30% in the previous decade. But these much higher prices have not yet lead to an increased availability of scrap and as a result North American scrap markets, faced with increased exports demands from China and Turkey, have been extremely tight in recent years. One argument for why scrap markets have been slow to respond is that much of the obsolete scrap from economic sources in industrialised regions (i.e. North America, EU-15, and Japan) has already been recovered. The rate at which scrap becomes available is limited by products becoming obsolete. In the United States, the world's largest exporter of scrap, the largest source of scrap is from obsolete automobiles and with the 2008 financial crisis recession-hit consumers have been holding onto their old cars (and appliances) rather than junking them and purchasing new ones (USGS, 2011a).

Figure 4. Average annual prices of metals and ferrous scrap, 1960-2010

Real price of zinc, iron ore, aluminium and copper | **U.S. composite price for No. 1 Heavy Melting Steel Scrap**

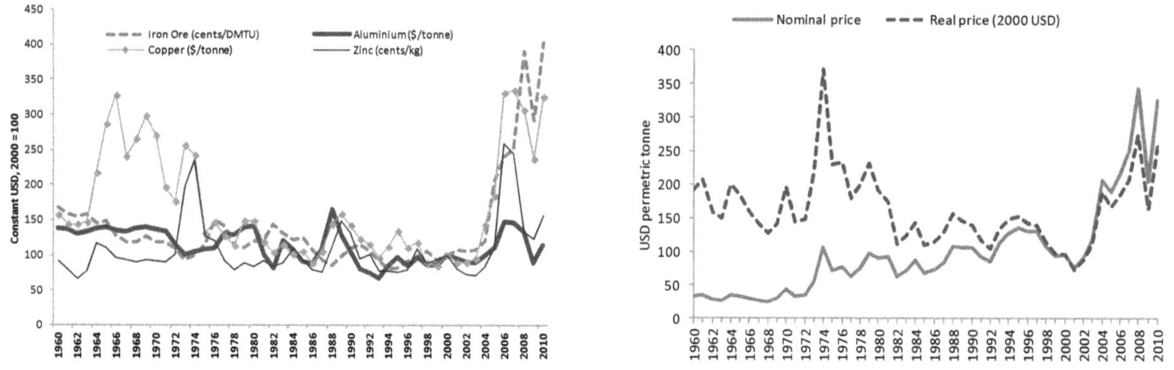

Source: World Bank Global Economic Monitor (Commodities) database

Source: Price data from U.S. Geological Survey based on American Metal Market; CPI from the OECD.

The stock of iron and steel currently in use in the economy represents an important future source of ferrous scrap. Recent studies have estimated the size this global 'urban mine' at around 12-18 billion tonnes, about 15-20% of iron ore reserves, or 2.2 – 2.7 tonnes per person (UNEP, 2010; Müller *et al.*, 2011; Hatayama *et al.*, 2010). Because of their long service lifetimes most of this stock is found in buildings and other large infrastructure (~60%), followed by vehicles, machinery and equipment, and appliances; although the relative size of the stocks found in these latter applications varies significantly from country to country. In absolute terms, the largest in-use stocks are found in the United States, China, Germany, Japan and Russia (Müller *et al.*, 2011).

Increasing attention is being focused on in-use stocks, not only as an indicator of future scrap supply, but also in forecasting future steel demand. The argument is that demand for steel increases when people feel a deficiency in the supply of steel-bearing products in society, but plateaus when the per capita stock reaches a saturation level. There is evidence that per capita iron stocks in the United States, France and United Kingdom have already reached a saturation point at around 8-12 tonnes/capita (Müller *et al.*, 2011). Future demand for iron will be driven by the large rapidly developing Asian economies, where per capita in-use stocks are low, around 2 tonnes/per cap in China and less than half a tonne per person in India (UNEP, 2010; Müller *et al.*, 2011). However, opportunities for these countries to fulfil their iron needs via domestic scrap will be limited because of the long service lifetimes associated with building construction, the largest end-use market for iron and steel. Nor will scrap imported from industrialised countries be able to completely substitute for iron ore; in 2010 scrap exports worldwide were 100 Mt while Chinese crude steel production reached 630 Mt.

Outlook

- Global demand for iron and steel is closely linked to economic growth. Although the recovery from the deepest recession in decades is becoming more broadly based, progress remains uneven across economies. Global growth has picked up since last year and is expected to be close to 4.25% in 2011 and 4.5% in 2012 (OECD, 2011). Demand is expected to remain robust in non-OECD countries, but economic growth moderated by inflation and rising commodity prices. The World Steel Association forecasts 6% growth in apparent steel use in 2011 and 2012, a rate on par with the average rate of growth between 2001 and 2010.[2] But demand will be almost exclusively driven by growth in steel use in emerging and developing economies, which are expected to account for over 70% of global steel demand by 2012 (World Steel Association, 2011b). Consumption in North America and Europe is also expected to grow, but remain well below pre-crisis levels.
- Despite continued growth in demand for steel, a future global shortage of iron ore is not a concern. Iron is one of the most abundant elements in the earth's crust, with identified reserves of over 180 Mt. The primary production of steel however is extremely energy intensive. The blast-furnace to basic oxygen furnace production path to convert iron into steel uses large amounts of coal, contributing to global CO_2 emissions.
- The secondary (recycled) production of steel offers important opportunities to improve resource productivity, decreasing pressures on the environmental and on virgin iron ore resources. But steel is already the most recycled material on the planet, with well-established and efficient scrap markets. The largest stocks of iron and steel in-use tend to be located in mature industrialised economies, locked in products with relatively long lives such as buildings and infrastructure. Junked cars, appliances and machinery make up the bulk of discarded scrap flows, but the iron content in these products has been decreasing, as steel is being increasingly replaced by aluminium, plastic and other materials. As a result, in the near term scrap flows have limited capacity to meet growing global steel demand. The recent tightness experienced in North America scrap markets may be a sign that many of the economic scrap stocks in mature industrialised economies have already been recovered.
- This tightness is likely to continue in the near term. The domestic flow of scrap in developing and emerging economies is very low as these countries build up their iron stocks, therefore it will be some time before discarded flows are large enough to contribute meaningfully to steel production. However, evidence that per capita iron stocks reach a saturation point in post-industrial economies offers the long-term possibility of transforming the global iron and steel industry from one that relies predominantly on primary (iron ore) sources to one that relies predominantly on secondary (ferrous scrap) sources, assuming the world's population also stabilises.

Figure 5. World map of per capita iron ore reserves versus per capita in use iron stocks, 2005

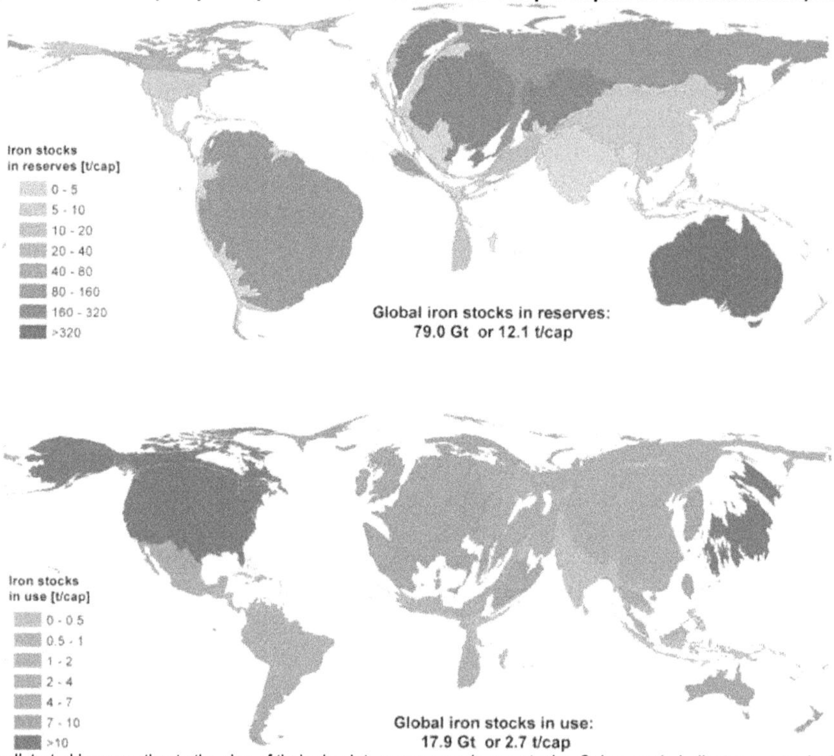

Note: Country sizes are distorted in proportion to the size of their absolute reserves or in use stocks. Colour scale indicates per capita levels.
Source: Müller *et al.* (2011).

ENDNOTES

1 Although no global slag production data are unavailable, based on typical ratios of slag to crude iron and steel output the U.S. Geological Survey estimates that world iron slag output in 2010 was around 230 to 270 million tonnes, and steel slag about 120 to 180 million tonnes.

2 This forecast was released in April 2011 and was not revised to take into account the potential global economic effects of the Great East Japan Earthquake.

REFERENCES

- EPA (U.S. Environmental Protection Agency) (1994), "The Extraction and Beneficiation of Ores and Minerals: Iron", *Technical Resource Document*, EPA 530-R-94-030, Vol. 3, EPA, Washington, D.C.
- Fenton, M. D. (2007), "Mineral Resource of the Month: Steel," Geotimes, June, American Geological Institute, Alexandra, VA.
- Fenton, M. D. (2005), *Mineral Commodity Profiles – Iron and Steel*, Open-file Report 2005-1254, U.S. Geological Survey, Reston, VA.
- Geoscience Australia, Mineral Resources website, *www.ga.gov.au/minerals/mineral-resources.html* [Accessed 24 August 2011].
- Hatayama, Hiroki *et al.* (2010), "Outlook on the World Steel Cycle Based on Stock and Flow Dynamics," *Environmental Science and Technology,* Vol. 44, No. 16, pp. 6457-6463.
- Mackerel, Steve (2006), "Your steel trash, China's treasure," *Asia Times Online,* 21 January 2006, *www.atimes.com/atimes/China_Business/HA21Cb05.html* [Accessed 1 September 2011]
- Müller, D., Wang, T., and Duval, B. (2011), "Patterns of Iron Use in Societal Evolution," *Environmental Science and Technology*, Vol. 45, No. 1, pp. 182-188
- Müller, D., *et al.* (2006), "Exploring the engine of anthropogenic iron cycles," *PNAS,* Vol. 104, No. 33, pp. 16111-16116, doi:10.1073/pnas.0603375103.
- OECD (2011), *OECD Economic Outlook*, Vol. 2011/1, OECD Publishing, Paris, *http://dx.doi.org/10.1787/eco_outlook-v2011-1-en.*
- OECD (2008), "Selected Industries: Mining," *OECD Environmental Outlook to 2030*, OECD Publishing, Paris, *http://dx.doi.org/10.1787/9789264040519-en.*
- UNEP (2010), *Metal Stocks in Society: Scientific Synthesis*, A Report of the Working Group on the Global Metal Flows to the International Panel for Sustainable Resource Management, UNEP, Paris.
- USGS (U.S. Geological Survey) (2011a), *2011 Mineral Commodity Summaries*, U.S. Geological Survey, Reston, VA.
- USGS (2011b), *2009 Minerals Yearbook*, U.S. Geological Survey, Reston, VA.
- USGS (2006), *Steel Stocks in Use in Automobiles in the United States*, Fact Sheet 2005—3144, January, U.S. Geological Survey, Reston, VA.
- USGS (1999), *Metal Prices in the United States through 1998*, U.S. Geological Survey, Reston, VA.
- Wang, T., Müller, D., and Graedel, T.E. (2007), "Forging the Anthropogenic Iron Cycle," *Environmental Science & Technology,* Vol. 41, No. 14, pp. 5120-5129
- World Bank (n.d.), Global Economic Monitor (Commodities) database, *http://data.worldbank.org/data-catalog/global-economic-monitor*
- World Coal Association. World Coal Association website, *www.worldcoal.org.*
- World Steel Association (2011a), *2011 Steel Statistical Yearbook*, World Steel Association, Brussels.
- World Steel Association (2011b), *Worldsteel Short Range Outlook,* 18 April 2011, *www.worldsteel.org/?action=newsdetail&id=322* [Accessed 1 September 2011]
- World Steel Association (2009), *2008 Sustainability Report of the World Steel Industry,* World Steel Association, Brussels.
- World Steel Association (2008), *Fact Sheet: Energy,* World Steel Association, Brussels.
- World Steel Association (n.d.), World Steel Association website, *www.worldsteel.org.*

PAPER FACTSHEET

Paper was one of the first products made by humans. Originally fabricated from plant fibre exclusively for writing, today paper is made mainly from wood fibre and is used in a variety of applications, ranging from packing boxes to personal hygiene. Despite challenges from new media and alternative materials, global demand for paper products continues to grow particularly in China and other non-OECD economies. Although the pulp and paper industry produces 50% of its own energy from biomass, production remains energy intensive and contributes to global greenhouse gas emissions. Water use and timber harvesting methods are other core environmental sustainability issues. The use of recovered fibre can reduce these environmental pressures to some extent, but there are signs that recycling rates may soon reach their natural and practical limits in some countries that are important global suppliers. Further energy and material efficiency gains will require focusing paper collection efforts in new supplier countries and expanding the use of best available technologies.

See the Reader's guide for information about the selection of key material resources.

Overview

Characteristics and Uses

Paper is made from naturally occurring plant fibres called cellulose that have been separated and reorganised. Although originally created solely for writing and printing, today a wide range of paper products have been developed for different applications across various industries. Paper can be made thin and soft for use as tissue, laminated and water-proofed for food and beverage containers, or strong and durable for corrugated cardboard boxes. In general paper products fall into five broad end-use categories: packaging and wrapping (52% of global production in 2010 according to FAO data), printing and writing (28%), newsprint and magazine (9%), household and sanitary (7%), and specialised and other (4%).

Figure 1. End-uses for the world's paper, 1990 and 2010

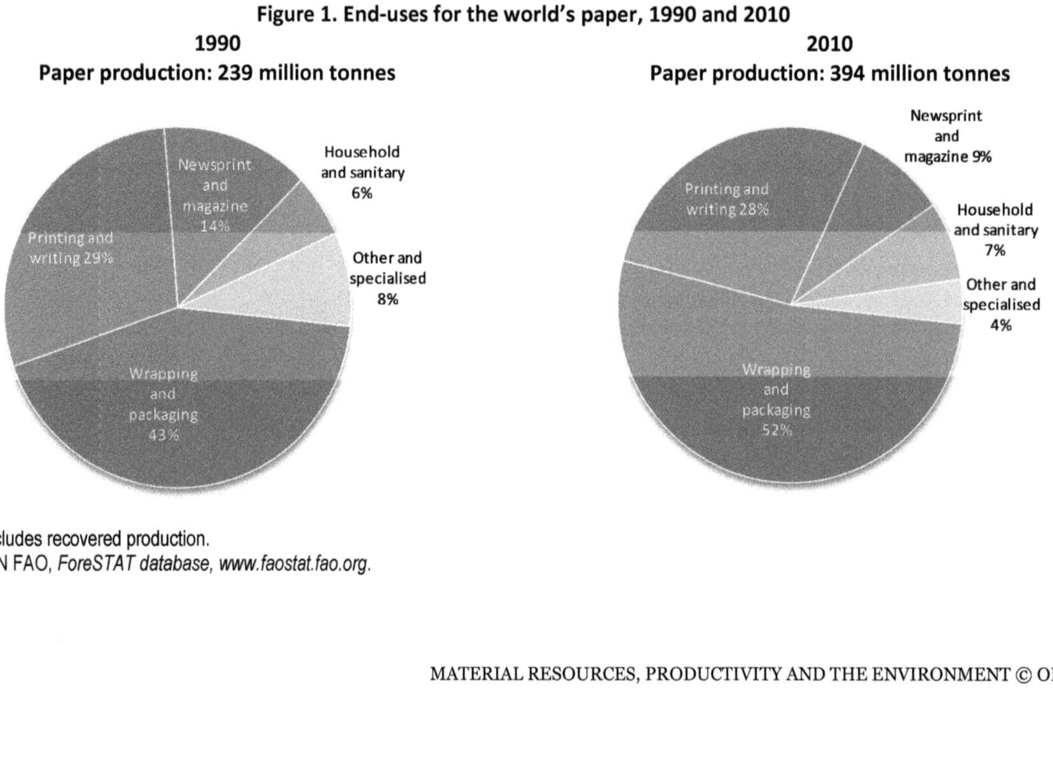

Notes: Includes recovered production.
*Source:*UN FAO, *ForeSTAT database, www.faostat.fao.org.*

Production, Recycling and Substitution

Paper can be made from primary raw materials, using wood pulp from hardwood and softwood trees and non-wood pulp from agricultural crops and residues, or from secondary raw materials, using pulp from recovered paper. Whether made from primary or secondary raw materials, wood provides the basis of 95% of the fibre in paper products today with agricultural materials such as flax, hemp, bamboo and grasses making up the remainder (OECD, 2010).

Wood is obtained by harvesting timber from forests and recovering wood chips and saw dusts from sawmill operations. Coniferous trees (softwood trees) are generally preferred over non-coniferous trees (hardwood trees) because they have longer fibres, producing stronger paper. Paper made from shorter hardwood fibres is weaker, but smoother. Soft- and hardwood fibres are typically blended to the desired combinations of characteristics (e.g. strength, softness, brightness, opacity, smoothness).

Once extracted, the wood then undergoes either a mechanical or chemical pulping process to separate the wood fibres held together by a natural adhesive material called lignin. As its name would imply, mechanical pulping is a physical separation process whereby the wood chips are ground in order to separate the fibres. Mechanical pulping is less common at the global scale, accounting for under 20% of wood pulp production worldwide in 2010, but is more efficient than chemical pulping in terms of material conversion because it uses the entire log (except for the bark), resulting in only a 5% material loss. Generally in chemical (or Kraft) pulping, wood chips are heated with chemicals under high pressure to remove the lignin completely, leaving the wood fibres intact. During this process, approximately half of the wood dissolves into a by-product of the cooking process called black liquor, which is used to generate heat and electricity for the mill and is recovered for re-use in the cooking liquor. Chemical pulping is the predominant process used worldwide, accounting for 73% of global wood pulp production in 2010 according to FAO data.[1] The chemical pulping process produces higher quality pulp than the mechanical process because the fibres are longer and more uniform, but the material yield is significantly lower (45-50%). Depending on the type of paper being produced, the pulp may need to be bleached. This is usually done with hydrogen peroxide or chlorine dioxide during the pulp making process. Bleaching removes the remaining lignin to whiten the pulp, prevent discolouration and strengthen the paper.

The process for making pulp from recovered paper requires begins with collecting, sorting and grading the recovered paper. Large non-fibre contaminants (e.g. staples, plastic, and glass) are then removed by dissolving the paper in water and passing the pulp through filters and screens. To produce paper, the pulp is de-inked using mechanical or chemical techniques.

The dried pulp (mechanical, chemical or recovered) is shipped to paper mills in the form of thick sheets in compressed bales, where it is mixed with water and agitated to separate the individual fibres. Chemicals and additives, such as kaolin clay or chalk, are added to the pulp-water slurry (called paper stock) to improve the papers characteristics. The paper stock is passed through a series of mechanical rollers and dryers to remove excess water and smooth the paper. The paper is wound onto a reel for further finishing (e.g. coating, super-calendaring).

Paper is one of the most commonly recycled materials. Pulp from recovered paper has become integral to the papermaking process; in the United States a third of fibre input comes from recovered paper. Unlike metals, paper cannot be infinitely recycled. With each round through the pulp making process the cellulose fibres are broken and become shorter and less uniform. As a result, paper can only be recycled 4-6 times. Using recovered fibre extends the life cycle of wood fibre, reducing the need for virgin fibre. It also uses less water and energy than making paper from virgin fibre. But the collection and transportation of recovered paper to recycling mills, which often involves significant distances (e.g. United States to China), can result in significant transportation fuel emissions.

Because recovered fibres are typically mixed with virgin fibres to improve the strength of the pulp, any paper products containing recovered fibre are labelled 'recovered paper,' making it difficult to estimate recycled production.[2] In 2009 over 211 million metric tonnes (Mt) of paper was collected for recycling worldwide compared and 373 Mt of paper produced, of which nearly 200 Mt contained some recovered fibre (BIR, 2010; FAO ForeSTAT). The most common applications for recovered paper are newsprint, packaging and tissue.

There are various substitutes available for paper products. In recent years, paper has faced strong competition from new media. Newspapers, magazines, books and other printed reading materials can be digitised and read electronically. Textiles, agricultural crops and other sources of non-wood fibre can be (and are still) used to make paper and paper products. Plastics and to a lesser extent glass and lightweight metals can substitute for paper in packaging. For some household and sanitary products, paper fills a niche market and substitution is less straightforward.

Supply and demand

Despite growing use of recovered paper pulp and because of limitations on the number of times recovered fibre can be recycled, the main source of the world's wood fibre today remains wood harvested from forests. In 2010 global forest cover exceeded 4 billion hectares, covering 31% of the earth's land (FAO, 2011). The world's five largest countries in terms of geographic size are also the most forest-rich countries; Russia, Brazil, Canada, the United States and China have more than half of the world's forest area (FAO, 2010).

About 30% of the world's forests are used primarily for the production of wood-based and non-wood-based products (FAO, 2010). According to data in the FAO's ForeSTAT database 518 million cubic metres of roundwood was removed worldwide for making wood pulp in 2010. The United States is the leading producer of pulp wood, accounting for over 26% of global removals, followed by Brazil (13%) and Russia (8%). OECD countries are important global producers; together they represent over two thirds of global pulpwood removals.

Examining the stages of production evolved in transforming pulpwood into finished paper provides important insight into the global flows of raw material used in papermaking. Not surprisingly, the world's largest pulp wood producers tend to also be the leading producers of primary pulp. But papermaking is also a heavy manufacturing process, with production also taking place in large industrialised economies that are relatively poorly endowed with forest resources, such as China and Japan. Although the United States remains the world's top primary pulp producer, accounting for 27% of global production in 2010, Chinese pulp production has grown rapidly. Since 1980 China has surpassed Finland, Japan, Sweden, and more recently Canada to become the second leading producer in the world.

In 2010 the largest exporters of primary pulp for paper were Canada, Brazil and the United States, respectively (FAO ForeSTAT database). Exports from these three countries represent half of the world's exports. OECD countries supply 70% of the world's virgin pulp exports, with the bulk of the area's exports coming from the OECD Americas (43% of global exports) and OECD Europe (24%) regions. Although Chinese production capacity has grown significantly over the last 20 years, domestic pulp production is insufficient to meet demand. Last year China imported more primary pulp than any other country in the world – 13.5 Mt or 27% of the world's imports. The United States is the second largest importer (11% share), followed by Germany (10% share). OECD countries export slightly more primary pulp than they import, resulting in a small negative physical trade balance (i.e. net exporter). OECD Europe is the main importing region in the OECD area, accounting for 41% of world imports in 2010.

A quarter of the world's paper and paperboard is made in China, 96 Mt in 2010. The United States produced 76 Mt (19% global share), Japan 24 Mt (6%), Germany 22 Mt (5.5%) and Canada 13 Mt (3%) (FAO ForeSTAT database). OECD countries dominate global trade in paper and paperboard, accounting for 84% of global exports and over 70% of imports in 2010. Germany, an important pulp importer, is the world's largest exporter of paper and paperboard. German exports reached 14 Mt 2010, ahead of the United States (12 Mt), Finland (11 Mt), Sweden (10 Mt) and Canada (under 10 Mt). The United States and Germany are also the biggest importers of paper and paperboard. Each imported 10.5 Mt in 2010, a 10% global share. The United Kingdom, France and Italy are the next largest importers.

Figure 2. Top 15 global producers: Pulpwood, virgin fibre pulp, paper and paperboard, and recovered paper

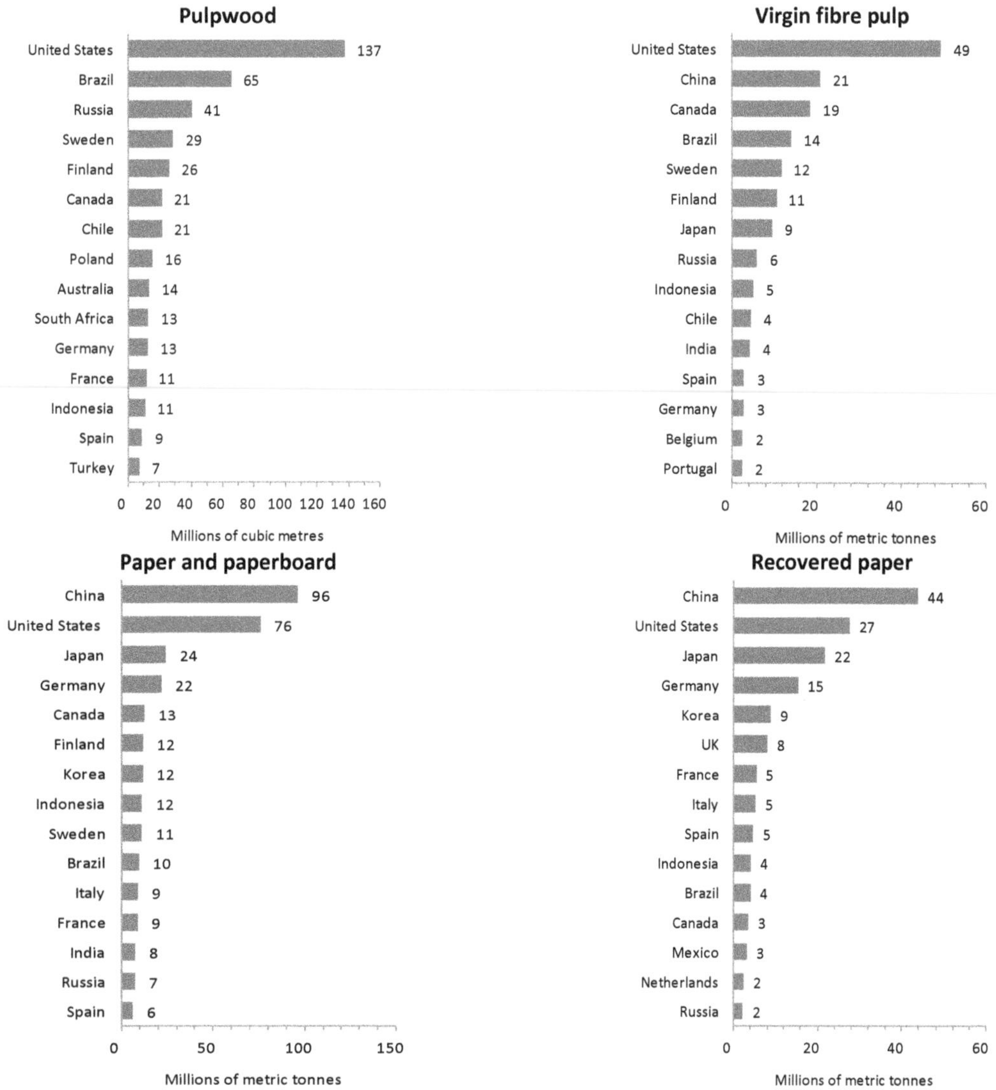

Source: UNFAO, ForeSTAT database, *www.faostat.fao.org*.

China is the largest consumer of paper and paperboard in absolute terms. Chinese consumption doubled over the last decade thanks to rising domestic production and increased imports, reaching

97 Mt in 2010. The United States remains the second largest consumer of paper, but consumption has been declining since 2000 due to lower production and imports, and increased exports. This is reflective of a general global trend in recent years of rising paper consumption in emerging and developing economies and declining or stable consumption in the OECD member countries. While OECD countries still account for the majority of global paper consumption, their share of consumption has decreased from 75% in 2000 to 57% in 2010 according to FAO data.

Production and consumption patterns of recovered fibre and paper are similar to those for virgin fibre and paper. China consumes the most recovered paper in the world (62 Mt in 2009) and is the dominant producer of recovered fibre pulp and recovered paper, with a 73% and 24% share of global production, respectively, in 2010 (BIR, 2010; FAO ForeSTAT). The United States however collects the most paper for recycling worldwide and is China's main source of imported recovered paper (OECD, 2010; BIR, 2010). U.S. net exports of paper for recycling reached over 19 Mt in 2009, of which some 10 Mt was destined for China (BIR, 2010). With the exception of flows of collected paper to China from the U.S., Canada, Europe and Japan, and trade within Europe, recovered fibre tends to be consumed in the country where it was collected. As a result, the largest paper collectors are generally also the largest producers of recovered paper: Japan, Germany, the United Kingdom, Korea, France, Italy and Spain.

Economic and environmental sustainability

Environmental implications

The pulp and paper industry consumed an estimated 4.5 exajoules (10^{18} J) of energy in 2005, making it the fourth largest industrial energy consumer (IEA, 2008). Approximately two-thirds of final energy consumption is fuel that is used to produce heat, while the remaining third is electricity. Energy consumption varies depending on the pulping process, type of paper being produced, and numerous plant specific characteristics (e.g. age, integrated or stand-alone, distance to markets and from electricity supply). In general, mechanical pulping and paper drying are the processes with the highest energy demands (IEA, 2007). Papermaking requires heat (steam) for drying and electricity is needed throughout the process. Mechanical pulping uses large amounts of electricity compared to chemical pulping, where black liquor is recovered and incinerated to produce heat and electricity, reducing the need for outside energy input. In some cases, pulp mills that use chemical pulping are net energy producers, selling electricity back to the grid. The ability to generate 50% of its own energy needs from biomass residues makes the pulp and paper industry unique from other industrial sectors and significantly lowers the industry's CO_2 intensity of production.

Greenhouse gas emissions from the pulp and paper source category are predominantly carbon dioxide (CO_2) with smaller amounts of methane (CH_4) and nitrous oxide (N_2O). It is estimated that the production and consumption of pulp and paper contributes approximately 570 million tonnes of CO_2 equivalent emissions per year (Mt CO_2e), which represents roughly 2% of global GHG emissions. The majority of these emissions (240 Mt CO_2e) are produced directly from the combustion of fossil fuels in the manufacturing process. Another 330 Mt are produced indirectly through electricity consumption, transportation and end-of-life methane emissions from landfills (OECD, 2008).

Timber harvesting for paper production has other indirect greenhouse gas implications. Forests play an integral role in regulating the level of carbon in the atmosphere through photosynthesis. In well-managed forests, the removal of forest wood is GHG-neutral as trees planted or regenerated absorb an amount equivalent to the CO_2 and methane released from the conversion of the carbon in wood products. In addition, stored CO2 is slowly released as paper products disposed of in landfills decompose.

Harvesting timber from forests also has an impact on ecosystems and biodiversity, depending on how forests are managed and, in plantations, which species are used. Although only a small portion of the timber harvested worldwide is used for papermaking, the pulp and paper industry contributes to the conversion of high conservation natural forests to managed forests (plantation or natural regeneration systems) in some regions and countries (e.g. Australia, Indonesia) (OECD, 2008). The environmental impact can be reduced and resource use efficiency increased through sustainable forest management.

Another environmental concern is water use and pollution. Water is an integral input to the pulp and paper making process, but usage varies according to the specific manufacturing processes in place and the type of paper being produced. In Canada, where mechanical pulping is more common, 32 cubic metres of water is used per tonne of paper on average while in Europe approximately 30 cubic metres of water are consumed per tonne of mechanical pulped printing paper (OECD, 2010). Waste water from mill operations is collected, treated and circulated within the mill (if possible) or discharged back to its source, which in most cases are surface waters. Waste water effluents from pulp and paper mills contain mainly: suspended solids, nutrients, such as nitrogen and phosphorus; oxygen-consuming organic substances (measured as biological oxygen demand, BOD; and chemical oxygen demand, COD); organically-bound chlorine compounds (measured as adsorbable organic halogens, AOX); and metals and toxins, such as resin acids that leach from the wood (OECD, 2008; 2010). The declining use of chlorine-based bleaches around the world has significantly reduced AOX emissions. In Europe, where chlorine is no longer used, AOX emissions have declined by over 95% since 1990 (CEPI, 2011). In Canada, AOX emissions have declined by over 90% since 1990 (FPAC, 2007).

Security of supply

Paper production depends on the availability of three raw material inputs: virgin wood fibre, virgin non-wood fibre and recovered paper fibre.

Forests are the only source of virgin wood fibre therefore sustainable forest management is critical to ensuring an adequate supply of wood fibre to meet paper demand. Between 2000 and 2010 the world lost 5.2 million hectares of forest area, mostly due to the conversion of forest land to agricultural land (FAO, 2011). Global deforestation has slowed over the last ten years, but some regions and countries have experienced significant losses of forest land (Africa, South America, Australia) that were only partly offset by the expansion of planted forests in others (Europe, China).

Paper can also be made from other types of plant fibre, but large scale production is considered unfeasible because enormous volumes of plant fibre would be required to meet current papermaking demand. Using alternative fibre for papermaking could also have greater adverse effects on the environment than using wood fibre. For example, in a life cycle analysis of Portuguese paper production da Silva Vieira *et al.* (2010) found that using hemp fibre produced greater environmental impacts than eucalyptus fibre because more mechanical pulping, fertilizer and chemical additives were required.

Recycling paper reduces the need for virgin fibre. Global paper recycling and recovery rates have been increasing steadily. In 2009 the amount of recovered paper used in the production of new paper reached 55.6%, up from 46.5% in 2000 (ICFPA, 2011). Europe is the global leader in the use of recovered paper; 66% of all paper consumed was recovered (CEPA, 2011). In the United States 63.5 % of consumed paper was recovered in 2010 according to the American Forest Paper Association; 40% of this paper was exported to China and other countries.

There are concerns that recycling and recovery rates may be nearing their practical limits in some regions and countries as high quality supplies are exhausted. In Europe high rates combined with

China's growing demand for recovered fibre has already created a tight supply situation that is expected to continue in the near term. There are also technical limits to paper recycling. Unlike metals, cellulose fibre cannot be infinitely recycled. There are also a significant percentage of paper that is not suitable for recovery because it is contaminated in use (tissue papers and certain food contact paper); it goes into permanent or semi-permanent use (libraries, archives and construction paper and paperboard); or is located in remote or sparsely populated areas not easily accessible by collection programs.

Demand for pulp and paper in OECD countries is mainly driven by demand for printing and writing paper, whereas in non-OECD countries consumption is driven by the need for other types of paper, paperboard in particular (OECD, 2010). Per capita paper consumption is increasing rapidly in the emerging and developing economies, but levels remain well below those in OECD countries. As incomes rise in countries such as China and India, it is expected that demand for printing and writing and speciality paper will also rise. The decoupling of per capita paper consumption from economic growth in OECD over the last decade points to the possibility of a threshold level income where paper consumption stabilises and even decreases. Increased used of new media at higher levels of income, which alters the paper demand mix, may be a factor behind this trend.[3]

Outlook

- After falling in the aftermath of the global financial crisis, pulp and paper production and prices have recovered in 2010 and the market for paper and board will continue to grow globally at 2.3% a year to 2030 (OECD, 2008). Demand will be driven by increasing consumption in developing and emerging economies, notably China and countries in the Middle East, Africa and Eastern Europe. Conversely, growth will be modest (less than 1% per year) in Western Europe and North America (Lombard, 2010). These important differences among world regions will continue to drive trade flows of paper and paperboard and the raw materials used in their production.
- Sustainable forest management, climate change and water use are among the core sustainability issues facing the pulp and paper industry. Technology will continue to play an important role in increasing energy and raw material efficiency and reducing negative environmental impacts.
- Given that the pulp and paper industry already produces half of its energy requirements from biomass, further reducing the CO_2 intensity of production will be challenging. Increasing the pace of diffusion of best available technologies, such as combined heat and power (CHP), particularly in emerging and developing economies; retrofitting existing mills with energy efficient technologies; and maximising economies of scale in production (e.g. integrating mills, larger paper machines) can result in significant energy savings. Mills in many OECD countries are nearing the end of their operating life and will need to be replaced or significantly upgraded over the next ten to fifteen years, affording an important opportunity for new technology deployment.
- Increased paper recycling and recovered paper use could help to further reduce energy consumption in pulp and paper production and the need for virgin wood fibre. However, the collection and transportation of recovered paper represent a significant component of the environmental footprint of paper recycling. While Europe, Japan and Korea appear to be close to their practical limits for paper recycling, North America and parts of Asia could benefit from more effective policies on waste disposal to encourage higher recycling rates.

Figure 3. Per capita consumption of paper and paperboard, OECD and BRIICS countries, 2010

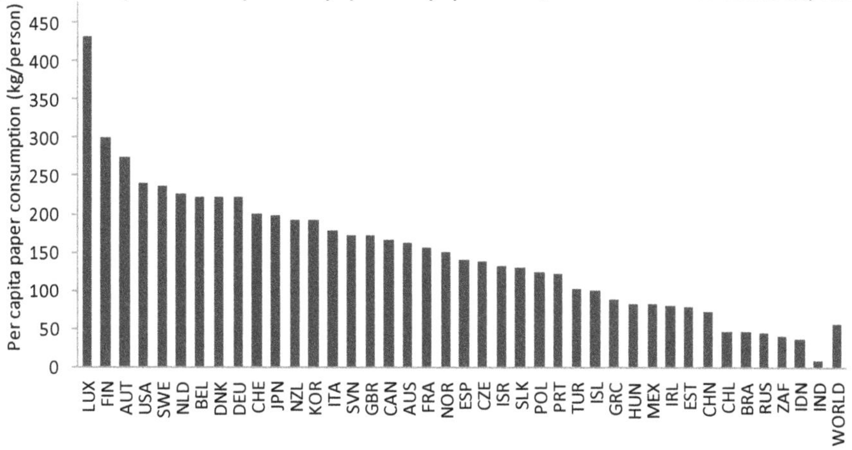

* The statistical data for Israel are supplied by and under the responsibility of the relevant Israeli authorities. The use of such data by the OECD is without prejudice to the status of the Golan Heights, East Jerusalem and Israeli settlements in the West Bank under the terms of international law.

Source: UN FAO, ForeSTAT database, *www.faostat.fao.org*; OECD; World Bank.

Figure 4. Change in per capita apparent consumption of paper versus GDP growth, 2000-2010

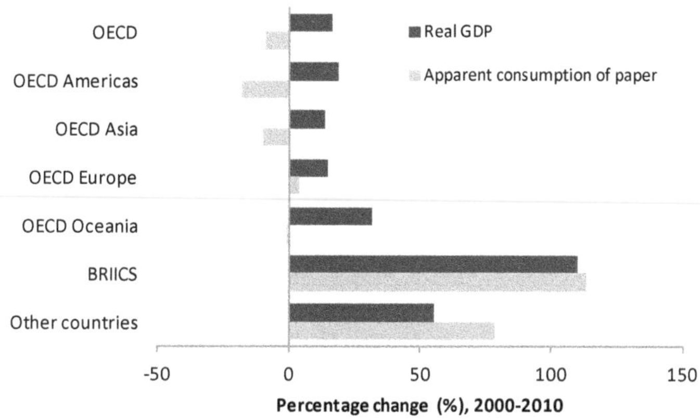

Notes: Real GDP in constant 2000 USD.

Source: UNFAO, *ForeSTAT database*, *www.faostat.fao.org*; World Bank.

ENDNOTES

1 Chemical pulping includes sulphate (kraft) and soda and sulphite wood pulp except dissolving grades. See faostat.fao.org.

2 Recovered paper and recycled paper are different. In general, paper can be called "recycled" only if it contains 100% post-consumer recovered fibre.

3 The increased use of computers and printers caused a change in consumer tastes with higher demand for printing and writing paper. The rapid uptake of the internet has reduced the demand for newsprint as electronic media replace traditional newspapers and periodicals.

REFERENCES

- BIR (Bureau of International Recycling), BIR website, *www.bir.org*
- CEPI (Confederation of European Paper Industries) (2010), *Key Statistics 2011: European Pulp and Paper Industry*, CEPI, Brussels.
- da Silva Vieira, Ricardo *et al.* (2010), "Industrial hemp or eucalyptus paper? An environmental comparison using life cycle assessment," *International Journal of Life Cycle Assessment*, 15, pp. 368-375
- EPA (U.S. Environmental Protection Agency) (2010), Available and Emerging Technologies for Reducing Greenhouse Gas Emissions from the Pulp and Paper Manufacturing Industry, U.S. EPA, Research Triangle Park, NC.
- European Paper and Packaging Industries Association, Paper Online website, www.paperonline.org
- FAO (Food and Agriculture Organisation of the United Nations) (2011), State of the World's Forests 2011, FAO, Rome.
- FAO (2010), Global Forest Resources Assessment 2010, FAO, Rome.
- FAO, Forest Statistics (ForeSTAT) website, *www.faostat.fao.org* [Accessed 4 September 2011]
- FPAC (Forest Products Association of Canada) (2007), *FPAC Sustainability Report 2007*, FPAC, Ottawa.
- IEA (International Energy Agency) (2008), Worldwide Trends in Energy Use and Efficiency: Key Insights from IEA Indicator Analysis, IEA, Paris.
- IEA (2007), Tracking Industrial Energy Efficiency and CO2 Emissions, OECD Publishing, Paris, *http://dx.doi.org/10.1787/9789264030404-en.*
- ICPFA (International Council of Forest Product Associations) (2011), *2011 ICPRA Sustainability Progress Report*, ICFPA.
- Lombard, Bernard (2010), "Pulp and paper industry: Main Economic Developments," CEPI Presentation to the FBI Advisory Committee, 29 November 2010.
- OECD (2011b), Sustainable materials management: Case studies, *http://www.oecd.org/env/waste/smm-casestudies.htm*
- OECD (2008), "Selected Industries: Pulp and Paper," *OECD Environmental Outlook to 2030*, OECD Publishing, Paris, *http://dx.doi.org/10.1787/9789264040519-en.*
- TAPPI, *www.tappi.org.*
- The Paper Life Cycle, *www.paperlifecycle.org.*
- World Bank, World Development Indicators, *http://data.worldbank.org/data-catalog/world-development-indicators.*

PHOSPHORUS FACTSHEET

One of the three macronutrients essential for plant growth, phosphorus is fundamental to sustaining human life. But the lack of substitutes in agriculture and the concentration of the earth's finite phosphate mineral reserves in a handful of countries are raising questions about future global food security. At the same time, eutrophication – the harmful build up of excess nutrients in lakes, rivers and marine environments – is a growing concern. Ensuring that there will be enough phosphorus to feed a population that is expected to grow to over 9.2 billion by 2050, while limiting the load on the environment, will require an integrated approach that focuses on both supply and demand solutions. Closing the nutrient cycle loop by recovering phosphorus from organic sources and changes in food consumption patterns will be critical.

See the Reader's guide for information about the selection of key material resources.

Overview

Characteristics and uses

Without phosphorus, life would not exist. As a component of every living cell, phosphorus plays a vital role in the physiological and biochemical processes of plants, animals and humans. Although phosphorus is the 11th most abundant element in the earth's crust, its concentration in soil and rock is usually very small. Phosphorus is never found in nature in its elemental form because it is highly reactive.

The largest source of phosphorus is phosphate rock, a general term for minerals containing a high concentration of phosphates. The industrial exploitation of phosphate rock began around the 1860s in the United States. Prior to that crop production relied exclusively on natural levels of soil phosphorus and the addition of locally available organic matter (e.g. crop residue, crushed bones, ash, food waste, manure and human excreta) (Cordell, Drangert & White, 2009). Rapid population growth and increasing food demand required more plentiful, richer sources of phosphate. Eventually guano and phosphate rock replaced local organic matter, but with the depletion of guano resources by the end of the 19th century, phosphate rock became the world's dominant source of phosphorus.

Figure 1. The flow of phosphorus in the environment

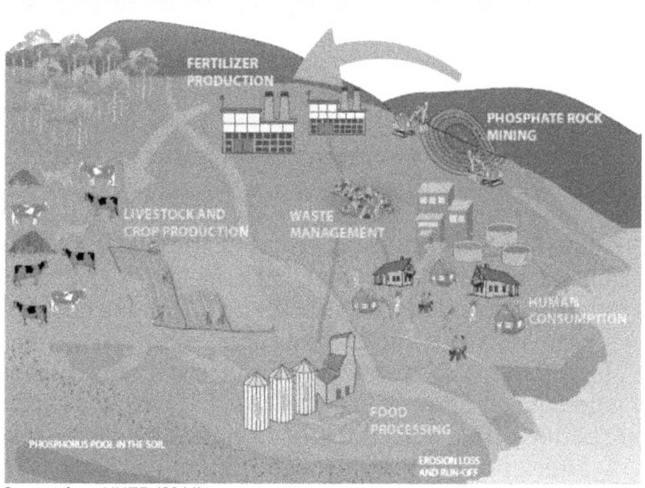

Source: from UNEP (2011).

Around 90% of phosphorus demand is used to produce food. The majority, over 80%, is used to make fertilizer while a smaller amount if goes toward making animal feed (7%) and food additives

(1-2%) (Schroder *et al.*, 2010). Phosphorus also has important industrial applications in the production of cleaners, detergents, food and beverages. Other less common applications include metal surface treatment, corrosion inhibition, flame-retardants, water treatment, ceramic production, explosives and pyrotechnics.

Production and processing

The primary production of phosphorus begins with mining phosphate rock and extracting the phosphate ore. Depending on the location and specific geological conditions, either surface or underground mining methods are used. Surface mining is common in parts of the United States, Morocco and Russia, while underground mining take place in Tunisia, Morocco, Mexico and India (UNEP and IFA, 2001). The mined ore is then upgraded via a beneficiation process to phosphate rock concentrate, whose characteristics are normally described by the concentration of phosphorus pentoxide (P_2O_5).[1] Most phosphate concentrate (80%) is converted into phosphoric acid, the precursor of many of the intermediate and end use products of phosphorus (Villalba, *et al.*, 2008).

Phosphoric acid is produced using one of two processes – wet or thermal – with each process producing a different grade of acid. Wet process phosphoric acids (merchant grade acids) are mainly used for fertilizers, industrial phosphates and animal feed supplements. In the wet process, sulphuric (most common), nitric or hydrochloric acids are reacted with phosphate rock to produce phosphoric acid and the calcium phosphate by-product, gypsum. In the thermal process, phosphoric acid is produced from elemental phosphorus that has been combusted and reacted with water (EPA, 1993). Thermal process phosphoric acid has a higher concentration of P_2O_5 and fewer impurities. Because of its higher grade, it is mainly used in the food industry or in specialised industrial applications. However, the thermal process is increasingly being replaced in favour of a purified wet process, which is more cost efficient and produces less negative environmental impacts. Today thermal acid is only being produced in China, the Netherlands and Kazakhstan. The wet phosphoric acid process is more far more prevalent globally (Villalba *et al.*, 2008); in the United States more than 95% of the phosphate rock concentrate produced is used to manufacture wet phosphoric acids (USGS, 2010a).

Recycling and substitutes

There are no substitutes for phosphorus in agriculture. Because phosphorus is an element it cannot be produced or synthesised in a laboratory.

Phosphorus is naturally recycled through a biochemical process: phosphorus flows from soil to plants and animals, and back again. But the advent of industrial agriculture disrupted the phosphorus nutrient cycle. Today the majority of food is transported and consumed far from where it was cultivated and the phosphorus extracted from the soil is not returned locally. Phosphorus can be recovered from the food production and consumption system and reused as a fertilizer either directly or after being processed through a variety of recovery methods (e.g. ploughing crop residues back into the soil; composting household, restaurant, and food processing plant food waste; and using human and animal excreta). The use and global flow of organic sources of phosphorus is not systematically tracked. Nearly all of the phosphorus that is consumed by animals and humans is excreted, but it is estimated that only 50% is returned to the agricultural system either formally or informally (Smil, 2000). The rate of recycling varies considerably between regions of the world. Some regions have soils that have already surpassed the critical phosphate level and have an oversupply of manure (e.g. the Netherlands and parts of North America) while there is a lack of manure in regions with phosphorus-deficient soils (e.g. sub-Saharan Africa and Australia) (Cordell, Drangert & White, 2009).

Organic phosphate sources can only partially offset demand for phosphate rock. They contain significantly lower concentrations of phosphorus (ranging from 0.1% P_2O_5 in cattle manure to 3.2% in activated sewage sludge), making them much bulkier to transport and store than fertilizers processed from phosphate rock. Consequently, organic phosphate sources are often disposed of as waste rather than recycled.

Supply and demand

Although phosphorus is one of the most common elements on earth only a small fraction – between 1.8 and 3 billion tonnes (Gt) – is available for use by living organisms.[2] Phosphate rock principally forms in ancient sedimentary marine basins. The largest sedimentary deposits are found in northern Africa, China, the Middle East, and the United States. Significant igneous occurrences are found in Brazil, Canada, Russia, and South Africa. Large phosphate resources have also been identified on the continental shelves and on seamounts in the Atlantic Ocean and the Pacific Ocean (USGS, 2011a).

Global phosphate rock reserves have recently been revised and are now reported at over 65 billion metric tonnes (Gt) (USGS, 2011a).[3] Significant revisions were made to reserves data for Morocco, using information from the Moroccan producer and a report by the International Fertilizer Development Centre. Morocco and the Western Sahara hold the largest share of global reserves, 50 Gt or 77%, followed by China (3.7 Gt or 6%), Algeria (2.2 Gt or 3.5%), Syria (1.8 Gt or 3%), South Africa and Jordan (1.5 Gt each or 2.3% each), and the United States (1.4 Gt or 2.2%). Smaller deposits are also found in Russia, Brazil, Israel, Senegal, Egypt, Tunisia, Australia, Togo and Canada.

Figure 2. Global distribution of phosphate rock reserves, 2010

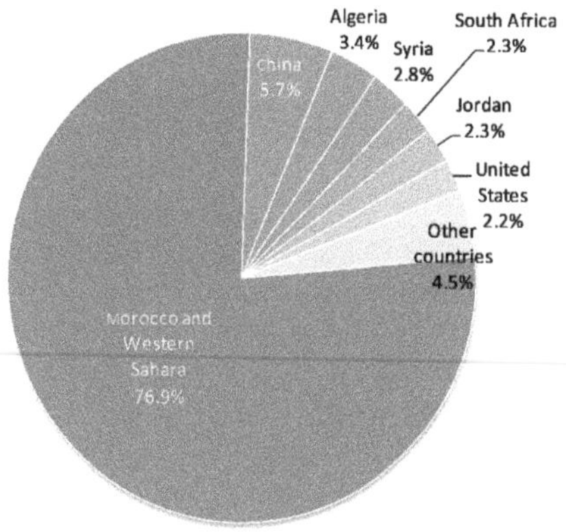

Source: U.S. Geological Survey.

Global extraction of phosphate rock climbed steadily from the Second World War, with growth accelerating in the 1960s with the Green Revolution, until 1988 when annual production peaked at 166 Mt. Extraction began to rise steadily again in 2001, driven predominantly by increased demand for fertilizer in East Asia (especially China). Global extraction of phosphate rock has made a strong recovery following the financial crisis and is estimated to have reached a new peak of 176 Mt in 2010 according to USGS production data (USGS, 2011a).

China has overtaken the United States to become the world's top phosphate rock producer, producing over an estimated 65 Mt in 2010 or nearly 37% of global production. The vast majority of China's mined phosphate rock production is consumed domestically with only a small fraction being exported (accounting for roughly 7% of total world exports according to the Potash Corporation). The United States is the world's second largest producer (over 26 Mt in 2010 or 15% of world production), but production has declined significantly over the last decade.

The African continent has emerged as an important producing region, with Morocco, the Western Sahara, Algeria, Egypt, Tunisia, Togo, Senegal and South Africa accounting for over one quarter (over 44 Mt) of global production in 2010 (USGS, 2011a). Other major global suppliers are the Middle

East (mainly Jordan, Israel and Syria), Russia and Brazil. Phosphate rock extraction also takes place in Australia, Canada, Finland and India.

Globally 80% of the total production of phosphate rock concentrate is consumed domestically and 20% is exported. Africa and the Middle East are the key exporting regions, accounting for more than 80% of the total world exports. Western Europe and Latin America, together with India, are the main importing regions (Potash Corporation, 2009).

Figure 3. Global phosphate rock production

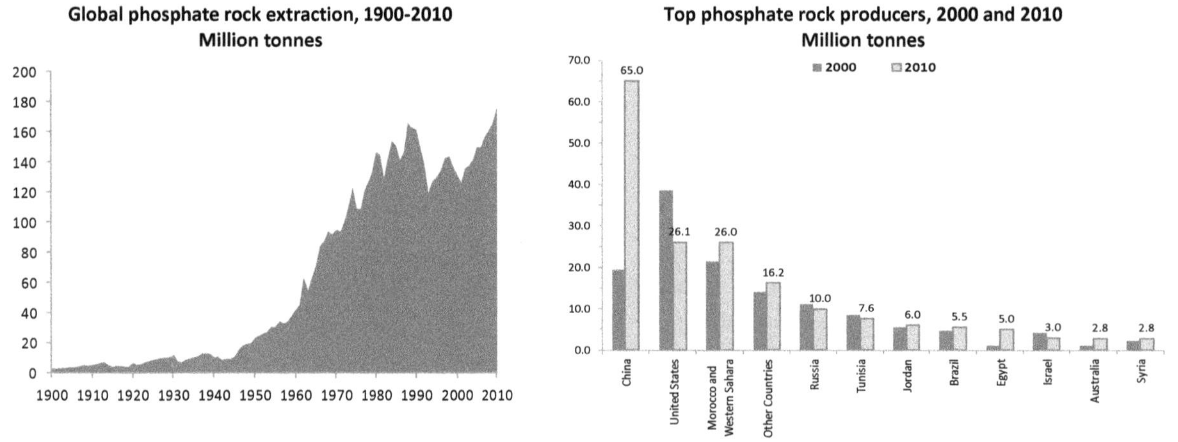

Note: Figures for 2010 are estimates.
Source: U.S. Geological Survey

* The statistical data for Israel are supplied by and under the responsibility of the relevant Israeli authorities. The use of such data by the OECD is without prejudice to the status of the Golan Heights, East Jerusalem and Israeli settlements in the West Bank under the terms of international law.

Economic and environmental sustainability

Security of supply

Identified reserves of phosphate rock are believed to be sufficient to meet demand in the long term. But in the near term there are concerns over potential supply disruptions due to the strong geographic concentration of reserves. Six countries – Morocco (and Western Sahara[4]), China, Algeria, Syria, South Africa and Jordan – hold over 90% of global reserves. Beyond the United States, there are no major phosphate rock producers in the OECD area although some extraction also takes place in Australia, Canada, Chile, Finland and Israel. Together these countries accounted for only 4% of global phosphate rock production in 2009.

Many countries are virtually completely dependent on imports of phosphate rock (e.g. India and the European Union) and some are taking steps to secure supplies. In 2004 the United States signed a free trade agreement with Morocco effectively guaranteeing it extended access to phosphorus (Schroder *et al.*, 2010). In 2008 China imposed a 135% export tariff in an effort to secure domestic supplies for food production (Schroder *et al.*, 2010; USGS, 2009b). This tightening of supplies combined with high demand from the agricultural sector caused the price of phosphate rock to increase sharply in 2008. The average U.S. price doubled from 2007 to 2008, while prices in North Africa and other exporting regions increased by a factor of 5 (USGS, 2009b). Prices dropped in 2009 with following the financial crisis, but remain historically elevated.

Figure 4. Real price phosphate rock, fertilizers, wheat, 1960-2010

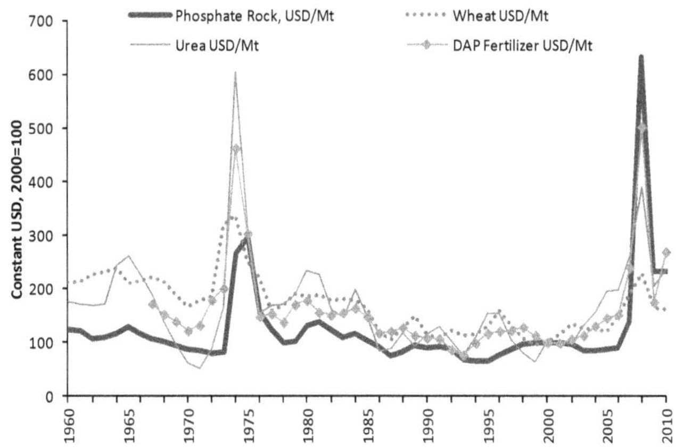

Source: World Bank (2011).

In 2010 two new phosphate rock mines began operation – one in northern Peru and one in Saudi Arabia – adding an additional 9 million tonnes to global mine capacity (USGS, 2011a). World mine production capacity is projected to increase to from 190 to 228 Mt by 2015 with expansion projects in Algeria, Brazil, China, Israel, Jordan, Syria, and Tunisia, and the development of new mines in Australia, Kazakhstan, Namibia, and Russia (USGS, 2011b).

Environmental implications

Phosphate rock mining

As with all mining activities, the extraction and beneficiation of phosphate rock has the potential to cause negative environmental impacts. These impacts can take the form of changes to the landscape, water contamination, excessive water consumption, air pollution and greenhouse gas emissions from the combustion of fossil fuels. The landscape may be disturbed through the removal of topsoil and vegetation, excavation and deposition of overburden, and disposal of processing wastes (UNEP and IFA, 2001). These potential impacts tend to be localised and depend on the processes and practices in place.

The amount of unused extraction associated with phosphate rock mining, like all mining activities, is significant. Mining overburden makes up over half of the raw materials handled. Extracted phosphate rock has an average phosphorus concentration of 13% and contains many impurities. As a result, a significant amount of solid waste is generated. The production of 1 tonne of P_2O_5 requires over 9 tonnes of ore, some 1 700 mega joules of electricity, as well as diesel fuel and water; and produces over 21 t of solid waste, including over 6 tonnes of tailings (Villalba, *et al.*, 2008). Resource efficiency is also of concern. Under current mining methods, some estimate that 20% of the resource is not extracted or recovered from reserves (Van Vuuren, Bouwman & Beusen, 2010). Other estimates suggest that a third of the phosphates are lost in mining, processing, and other metallurgical operations and that up to 10% is lost in transportation and handling (Villalba *et al.*, 2008).

Phosphoric acid production

In the wet process, the fluorine compounds, hydrogen fluoride (HF) and silicon tetra fluoride (SiF_4) form as by-products of the phosphate-acid reaction. The compounds are volatised to remove them from the final product, producing environmentally harmful fluorine emissions. In modern plants, fluorides are recovered and used to produce commercial products such as fluosilicic acid. Currently this is only taking place in the United States. Increased recovery of fluorine during wet-process could drastically reduce pressure on non-renewable sources of fluorine (i.e. fluorspar) (Villalba *et al.*, 2007).

Phosphogypsum (PG) is a toxic by-product of the wet process. In addition to fluorine, PG can also contain traces of heavy metals (cadmium) and radio nuclides (uranium and thorium). An estimated four to six tonnes of PG are produced for every tonne of wet process phosphoric acid. PG is usually disposed of as waste in settling ponds or at sea (Villalba *et al.*, 2008), but when levels of radioactivity are unacceptably high, the material is stockpiled. Global stockpiles of PG are estimated at over 3 Gt and growing by over 110 tonnes a year, presenting a risk of groundwater contamination (Cordel, Drangert & White, 2009; Stackfree.com, n.d.). Industry, regulatory agencies and research institutions are working together to develop beneficial uses of PG, including applications in agriculture, construction, landfill management, and road construction.

Phosphoric acid mist is the main atmospheric emission resulting from the production of thermal phosphoric acid. Although most of the mist is captured some emissions are released into the atmosphere.

Phosphate fertilizer use

Phosphorus concentrations in freshwater and terrestrial systems have increased by at least 75 per cent over the last 50 years while the estimated flow of phosphorus to the ocean from land has risen to 22 million tonnes per year – an amount that exceeds the world's annual consumption of phosphorus fertilizer (UNEP, 2011). Excess phosphorus and other nutrients in aquatic systems can lead to eutrophication, or nutrient over enrichment. Eutrophication can promote the excessive growth of algae and other undesirable aquatic plant species, which can alter aquatic ecosystems and destroy aquatic species. Algal blooms in some species can produce toxins that are harmful to both humans and animals (e.g. blue-green algae or cyanobacteria). Increased decomposition of aquatic plants can decrease oxygen levels (hypoxia) for fish. Agricultural runoff and municipal and industrial wastes are mainly responsible for phosphate loading of surface waters (Maene, 2000; Liu *et al.*, 2008). The problem is exacerbated in large urban areas where phosphorus form human excreta and detergents become concentrated in wastewater streams and is discharged along with nitrogen and other nutrients. Around the world 415 eutrophic and hypoxic coastal areas have been identified (Selman, *et al.*, 2008).

Outlook

- Pressure on the earth's limited phosphorus-rich resources is unlikely to diminish in the foreseeable future. Although decreasing in developing countries, global phosphorus fertilizer demand is expected to grow, led by the highly populated and increasingly affluent countries of East and South Asia. By 2050, world agriculture production is expected to have increased by 70% to feed a population that will have grown to over 9 billion (from 7 billion today) (FAO, 2009; OECD; 2011). The share of biomass in the total energy supply is expected to increase by at least 10% by 2050, placing additional pressure on land use and agricultural resources, including fertilizers (IEA, 2009).
- Given the lack of substitutes for phosphorus in agriculture, maintaining a sustainable supply is essential for global food security. Reducing phosphate losses during mining, processing and transport, which range between 20-40%, can help extend the life expectancy of phosphate rock resources. As can measures to increase the efficacy of phosphate fertilizer use in agriculture (e.g. precision agriculture, organic farming, and microbial inoculants).
- The recovery and recycling of phosphorus from organic sources can alleviate some of the pressure on inorganic sources while at the same time help address the problem of eutrophication. However, establishing large scale phosphorus recovery programs will require

fundamental changes in the way organic waste if perceived and managed, in particular waste water, sewage and manure from intensive livestock facilities. The necessary infrastructures will also need to be built. Some OECD member countries are already moving forward with measures to capture and recover nutrients from waste water and sewage (i.e. "econsan" or ecological sanitation systems). Sweden has also proposed that 60% of phosphorus in sewage should be returned to land by 2015 (Cordell, Drangert and White, 2009).

- Beyond the problem of eutrophication, reducing the environmental impacts associated with the production and use of industrial phosphate fertilizer, including the production of solid wastes such as PG, will remain a priority. Japan has demonstrated that process improvements can produce higher-quality PG, which can be reused for wallboard, cement, sulphuric acid, fertilizer, or conditioners for certain types of soils (Villalba *et al.*, 2008). Expansion of fluorine recovery activities can reduce environmentally harmful emissions and demand for fluorspar, an industrial mineral used in the manufacture of products such as aluminium, gasoline, insulating foams, plastics, refrigerants, steel, and uranium fuel (USGS, 2010b). The development of new technology, such as the low intensity thermal process, can increase the energy efficiency of phosphoric acid production.
- Future demand for phosphorus will also depend heavily on food consumption patterns. As incomes rise the global food basket is shifting from staple foods towards more processed and prepared food products that contain a greater proportion of animal protein. Meat- and dairy-based diets are more phosphate intensive and it is estimated that changing from the average western diet to a vegetarian diet could decrease phosphorus fertilizers demand by at least 20-45% (Cordell, Drangert and White, 2009). Global per capita meat consumption is expected to increase by 9% (or 60 Mt), led by consumption growth in Asia (OECD-FAO, 2011). Although per capita consumption levels are largely stable in OECD countries, they are relatively high and are expected to remain well above levels in non-OECD countries for the foreseeable future.[5]

ENDNOTES

1 The P_2O_5 content of phosphate normally ranges between 25 and 40% and is on average close to 30-35% (USGS, 2001).

2 The largest amount of phosphorus, 27 to 840 peta (10^{15}) tonnes, is stored in oceans (80 to 120 Gt in sea water and the remainder in the sea bed in the form of insoluble calcium phosphate) (Liu *et al.*, 2008).

3 In 2010, the U.S. Geological Survey reported global phosphate rock reserves of 16 Gt. Figures for Morocco were revised in 2011 using new information from the Moroccan producer and a report by the International Fertilizer Development Centre.

4 The Western Sahara is a disputed territory currently administered by Morocco.

5 For example, in 2020 per capita beef consumption in non-OECD countries is expected to be 5.0 kg/person compared to 14.9 kg/person on average in OECD countries (OECD-FAO, 2011).

REFERENCES

- BGS (British Geological Survey) (2010), *World mineral production 2004-08*, British Geological Survey, Keyworth, Nottingham.
- BGS (2008), *World mineral production 2002-06,* British Geological Survey, Keyworth, Nottingham.
- Cordell, D., Drangert, J. O., and White, S. (2009), "The story of phosphorus: Global food security and food for thought," *Global Environmental Change*, 19, pp. 292-305.
- Cordell, D., *et al.* (2009), "Preferred future phosphorus scenarios: a framework for meeting long-term phosphorus needs for global food demand," in D. Mavinic, K. Ashley and F. Koch (eds.), *International Conference on Nutrients Recovery from Wastewater Streams*, 10-13 May 2009, , IWA Publishing, London.
- EC (European Commission), *Use of Phosphorus and its resource availability*, website *www.ec.europa.eu/environment/natres/phosphorus.htm*
- EPA (U.S. Environmental Protection Agency) (1993), *Phosphoric Acid and Phosphoric Fertilizers*, RTI Project Number 5428-49 DR, EPA, Triangle Research Park, North Carolina.
- FAO (Food and Agriculture Organisation of the United Nations) (2009), "Global Agriculture Towards 2050," *How to Feed the World 2050*, High-Level Expert Forum, Rome, 12-15 October 2009, FAO, Rome.
- FAO (2004), Use of Phosphate Rocks for Sustainable Agriculture, FAO, Rome.
- Heffer, S. and Prud'homme, M. (2009), "Fertilizer Outlook 2009-2013," *77th International Fertiliser Association Annual Conference*, 25-27 May 2009, Shanghai, People's Republic of China, IFA, Paris.
- IEA (International Energy Agency) (2009), Energy Technology Perspectives 2010: Scenarios and Strategies to 2050, OECD Publishing, Paris, *http://dx.doi.org/10.1787/energy_tech-2010-en.*
- IFA (International Fertilizer Industry Association) (2010), Production and trade statistics website, *www.fertilizer.org/ifa/Home-Page/STATISTICS/Production-and-trade* [Accessed September 2010].
- Liu, Y., *et al.* (2008), "Global phosphorus flows and environmental impacts from a consumption perspective," *Journal of Industrial Ecology*, 12(4), p. 229-247.
- Maene, L.M. (2000), "Efficient Fertilizer Use and its Role in Increasing Food Production and Protecting the Environment," *6th AFA International Annual Conference*, 31 January to 3 February 2000, Cairo.
- Morrison, L. (2009), "Enough Phosphorus for the Future" *Corn and Soybean Digest* online, February 15, *http://cornandsoybeandigest.com/inputs/fertilizer/0215-enough-future-phosphorus/* [Accessed 26 January 2011].
- OECD-FAO (2011), *Agricultural Outlook 2011-2020*, OECD, Paris. *http://dx.doi.org/10.1787/agr_outlook-2011-en*
- OECD (2011), *OECD Environmental Outlook to 2050: The Consequences of inaction,* OECD, Paris. *http://dx.doi.org/10.1787/9789264122246-en*
- OECD-FAO (2010), *Agricultural Outlook 2010-2019*, OECD, Paris. *http://dx.doi.org/10.1787/agr_outlook-2010-en*
- Potash Corporation (2009), *Phosphate*, *www.potashcorp.com/industry_overview/2009/media/pdf/POT_OB_Phosphate_09.pdf* [Accessed 25 January 2011]
- Schröder, J.J. *et al.* (2010), *Sustainable Use of Phosphorus,* Report 357, Plant Research International, Wageningen, the Netherlands.
- SEI (Stockholm Environment Institute) (2008), "Closing the Loop on Phosphorus," *EcoSanRes,* Factsheet 4, *www.ecosanres.org/pdf_files/ESR-factsheet-04.pdf.*
- Selman, M., *et al.* (2008), "Eutrophication and Hypoxia in Coastal Areas: a Global Assessment of the State of Knowledge," *Policy Note on Water Quality: Eutropication and Hypoxia*, No. 1, World Resources Institute, Washington, D.C.
- Smil, V. (2000), Feeding the World: A Challenge for the 21st Century, MIT Press, Cambridge, MA.
- Stackfree.com (n.d.), *www.stackfree.com* [Accessed: 25 January 2011]

- UNEP (United Nations Environment Programme) and IFA (2001), Environmental Aspects of Phosphate and Potash Mining, UNEP & IFA, Paris.
- UNEP and IFA (2000), *Mineral Fertilizer Use and the Environment*, Revised edition, UNEP & IFA, Paris.
- UNEP (2011), "Phosphorus and Food Production," *UNEP Yearbook 2011*, UNEP, Paris.
- USGS (U.S. Geological Survey) (2011a) *Mineral commodity summaries 2011*, USGS, Reston, VA.
- USGS (2011b) 2009 Minerals Yearbook: Phosphate Rock [Advance Release], USGS, Reston, VA.
- USGS (2010a), *Mineral commodity summaries 2010*, USGS, Reston, VA.
- USGS (2010b), 2008 Minerals Yearbook: Fluorspar [Advance Release], USGS, Reston, VA.
- USGS (2009a), "Phosphate rock statistics," in Kelly, T.D., and Matos, G.R., comps., *Historical statistics for mineral and material commodities in the United States*, USGS Data Series 140[Accessed 17 September 2010].
- USGS (2009b), *Mineral commodity summaries 2009*, USGS, Reston, VA.
- Van Kauwenbergh, S. J. (2010), *World Phosphate Rock Reserves and Resources*, International Fertilizers Development Centre (IFDC) Publications, Muscle Shoals, AL.
- Van Vuuren, D. P., Bouwman, A. F. and Beusen, A. H. W. (2010), "Phosphorus demand for the 1970–2100 period: A scenario analysis of resource depletion," *Global Environmental Change*, Volume 20, pp. 428–439.
- Villalba, G., *et al.* (2008), "Global Phosphorus Flows in the Industrial Economy from a Production Perspective," *Journal of Industrial Ecology*, 12(4), p. 557-569, doi:10.1111/j.1530-9290.2008.00050.x.
- Villalba, G., Schroder, H., and Ayres R. U. (2007), "Accounting for fluorine: Production, use, and loss," *Journal of Industrial Ecology*, 11(4), pp. 85–101.
- World Bank (2011), Commodity Price Data (Pink Sheet) website, *econ.worldbank.org/WBSITE/EXTERNAL/EXTDEC/EXTDECPROSPECTS/0,,contentMDK:21148472~menuPK:556802~pagePK:64165401~piPK:64165026~theSitePK:476883,00.html* [Accessed 25 January 2011].

RARE EARTH ELEMENTS FACTSHEET

From relatively obscurity rare earth elements have grown to become essential components in a wide range of high tech, alternative energy and military applications. Although crustally abundant, concentrations that can be economically extracted are rare. China's dominance over global supplies in the face of rising global demand are raising fears of shortages that risk disrupting economies and derailing green growth plans. As with other metals, refining rare earths is energy- and water-intensive, with added complexity due to their similar chemical properties. While there is renewed interest in 3R and circular economy approaches, the recycling and reuse of rare earths remains uneconomic and remains near zero.

See the Reader's guide for information about the selection of key material resources.

Overview

Characteristics and uses

Rare earths are not a single element, but a group of 17 chemically similar metallic elements found in the lanthanides series in the periodic table. Yttrium and Scandium are considered rare earth elements (REE); they are often recovered with REE and share many of the same chemical properties. Despite their name some rare earths are as abundant in the earth's crust as major industrial metals such as copper, nickel, zinc, tin or lead. Unlike other metals REE tend not to form in concentrations that can be economically extracted. Crustal abundance varies widely by REE, from cerium, the most abundant REE and the 25th most abundant element in the earth's crust at 60 parts per million, to thulium and lutetium, the least abundant REE at about 0.5 part per million (USGS, 2010c).[1]

Unique magnetic, catalytic, metallurgical, electrical, optical and nuclear properties have led to the use of REE in a number of highly specific applications. Established end-uses, such as glass-making, catalysts, lighting and metallurgy (excluding batteries), account for 59% of global consumption of REE and developing, high-growth applications, such as batteries, ceramics and permanent magnets, account for the remaining 41% (Goonan, 2011).[2] Without REE many of the electronics consumers enjoy today – smart phones, laptops, and home entertainment systems – would not be possible. REE are integral components in a wide variety of energy efficiency and alternative energy technologies. Wind turbines and hybrid and electric vehicles use powerful neodymium-based permanent magnets to reduce weight and increase efficiency. REE phosphors are used in energy-saving compact fluorescent and light-emitting diode (LED) light bulbs. REE are also used in hydrogen and solid oxide fuel cell technology. The number of environmental applications of REE continues to expand.

Figure 1. End-use markets and applications for rare earth elements

Names and symbols of the rare earth elements

Lanthanides					
Light REE		Heavy REE		Others	
Lanthanum	La	Gadolinium	Gd	Scandium	Sc
Cerium	Ce	Terbium	Tb	Yttrium	Y
Praseodymium	Pr	Dysprosium	Dy		
Neodymium	Nd	Holmium	Ho		
Promethium	Pm	Ebrium	Er		
Samarium	Sm	Thulium	Tm		
Europium	Eu	Ytterbium	Yb		
		Lutetium	Lu		

Global distribution of rare earth oxides by end-use, 2008

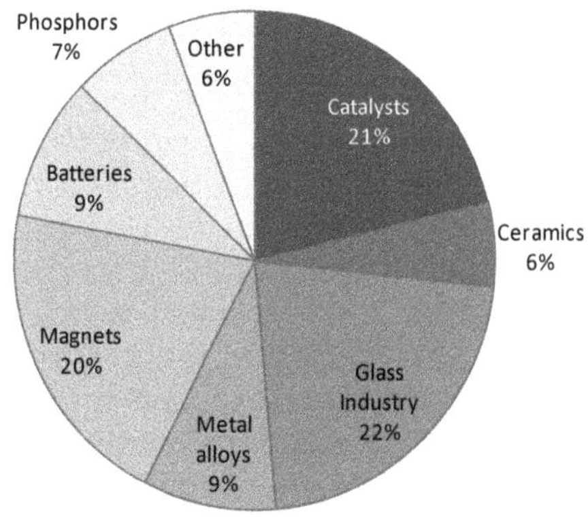

Source: Goonan (2011).

End markets and applications for rare earth elements

End-Use Market	Applications	Rare Earth Elements
Magnets	Electric and hybrid motors, disc drives, power windows in vehicles, magnetic resonance imaging, wind turbines, microphones and speakers, magnetic refrigeration	Nb, Pr, Tb, Dy
Catalysts	Petroleum refining (fluid cracking), automobile catalytic converters, diesel additives, chemical processing	La, Ce, Pr, Nd
Metallurgy	Alloys, lighter flints	La, Cr, Pr, Nd
Glass Industry	Polishing compounds, decolourisers/colourisers, UV resistant glass, x-ray imaging, lasers	Ce, La, Pr, Nd, Gd, Er, Ho, Y
Batteries	Rechargeable batteries (electric and hybrid vehicles)	
Phosphors	Cathode ray tubes, liquid crystal display and plasma display panels, energy efficient lighting, fibre optics	Eu, Y, Tb, Nd, Er, Gd, Ce, Pr
Ceramics	Colorants, refractories, capacitators, semiconductor sensors	La, Ce, Pr, Nd, Y, Eu, Gd, Lu, Dy
Others	Nuclear energy, defence applications, water treatment, fertilizers, other chemical applications	Eu, Gd, Ce, Y, Sm, Er, Nd, Pr, Dy, Tb, La, Lu, Sc

Source: Adapted from BGS (2010) and Goonan (2011).

Production, recycling and substitution

Owing to their chemical similarities, REE usually occur together in rock-forming minerals. They are often mined as the by-product (rather than the primary product) of a mine, like at Bayan Obo in China where REE were originally mined as an iron by-product. Depending on the deposit's characteristics either conventional surface or underground mining methods are used. Once extracted the mined ore is crushed and screened before undergoing a series of physical and chemical beneficiation processes in order to separate the REE and gangue minerals. Separating out individual REE to produce high purity compounds is complex because they are so chemically similar to one another, requiring significant amounts of energy and water.

Substituting a REE with another compound is rarely straightforward. Although substitutes are available for many applications, they are generally less effective, more costly (i.e. platinum-group elements), other rare earth elements or require a complete product re-design (Schüler *et al.*, 2011). In some cases, REE are already substitutes for other more toxic materials, such as cadmium in rechargeable batteries or heavy metals in colorants. For end-uses based on specific optical, chemical and magnetic properties substitution is particularly challenging and, in some cases, simply not possible with current technology. Despite decades of research efforts no alternative have been found for the neodymium magnet and no substitute currently exists for europium, which is used in colour televisions and computer monitors (BGS, 2010).

The level of rare earth recycling is virtually zero. End-uses for rare earth oxides are generally dissipative and highly specialised. The relatively small amounts of rare earth oxides used in an application combined with their chemical complexity making recycling technically challenging and, with the generally low prices of REE, uneconomic. When REE-bearing products or scrap are being recycled, recovery activities tend to focus on other materials that are available in much larger quantities or more valuable (e.g. palladium and platinum in automobile catalytic converters, nickel and cobalt in rechargeable batteries, coloured glass bearing REE is converted to coloured tile or glass fibre). It is estimated that less than 1% of REE-bearing scrap is currently being recycled (USGS, 2011a). Most of the REE-bearing scrap that is being recycled is new (pre-consumer) scrap generated during the production of permanent magnets. There is currently little recycling of REE from old (post-consumer) scrap taking place (Schüler *et al.*, 2011). Generally REE-bearing scrap is disposed of as waste in landfills or converted to construction aggregate.

The recycling of REE from permanent magnets (pre- and post-consumer) shows the greatest potential from a technical point of view and is the focus of a number of research activities, particularly in China and Japan.[3] Hitachi recently developed technologies to recycle rare earth magnets from hard disk drives and has successfully extracted rare earths from rare earth magnets (Goonan, 2011). Permanent magnets and batteries also have strong potential for re-use because their lifetimes often exceed that of the device for which they were used.

Supply and demand

World rare earth resources are difficult to accurately estimate due to the quality and availability of data. Global reserves have been estimated by the U.S. Geological Survey (USGS) at over 110 million tonnes (Mt).[4] Exploitable REE deposits are concentrated in a few countries. China holds the largest reserves (55 Mt), followed by the Commonwealth of Independent States (19 Mt), the United States (13 Mt), India (3.1 Mt) and Australia (1.6 Mt). Remaining reserves are found in Brazil, Malaysia, Canada, Greenland, South Africa, Namibia, Mauritania, Burundi, Malawi, Vietnam and Thailand (USGS, 2010a; BGS, 2010).

Although China holds 48% of global reserves, it virtually dominates world REE production. In 2010 of the 130 000 t of REE produced, 97% was produced in China. China's share of global production has been increasing steadily since it began to extract rare earths in the late 1970s. Prior to the 1940s small quantities were produced in India, Brazil, Australia and Malaysia, but commercial production did not take off in earnest until the 1960s following the discovery of a large deposit in Mountain Pass, California and the popularisation of colour television. The Mountain Pass reserves helped the United States become predominant producer of REE until the late 1980s when it was overtaken by China (BGS, 2010). REE mining operations at Mountain Pass were subsequently halted in 2002 because of low market prices due to abundant, low cost Chinese production. Today no active mining is taking place at Mountain Pass, but moderate amounts of rare earth concentrates are being produced from mine stocks. Beyond China, lesser quantities of REE are being mined in Brazil (550 t), Malaysia (30 t) India (25 t) (USGS, 2011b). It is estimated that Russia produced around 2 500 t in 2009 and that some extraction is also taking place in Indonesia, Kazakhstan, North Korea, South Korea, Kyrgyzstan, Mozambique, Nigeria and Vietnam (BGS, 2010).

China is also a global leader in rare earth processing technology. It produces both intermediate products such as rare earth metals, alloys or carbonates and also manufactures many of the rare earth-bearing end products (e.g. phosphors, LEDs, catalysts, batteries, magnets). China exported 44 000 t of rare earth compounds and metals in 2009 – over 55% of the total export market. [5] Some OECD member countries are also important suppliers. Austria produces a number of REE products and is the world's second leading exporter (11 000 t) followed by Japan (6 000 t) and the United States (5 500 t). OECD countries represented over 40% of REE exports in 2009.

Over 85% of rare earth exports are destined for OECD countries. Member countries are the leading importers of rare earth compounds and metals, lead by Japan (18 300 t in 2009), the United States (16 600 t), Germany (8 300 t), France (7 400 t) and Austria (4 700 t).

Figure 2. Reserves and mine production of rare earth elements

Global shares of reserves, 2010 | **Mine production, Total, U.S. and China, 1988-2010**

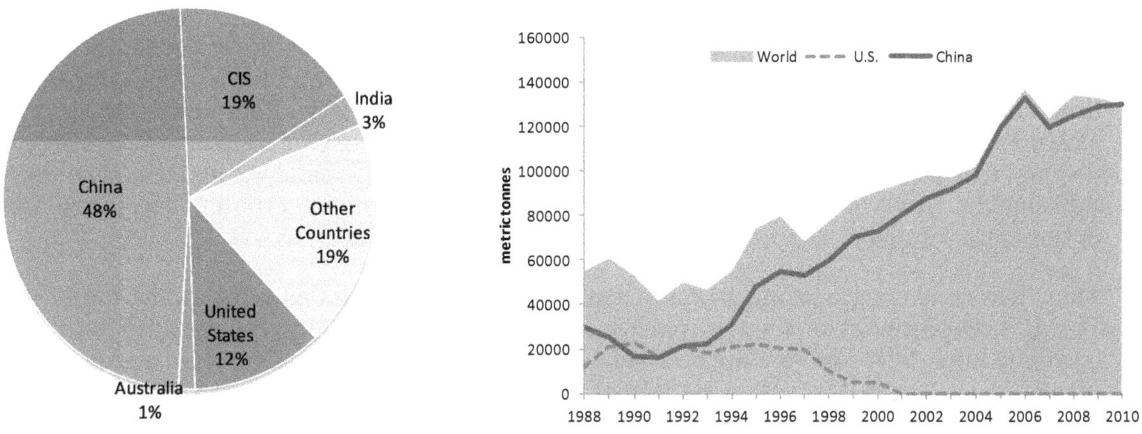

Source: U.S. Geological Survey

Economic and environmental sustainability

Security of supply

In the long-term REE reserves are thought to be large relative to demand (USGS, 2010a). In the short term, supply chain issues may give rise to tight supplies of certain REE (particularly heavy REE, which are predominantly produced in China). The REE market has already witnessed a dramatic change from a situation of oversupply to one of over demand in the last three years due to the explosion of rare earth applications and rising demand for alternative energy and consumer technologies. For several years now, China has been strengthening policies and regulations governing the rare earth industry in order to ensure sufficient supplies to meet its own growing domestic demand and to protect the resource and the environment. Some of the measures introduced include export restrictions, a moratorium on new mining licences and restrictions on foreign investment in mining and extraction (Schüler *et al.*, 2011). The Chinese government has also been cracking down on illegal mining and smuggling resulting in the closure of several operations. It is estimated that at least 20 000 t of rare earths were smuggled out of China in 2009 (Schüler *et al.*, 2011).

The contraction in exports from the world's dominant supplier coupled with continued strong global demand have contributed to sharp increases in prices of many rare earth oxides. The price outside of China for lanthanum oxide had reached over 150 USD per kilogram in July 2011 compared to 50 USD/kg at the beginning of 2011 and less than 10 USD/kg in 2001. Dysprosium oxide has jumped to 3 300 – 3 500 USD/kg compared to less than 50 USD/kg in 2001 (Montgomery, 2011; Schüler *et al.*, 2011).

Concerns over supplies have spurred exploration and development of REE resources in various parts of the world. Over 100 deposits are being investigated and some projects in Australia, Greenland, Canada, South Africa, the U.S., Namibia and Malawi are undergoing feasibility studies or are in the exploration stage. The Mountain Pass mine in California has been reopened and production is expected to expand in 2012 and 2013. The Mount Weld mine in Australia is expected to begin production sometime in 2011 (European Commission, 2010). Starting up a mining operation is a lengthy process, which often takes decades between discovery and commercial production. As a result, supplies are expected to be tight for the several years, placing upward pressure on the prices of rare earth metal alloys and oxides.

Predicting future demand for REE is challenging given the number of elements and their broad range of applications, many of which are technology driven. Demand for REE has fluctuated over time and demand for individual elements has varied considerably. Some estimates predict that global REE demand will reach 190 000 to 210 000 tonnes per year by 2015 (BGS, n.d.). Strong demand for specific end-uses (i.e. magnets, batteries, automotive catalysts and display monitors) is expected to result in particularly tight supplies of neodymium, erbium, europium, terbium, dysprosium, lanthanum, yttrium, and praseodymium (Schüler *et al.*, 2011).

Many governments are taking action to response to the uncertainties surrounding future supplies. The U.S. Department of Energy released a *Critical Materials Strategy* in 2010 and there are currently four bills before Congress related to REE supply security.[6] Rare earths have been identified as one of the raw materials of critical importance to European industry under the framework of the Raw Materials Initiative (European Commission, 2010). In October 2010, the Government of Austria organised the conference "How safe is the raw material supply for the energy technologies of the future?" to discuss strategies to secure the supply of raw materials, in particular metals, that are critical to making the transition to a clean energy society. Japan and South Korea have recently issued REE policies. The UK Government commissioned a report entitled 'Lanthanide Resources and Alternatives,' which concluded that shortages are expected for key heavy elements.

Tight supplies and rising prices have also increased interest in the secondary production of rare earths. As discussed earlier there are numerous challenges to recycling REE. Estimating the in-use stock of REE is difficult because most uses are dissipative, resulting in very small quantities being present in some products. The Toyota Prius is believed to be the product that is the single largest consumer of REE (BGS, 2010). Each vehicle contains approximately 30 kilograms of REE, including 1 kg of neodymium and 10 kg of lanthanum (Avalon Rare Metals, Inc., 2010b; Hilsum, 2009).[7] A wind turbine requires an estimated 0.6 to 0.9 tonnes of neodymium iron boron magnets per megawatt, with each magnet containing up to 30% REE (Avalon Rare Metals, Inc., 2010b). Computer hard drives, DVD players, earphones and high performance speakers use REE magnets, but the volume of REE in these consumer electronics is small relative to other materials, such as plastic. A typical desk top computer contains less than 0.1 grams of each of terbium, europium and yttrium (Basel Action Network, 2002).

Man-made stocks will likely increase significantly over the next few years as consumers continue to demand the latest in high tech gadgetry and the desire to reduce carbon emissions from fossil fuel combustion drive the development and adoption of cleaner energy technologies. But the rate at which those stocks become available for recovery will depend on a number of factors, including the length of the in-service period associated with different applications. For some applications, such as consumer electronics where turnover is driven by technological change rather than product obsolescence, the in-service period is relatively short and decreasing over time. For example, the average lifespan of a cell phone for the first user was 4 years in the 1990s, but today stands at about 18 months (OECD, 2009). Many electronics are discarded when they are still functional and are often reused, but a large portion also ends up as e-waste. Many applications that use larger volumes of REE have long in-service lifetimes. Vehicles, including hybrid and electric vehicles, remain in service for 10-15 years while the lifetime of an individual wind turbine is 20-25 years. As a result, scrap from these end-uses is not expected to substantially increase until well into the next decade.

Environmental implications

Extracting and processing REE requires many of the same inputs (e.g. water, chemicals, and energy) and produces many of the same outputs (e.g. air emissions, tailings, waste water) as production of major metals. Because REE share similar properties and tend to form together along with other metallic elements, separating out individual rare earth elements is extremely complex and requires an intensive chemical process. Toxic chemicals like ammonium carbonate and oxalic acid are often used (Seaman, 2010). It is estimated that producing one tonne of rare earth oxide produces 63 000 cubic metres of air emissions containing sulphuric and hydrofluoric acid, 200 cubic metres of acidic wastewater and 1.4 tonnes of radioactive waste (Li and Lie, 2009). REE production, like other extractive operations, is energy-intensive and depending on the primary energy source can produce significant carbon emissions (e.g. coal-fired electricity generation).

Radioactivity is an inherent concern associated with the extraction and production of REE. Many of the same minerals that hold REE often also contain varying levels of thorium. Naturally occurring radioactive material makes the extraction and processing hazardous and, in some cases, has prevented REE deposits from being exploited (e.g. beach sand in Australia, China and Europe). Radioactive waste can be generated at any stage of the refinement process (e.g. milling, flotation) and must be properly disposed of.

The poor or insufficient environmental regulation and enforcement related to REE production has led to localised problems. A series of leaks of radioactive wastewater from the main pipeline from the REE separation plant contributed to the eventual closure of the Mountain Pass mine. In China, the rapid expansion of the rare earth industry took place under little regulatory oversight with serious consequences for the environment and the surrounding communities. At the world's largest REE mine, Bayan Obo, tailings ponds are reported to be leaching into groundwater and occupational poisoning from lead, mercury, benzene and phosphorous have increased sharply (Hilsum, 2009; Li and Liu, 2009). There is also evidence of radioactive contamination in plants and soils around the mine site (Schüler *et al.*, 2011). The Chinese government has taken a number of steps to improve the environmental performance of its domestic rare earth industry, including issuing revised pollution emission standards, establishing enhanced monitoring, encouraging improved management practices and mining techniques, and closing illegal mining operations.

Outlook

With lingering uncertainty over the stability of overall supply and shortages forecasted for certain key individual elements, ensuring that rare earth resources are being used efficiently will be vitally important to achieving green growth objectives.

Increased recycling and reuse of REE has the potential to alleviate some of the pressure on tight supplies from virgin resources, but technical challenges will have to be overcome and costs decreased significantly for robust secondary markets to develop. The constant stream of new applications and new REE-bearing products being developed and brought to market, provides important opportunities for manufacturers to design products to facilitate recyclability and re-use (i.e. cradle-to-cradle approaches) going forward. Given the length of time before any new rare earth resource are expected to come online, developing and securing effective substitutes will be important.

With several mining projects in the pipeline and over 100 deposits being investigated, it will also be important to ensure that the potential environmental impacts of REE extraction and processing are not overlooked in the race to meet growing demand. As with other metals, air pollution, water contamination, habitat destruction and carbon-based gas emissions can result from REE production. But for rare earths, the refinement process is made all the more complex (and risky from an environmental impacts point of view) due to their chemical and radioactive properties. A detailed material flow analysis of rare earths would help to better understand the environmental implications of their different end uses.

Endnotes

1 The abundance of individual REE depends on the element's atomic number (even numbers are more abundant) and whether the element is light or heavy (light REE are more abundant).

2 REE figures refer to rare earth oxide (REO) equivalents. The REE-to-REO ratio for each of the REEs is around 1:0.85. The relative fractions of REOs by end-use closely approximate the relative REE end uses.

3 See Schüler *et al.*, (2011) for a detailed list of research activities on recycling REE by end-use.

4 "Reserves" are defined by USGS as the estimated amount of the material in such a form or amount of concentration that economic extraction is currently or potentially feasible.

5 Rare earth elements are rarely traded as ores or concentrates. In 2009 rare earth compounds accounted for nearly 90% of total world exports. REE metals and alloys made up 10% of exports.

6 The four bills are: The Rare Earths and Critical Materials Revitalization Act of 2011 (H.R. 618), the RARE Act of 2011 (H.R. 1314), the Rare Earths Supply Chain Technology and Resources Transformation Act of 2011 (H.R. 1388) and the Rare Earth Policy Task Force and Materials Act (H.R. 2184).

7 Toyota and Honda have established recycling programmes, offering customers 200 USD for each battery returned at the end of its life. Toyota also owns a company with an interest in an REE mine under development in Vietnam (BGS, 2010).

REFERENCES

- Areddy, James T. (2010), "U.S. Congress Spurs Rare Earth Race," The Wall Street Journal (Online), 1 October, available at: *blogs.wsj.com/chinarealtime/2010/10/01/us-congress-spurs-rare-earth-race/tab/print/* [Accessed 18 October 2010]
- Avalon Rare Metals, Inc. (2010a), "The Delicate Supply Balance and Growing Demand for Rare Earths," presentation by Ian London at Magnetics 2010, 27 January 2010.
- Avalon Rare Metals, Inc. (2010b), *Rare Earth Elements and the Green Energy Economy*, available at: *www.avalonraremetals.com/_resources/REE_101_web.6_2010.01.18.pdf* [Accessed 29 September 2010]
- Basel Action Network (2002), *Exporting Harm: The High Tech Trashing of Asia,* Basel Action Network, Seattle, WA.
- Bradsher, K. (2010a), "Challenging China in Rare Earth Mining," The New York Times, 21 April.
- Bradsher, K. (2010b), "Amid Tension, China Blocks Vital Exports to Japan," The New York Times, 22 September.
- Bradsher, K. (2009), "China Tightens Grip on Rare Minerals," The New York Times, 1 September.
- BGS (British Geological Survey) (2010), *Commodity Profile: Rare Earth Elements,* BGS, Keyworth, Nottingham.

- BGS (n.d.) Rare earth elements: a beginner's guide from the BGS website, BGS, Keyworth, Nottingham, *www.bgs.ac.uk/research/highlights/rare_earth_elements.html* [Accessed 31 January 2011]
- European Commission (2010), Report of the Ad-hoc Working Group on Defining Critical Raw Materials, European Commission, Brussels.
- Goonan, T.G. (2011), *Rare earth elements—End use and recyclability*, U.S. Geological Survey Scientific Investigations Report 2011–5094, 15 p.
- Haxel, Gordon B., Hedrick, James B., and Orris, Greta J. (2002), *Rare Earth Elements – Critical Resources for High Technology*, U.S. Geological Survey, Washington, D.C.
- Hilsum, Lindsay (2009), "Are Rare Earth Minerals Too Costly for Environment?" transcript from PBS Newshour, Air date 14 December 2009, available at: www.pbs.org/newshour/bb/asia/july-dec09/china_12-14.html
- Humphries, Marc (2010), *Rare Earth Elements: The Global Supply Chain*, Congressional Research Service, Washington, D.C.
- ITU (2009), The World in 2009: ICT Facts & Figures website, www.itu.int
- Li, Jiabao and Liu, Jie (2009), "Rare earth industry adjusts to slow market," China Daily Online, updated 7 September 2009, www.chinadaily.com.cn/bw/2009-09/07/content_8660849.htm
- Loveday, Eric (2010), "Toyota's hybrid sales eclipse 2.5M mark, now climbing at 2,000 per day", AutoblogGreen, 2 July 2010, green.autoblog.com/2010/07/02/toyotas-hybrid-sales-eclipse-2-5m-mark-now-climbing-at-2-000-p/
- Lusty, Paul (2010), "Critical Metals and Rare Earth Elements," *Mines and Money 2010*, British Geological Survey, Keyworth, Nottingham.
- Margonelli, Lisa (2009), "Clean Energy's Dirty Little Secret," The Atlantic Monthly, May 2009.
- Molycorp Minerals (2010), "Rare Earth Minerals: The Indispensable Resource for Clean Energy Technologies", presentation by Mark A. Smith to the Colorado Mining Association, 10 February 2010.
- Montgomery, Michael (2011), "Rare Earth Elements Monthly Recap: July," Rare Earth Investing News, 1 August 2011, *http://rareearthinvestingnews.com/4463/rare-earth-elements-monthly-recap-july/*
- OECD (2012a), *Case Study on Critical Metals in Mobile Phones: Final Report*, *http://www.oecd.org/env/waste/Case%20Study%20on%20Critical%20Metals%20in%20Mobile%20Phones.pdf.*
- Schüler, D. *et al.* (2011), "A Study on Rare Earth and Their Recycling," Final Report for the Greens/EFA Group in the European Parliament, Öko-Institut e.V., Freiburg.
- Seaman, John (2010), *Rare Earths and Clean Energy: Analyzing China's Upper Hand*, Institut français des relations internationales, Paris.
- U.S. Department of Energy (2010), *Critical Materials Strategy*, U.S. Department of Energy, Washington, D.C.
- USGS (2011a), *Mineral Commodity Summaries 2011*, USGS, Reston, Virginia.
- USGS (2011b), written communication, 3 October 2011.
- USGS (2010a), *Mineral Commodity Summaries 2010*, USGS, Reston, Virginia.
- USGS (2010b), "Rare earths statistics," in Kelly, T.D., and Matos, G.R., comps., *Historical statistics for mineral and material commodities in the United States*, USGS Data Series 140 [Accessed 28 September 2010].
- USGS (2010c), *2008 Minerals Yearbook: Rare Earths [Advance Release]*, U.S. Geological Survey, Reston, Virginia
- USGS (2010d), The Principal Rare Earth Elements Deposits of the United States—A Summary of Domestic Deposits and a Global Perspective, Scientific Investigations Report 2010–5220, USGS, Reston, Virginia.

GLOSSARY

Decoupling

The term decoupling refers to breaking the link between “environmental bads” and “economic goods.” Using this concept helps analyse and assess the linkages between environmental degradation and economic development.

In practice, the measurement of decoupling refers to the relative growth rates of a direct pressure on the environment and of an economically relevant variable to which it is causally linked. Decoupling occurs when the growth rate of the environmental pressure (EP) is less than that of its economic driving force (DF) over a given period. One distinguishes between absolute and relative decoupling. Decoupling is said to be absolute when the environmental variable is stable or decreasing while the economic variable is growing. Decoupling is said to be relative when environmental variable is increasing, but at a lower rate than the economic variable.

The decoupling concept has no automatic link to the environment’s capacity to sustain, absorb or resist pressures of various kinds (deposition, discharges, harvests). A meaningful interpretation of the relationship of EP to economic DF will require additional information. Also, the relationship between economic DF and EP, more often than not, is complex. Most DF have multiple environmental effects, and most EP are generated by multiple DF, which, in turn, are affected by societal responses. Changes in decoupling may thus be decomposed in a number of intermediate steps. These may include changes in the scale of the economy, in consumption patterns, and in economic structure — including the extent to which demand is satisfied by domestic production or by imports. Other mechanisms in the causal chain include the adoption of cleaner technology, the use of higher quality inputs, and the post facto clean up of pollution and treatment of waste.

Source: OECD (2002)

Domestic Extraction Used (DEU)

Domestic Extraction Used (DEU) is a variable used in material flow accounting. DEU measures the flows of materials that originate from the environment and that physically enter the economic system for further processing or direct consumption (they are "used" by the economy). They are converted into or incorporated in products in one way or the other, and are usually of economic value.

Source: OECD (2008)

Direct (material) flows

In material flow accounting, direct materials flows refer to flows of materials that physically cross the boundary of the economic system (at the level for which the accounts are made, i.e. the national economy in the case of national economy-wide material flow accounts) either as an input or as an output. Direct flows refer to the actual mass (weight) of the material or product that enters or leaves the system and do not take into account the life-cycle dimension of the production chain.

Source: OECD (2008)

Domestic Material Consumption (DMC)

Domestic Material Consumption (DMC) is a variable used in material flow accounting. DMC measures the mass (weight) of the materials that are physically used in the consumption activities of the domestic economic system (i.e. the direct apparent consumption of materials, excluding indirect flows). In economy–wide material flow accounting DMC equals DMI minus exports, i.e. domestic extraction plus imports minus exports.

Source: OECD (2008)

Domestic Material Input (DMI)

Direct Material Input (DMI) is a variable used in material flow accounting. DMI measures the direct flows of materials that physically enter the economic system as an input, i.e. materials that are of economic value and that are used in production and consumption activities. In economy–wide material flow accounting DMI equals domestic (used) extraction plus imports.

Source: OECD (2008)

Economy-wide Material Flow Accounts (EW-MFAcc)

The term "economy-wide" is used to qualify MFAcc that cover the national economy as a whole (black box), and that track the physical flows of the entire range of natural resources and materials exchanged at the boundary of the national economy. An important feature of EW-MFAcc is that they are complete as regards the materials covered, with the exception of water, and that all materials are recorded in a common physical unit. They thus usually provide a fairly detailed database that can be used to provide both an aggregate overview of annual material inputs and outputs of an economy, and a basis for in-depth MF studies and analyses.

Source: OECD (2008)

Hazardous waste

Hazardous waste refers to the categories of waste to be controlled according to the Basel Convention on the control of transboundary movements of hazardous waste and their disposal (Article 1 and Annex I).

Source: OECD Questionnaire on the state of the environment 2010

Hidden flows

The term "hidden flow" refers to a concept used in economy-wide material flow analysis and accounting. It is used to designate (i) the movements of unused materials associated with the extraction of raw materials from natural resources, both nationally and abroad, intended for use in the national economy; and (ii) the indirect flows of materials such as pollution or waste that occur upstream in a production process but that are not physically embodied in the product itself. The word "hidden" reflects the fact that these flows usually do not appear in traditional economic accounting. Since indirect flows are often difficult to estimate, the term "hidden flows" is sometimes used as a synonym for "unused extraction".

Source: OECD (2008)

Indirect flows

The term 'indirect flows' is used to designate the flows of materials that (i) are needed for the production of a product, (ii) have occurred up-stream in the production process, and (iii) are not physically embodied in the product itself. Indirect flows take into account the life-cycle dimension of the production chain, and encompass both used and unused materials.

In material flow accounting, indirect materials flows refer to flows of materials that are associated to direct flows, but that do not physically cross the boundary of the economic system (i.e. the national economy in the case of national economy-wide material flow accounts). They measure the mass (weight) of the 'cradle to border' material requirements necessary to make a product available at the border of a system either as an input or an output, minus the mass (weight) of the product itself. Such indirect flows are sometimes called "ecological rucksack".

Source: OECD (2008)

Mass balance principle

The mass balance principle is founded on the first law of thermodynamics (called the law of conservation of matter), which states that matter (mass, energy) is neither created nor destroyed by any physical process. When applied to material flow analysis and accounts, this leads to the following accounting identity: natural resource extraction + imports = residual output + exports + net addition to man-made stocks, i.e. the sum of material inputs into a system equals the sum of its material outputs, thereby comprising the materials_accumulated as changes in stocks.

Source: OECD (2008).

Material Flow Accounts (MFAcc)

Material flow accounts (MFAcc) are methodically organised accounts in physical units (usually in tonnes) that quantify the flows of different types of materials into, out of and possibly within a given system at different levels of detail and completeness, and by making reference to the material balance principle. They provide information on the material input from the environment into the system (e.g. resources extracted or harvested from the surrounding natural environment or imported from other systems), the transformation and use of that input in the system (from material production to final consumption) and the material outputs of the system in the form of returns to the environment as residuals (waste, pollutants) or in the form of exports to other systems.

Material flow accounts are part of environmental accounting and of the physical flow accounts family as described in the System of integrated Environmental and Economic Accounting (SEEA). An important feature of MFAcc is that they track both direct flows (i.e. flows of materials physically entering the economic process) and indirect and unused flows (i.e. flows of materials not entering the economic process, but associated to resource exploitation and to the up-stream production process of a product and of relevance from an environmental point of view).

The system to which the accounts apply is usually an economic system with its production and consumption activities, and its interactions with the surrounding environment and with other economic systems and their environment. It is these interactions that are of interest to MFAcc. The materials are recorded in physical units (usually tonnes). MFAcc can be established at various levels of scale (world regions, whole national economy, branches of production, firms, municipalities, etc.) and can be applied to materials at various levels of detail (all materials, groups of materials, individual materials or substances).

Source: OECD (2008).

Material Flow Analysis (MFA)

Material flow analysis (MFA) refers to the monitoring and analysis of physical flows of materials into, through and out of a given system (usually the economy) through the process chains, through extraction, production, use, recycling and final disposal. MFA is generally based on methodically organised accounts in physical units

(Material flow accounts). It helps identify waste of natural resources and materials in the economy which would otherwise go unnoticed in conventional economic monitoring systems.

The term MFA is used in a generic way to designate a family of tools encompassing different types of accounts, indicators and evaluation methods at different levels of ambition, detail and completeness. MFA can be applied to a wide range of economic, administrative or natural entities at various levels of scale (world regions, whole economy, industries, firms, plants, territories, cities, river basins, eco-zones, etc.) and can be applied to materials at various levels of detail (individual materials or substances, groups of materials, all materials).

Source: OECD (2008).

Materials or material resources

The term "materials" or "material resources" designates the usable materials or substances (raw materials, energy) produced from natural resources. These usable "materials" include energy carriers (gas, oil, coal), metal ores and metals, construction minerals and other minerals, soil and biomass.

In the context of Material Flow Analysis and Accounting, the term "materials" is used in a very broad sense so as to record all material related flows at all relevant stages of the material cycle. It designates materials from renewable and non-renewable natural resource stocks that are used as material inputs into human activities and the products that embody them, as well as the residuals arising from their extraction, production and use (such as waste or pollutant emissions to air, land, water) and the ecosystem inputs required for their extraction, production and use (such as nutrients, carbon dioxide required by plants and animals for growth and the oxygen necessary for combustion).

Source: OECD (2008).

Material productivity

Material productivity makes reference to the effectiveness with which an economy or a production process is using materials extracted from natural resources. The term also designates an indicator that reflects the output or value added generated per unit of materials used. This is typically a macro-economic concept that can be presented alongside labour or capital productivity. It should be noted that the term "resource productivity" is often used to designate material productivity though the latter does not cover all resources (e.g. water is usually not included).

Source: OECD (2008)

Municipal solid waste (MSW)

MSW refers to waste collected by or on behalf of municipalities from households, commerce and trade, small businesses, office buildings and institutions (schools, hospitals, government buildings), and selected municipal services if managed as waste (e.g. waste from street cleaning, parks and garden maintenance). It includes waste from these sources collected door-to-door through traditional collection operations and fractions collected separately for recovery operations (door-to-door and/or voluntary deposits). Municipal solid waste includes household and other similar waste, as well as bulky waste (e.g. old furniture, appliances), yard waste, leaves, grass clippings, street sweepings and the content of litter containers, if managed as waste.

Source: OECD Questionnaire on the state of the environment 2010

Natural capital

In environmental accounting, the term "natural capital" is used to designate all natural assets, also called environmental assets, whether they are economic assets or not. Natural capital is generally considered to comprise three principal categories: natural resource stocks, land and ecosystems. All are considered essential to the long-term sustainability of development for their provision of "functions" to the economy, as well as to humankind outside the economy and other living beings.

Source: SEEA 1.23

Natural resources

The term "natural resources" designates renewable and non-renewable resource stocks that are found in nature (mineral resources, energy resources, soil resources, water resources and biological resources). Natural resources are commonly divided into non-renewable and renewable resources:

Renewable natural resources

Renewable natural resources are resources from renewable natural stocks that, after exploitation, can return to their previous stock levels by natural processes of growth or replenishment. Conditionally renewable resources are those whose exploitation eventually reaches a level beyond which regeneration will become impossible. Such is the case with the clear-cutting of tropical forests. Examples of renewable resources include timber from forest resources, freshwater resources, land resources, wildlife resources such as fish, agricultural resources.

Source: OECD (2008), and UNSD, Environment Glossary

Non-renewable natural resources

Non-renewable natural resources are exhaustible natural resources whose natural stocks cannot be regenerated after exploitation or that can only be regenerated or replenished by natural cycles that are relatively slow at human scale. Examples include metals and other minerals such as industrial and construction minerals, and fossil energy carriers, such as oil.

Source: OECD (2008), and UNSD, Environment Glossary

In environmental accounting, the term "natural resources" is used to designate stocks of natural resources. It is defined as the natural assets occurring in nature that can be used for economic production or consumption, i.e. natural economic assets. Together with land and ecosystems, stocks of natural resources form what is called the natural capital.

Natural resource stocks are the naturally occurring assets that provide use benefits through the provision of raw materials and energy used in economic activity (or that may provide such benefits one day) and that are subject primarily to quantitative depletion through human use. They are subdivided into four categories: mineral and energy resources, soil resources, water resources and biological resources. Stocks of mineral and energy resources are also called mineral and energy reserves.

Source: OECD (2008)

Physical Trade Balance (PTB)

Physical Trade Balance (PTB) is a variable used in material flow accounting. It measures the physical trade surplus or deficit of an economy. In economy-wide material flow accounting, PTB equals imports minus exports. Physical trade balances may also be calculated for indirect flows associated to Imports and Exports.

Source: OECD (2008)

Productivity

Productivity is commonly defined as a ratio of a volume measure of output to a volume measure of input use. While there is no disagreement on this general notion, a look at the productivity literature and its various applications reveals that there is neither a unique purpose for measuring productivity nor a single measure.

The terms productivity and efficiency refer to different but related concepts. Productivity relates the quantity of output produced to one or more inputs used in the production of the output, irrespective of the efficiency of their use.

Reserves

Reserves refer to "that part of the reserve base which could be economically extracted or produced at the time of determination. The term reserves need not signify that extraction facilities are in place and operative. Reserves include only recoverable materials; thus, terms such as "extractable reserves" and "recoverable reserves" are redundant."

Source: U.S. Geological Survey.

Reserve Base

The reserve base is "that part of an identified resource that meets specified minimum physical and chemical criteria related to current mining and production practices, including those for grade, quality, thickness, and depth. The reserve base is the in-place demonstrated (measured plus indicated) resource from which reserves are estimated. It may encompass those parts of the resources that have a reasonable potential for becoming economically available within planning horizons beyond those that assume proven technology and current economics. The reserve base includes those resources that are currently economic (reserves), marginally economic (marginal reserves), and some of those that are currently subeconomic (subeconomic resources)."

Source: U.S. Geological Survey.

Resource

In geology, the term "resource" refers to "a concentration of naturally occurring solid, liquid, or gaseous material in or on the Earth's crust in such form and amount that economic extraction of a commodity from the concentration is currently or potentially feasible."

Source: U.S. Geological Survey.

Resource productivity

Resource productivity refers to the effectiveness with which an economy or a production process is using natural resources. It can be defined with respect to:

- the economic-physical efficiency, i.e. the money value added of outputs per mass unit of resource inputs used. This is also the focus when the aim is to decouple value added and resource consumption.
- the physical or technical efficiency, i.e. the amount of resources input required to produce a unit of output, both expressed in physical terms (e.g. iron ore inputs for crude steel production or raw material

inputs for the production of a computer, a car, batteries). The focus is on maximising the output with a given set of inputs and a given technology or on minimising the inputs for a given output.

– the economic efficiency, i.e. the money value of outputs relative to the money value of inputs. The focus is on minimising resource input costs.

The term also designates an indicator that reflects the output or value added generated per unit of resources used. This is typically a macro-economic concept that can be presented alongside labour or capital productivity.

Resource productivity would ideally encompass all natural resources and ecosystem inputs that are used as factors of production in the economy. The term is however often used as a synonym for material productivity.

Source: OECD (2008).

Total Material Consumption (TMC)

Total Material Consumption (TMC) is a variable used in material flow accounting. TMC measures the total mass (weight) of materials that are associated to the (apparent) material consumption of the domestic economic system, whatever their origin is (domestic, rest of the world). In economy-wide material flow accounting TMC equals DMC plus unused extraction plus indirect flows associated with imports minus indirect flows associated with exports.

Source: OECD (2008)

Total Material Requirement (TMR)

Total Material Requirement (TMR) is a variable used in material flow accounting. TMR refers to the total 'material base' of an economic system (i.e. the total primary material requirements of production activities). TMR measures the total mass (weight) of materials that are required to support an economic system, whether for use in production and consumption activities or not, and whatever their origin is (domestic, rest of the world). In economy-wide material flow accounting TMR equals TMI plus indirect (upstream) flows associated to imports. Adding indirect flows converts imports into their 'primary resource extraction equivalent'.

Source: OECD (2008)

TMR is an overall indicator developed by the Wuppertal Institute to describe, in terms of total tonnage, not only the amount of natural resources contained in the commodities produced by the economy, but also the indirect flows which are involved in such production. These material flows which remain outside of the economy include wood materials which are not used in logging (branches, needles, leaves and roots), earth and stone which is excavated in mining and quarrying along with usable ore and minerals, earthworks necessary in the construction of infrastructure systems (roads and communities) and erosion resulting from human activities (including intensive agriculture).

Source: Wuppertal Institute

Unused domestic extraction (UDE)

In material flow accounting, unused domestic extraction refers to materials that originate from the environment, but do not physically enter the economic system as input for further processing or consumption and return to the environment as residuals immediately after removal/displacement from their natural site. They are not incorporated in products at any stage and are usually without economic value.

It includes materials that (i) are extracted, moved or disturbed by economic activities on purpose and by means of technology, (ii) are not fit or not intended for use in further processing, and (iii) remain unused in the environment. This is the case when material must be extracted from the natural environment, along with the desired material, to obtain the desired material, or when material is moved or disturbed to obtain the natural resource, or to create and maintain an infrastructure,

Examples of unused extraction are soil and rock excavated during construction and not used elsewhere, dredged sediments from harbours, overburden from mining and quarrying and unused biomass from harvest.

Source: OECD (2008)

Waste

Waste refers to materials that are not prime products (i.e. products produced for the market) and for which the generator has no further use for his/her own purpose of production, transformation or consumption, and which he/she discards, intends to discard or is required to discard. Wastes may be generated during the extraction of raw materials during the processing of raw materials to intermediate and final products, during the consumption of final products, and during any other human activity. Waste does not include residuals directly recycled or reused at the place of generation (i.e. establishment) or waste materials that are directly discharged into ambient water or air.

Source: OECD Questionnaire on the state of the environment

REFERENCES

- OECD (2002), Indicators to measure decoupling of environmental pressure from economic growth; OECD (2008), Measuring material flows and resource productivity: The OECD Guide. , *www.oecd.org/environment/indicators-modelling-outlooks/MFA-Guide.pdf*
- OECD (2010), Questionnaire on the state of the environment, OECD.
- UN (2014), *System of Environmental-Economic Accounting 2012: Central framework*, European Commission, FAO, IMF, OECD, UN, the World Bank, United Nations, New York. *http://unstats.un.org/unsd/envaccounting/seeaRev/SEEA_CF_Final_en.pdf.*
- UNSD (n.d.), Environment Glossary, *http://unstats.un.org/unsd/environmentgl/*, UNSD.
- U.S. Geological Survey (n.d.), *www.usgs.gov/.*
- Wuppertal Institute (n.d.), *http://wupperinst.org/en/home/.*

ORGANISATION FOR ECONOMIC CO-OPERATION AND DEVELOPMENT

The OECD is a unique forum where governments work together to address the economic, social and environmental challenges of globalisation. The OECD is also at the forefront of efforts to understand and to help governments respond to new developments and concerns, such as corporate governance, the information economy and the challenges of an ageing population. The Organisation provides a setting where governments can compare policy experiences, seek answers to common problems, identify good practice and work to co-ordinate domestic and international policies.

The OECD member countries are: Australia, Austria, Belgium, Canada, Chile, the Czech Republic, Denmark, Estonia, Finland, France, Germany, Greece, Hungary, Iceland, Ireland, Israel, Italy, Japan, Korea, Luxembourg, Mexico, the Netherlands, New Zealand, Norway, Poland, Portugal, the Slovak Republic, Slovenia, Spain, Sweden, Switzerland, Turkey, the United Kingdom and the United States. The European Commission takes part in the work of the OECD.

OECD Publishing disseminates widely the results of the Organisation's statistics gathering and research on economic, social and environmental issues, as well as the conventions, guidelines and standards agreed by its members.

OECD PUBLISHING, 2, rue André-Pascal, 75775 PARIS CEDEX 16
(97 2013 06 1 P) ISBN 978-92-64-19049-8 – 2015-17

www.ingramcontent.com/pod-product-compliance
Ingram Content Group UK Ltd.
Pitfield, Milton Keynes, MK11 3LW, UK
UKHW051502290926
15471UKWH00008B/1370

9 789264 190498